Praise for *Back Seat with Fish*

"A really great book about the entangled bird's nest of relationships and pursuing one's passion—in this case fishing. Highly recommended!"

—Stephen Sautner, author of *Fish On, Fish Off* and *A Cast in the Woods*

"Like all good fishing stories, Hughes' memoir is full of deep contemplation, rakish humor, and moments of true drama. A personal history of a life defined by tight lines, both literal and literary, *Back Seat with Fish* lures us from coast to coast and beyond, baited by stories of big fish hooked and lost; youthful tales of sport, sometimes clean, sometimes bawdy; and an ongoing inquiry into the relationship between friends, family, mentors, lovers, and the waters that birth us all."

—Kim Barnes, author of *In the Wilderness* and *In the Kingdom of Men*

"The writing? Holy cow. Can Henry Hughes write! Among our "Best of the Year" choices, *Back Seat with Fish* is the ~~...~~ ughes draws from a foundation in poetr~~...~~ nviting imagery and provides an unde~~...~~ t to flow easily along."

—Ron Watters, editor ~~...~~ *utdoor Literature*

"*Back Seat with Fish* is finely written by a man with an appetite for the world. Henry Hughes is an absolute pleasure to read."

—Ted Leeson, author of *Habit of Rivers*

"This is a globe-spanning adventure story of love and fishing that I highly recommend to all anglers. It's a funny, provocative, philosophical page-turner that I couldn't put down."

—Cameron Pierce, editor of *Taut Lines*

"Along comes a gifted writer like Henry Hughes to remind us just how richly entertaining the intertwining obsessions of angling, life, and literature can truly be."

—James R Babb, editor emeritus, *Gray's Sporting Journal*

"It's written that fish are sacred, and the angler one lured by their mystery. That is Henry Hughes, and we are grateful for the beautiful stories he shapes from a fisher's life."

—Sandra Alcosser, author of *A Fish to Feed All Hunger* and *Except by Nature*

"Beautiful and wild. Imagine a contemporary Eden prior to and after The Fall, and Eve still unashamed, taking off her clothes before the very eyes of Adam, who has caught his limit for the day, and has no need to lie, except with her."

—Jim Hepworth, Fishtrap Writers Gathering

"*Back Seat with Fish* is enjoyable precisely because it lacks the pretense found in a lot of angling literature and delves into uncertain truths of lived experience. From his working-class family background to his university professorship, Hughes writes his story with a sense of awe and connectedness to the people and world around him."

—Craig Schuhmann, editor of *Flyfishing & Tying Journal*

"This literary, earthy memoir by Henry Hughes is a collection of funny, sexy, and heartbreaking tales about fishing, family, love, and life. It's a ranging coming-of-age read with a tang of sex, drugs, and rock n' roll mixed in with joyous, frustrating angling stories from the Long Island Sound to the Sea of Japan. Strong narrative voice, refreshingly honest, and a bit haunting."

—Margot Page, author of *Little Rivers*

"Hughes writes with a poet's pen, while drawing easily on his remarkable sense of fishing's literary and cultural past. This adventurer in "Angling and Romance" has a heart, too, and you'll feel the tug of it, or of his fine wit, as you would bumps on the end of your line."

—Bert Bender, author of *Sea-Brothers* and *Catching the Ebb*

"No one sucks the marrow quite like Hughes. Beginning in his childhood waters off New York, sensual romance and sensational fishing pulls the narrative across the country, overseas to Asia and back. Hughes is an angler in the finest regard. From bait and spin fishing in Long Island Sound to fly fishing for carp in China, his breadth of fishing expertise is one that every angler can admire. Also dealing honestly with issues of race, class, gender, and cross-cultural relations, *Back Seat with Fish* achieves what great memoirs all aspire to do—tell a story with passion and tenderness in a way that keeps the reader turning the page. This is a fishing life you'll want to read."

—Noah Davis, *Anglers Journal*

"Here is a writer who contemplates the deeper questions we longtime anglers think about in slower moments. Do the fish feel pain? Why is there such joy in feeling a fish struggle? Hughes looks fish in the eye and knows that he will kill and eat some of them. There's an honesty here that he carries through his Pacific travels in Japan, China, Indonesia, Malaysia, Alaska and his home waters of Oregon. Not only does he angle in these faraway places and eat some strange fish, he drinks in the culture like a parched explorer."

—Shannon Drawe, *Texas Fly Caster*

"Henry Hughes is a man who moves through the world obsessed with fish and fishing. His memoir is an incredible catalog of fish encountered, caught, released, eaten, as well as encounters of the amorous variety. You have to admire the gusto with which this man follows his natural attractions."

—Lorraine Anderson, editor of *Sisters of the Earth*
and *Earth and Eros*

"Henry Hughes' wonderful *Back Seat with Fish*, a memoir of obsessive angling that takes place amidst family, friends, work, loss, academics, partying and romance (lots of romance). The result is a far richer fishing life than anything I've seen portrayed in a glossy fly-fishing magazine. It's at times hilarious, at times heartbreaking, filled with both fishing triumphs and failures, all captured beautifully through Hughes' prose. I can't recommend this book highly enough."

—Matthew Miller, The Nature Conservancy

BACK SEAT *with* FISH

Also by Henry Hughes

Poetry
Men Holding Eggs
Moist Meridian
Shutter Lines
Bunch of Animals

Edited Collections
Art of Angling: Poems About Fishing
Fishing Stories

BACK SEAT

with

FISH

A Man's Adventures in Angling and Romance

Henry Hughes

Skyhorse Publishing

Skyhorse Publishing books may be purchased in bulk at special discounts for sales promotion, corporate gifts, fund-raising, or educational purposes. Special editions can also be created to specifications. For details, contact the Special Sales Department, Skyhorse Publishing, 307 West 36th Street, 11th Floor, New York, NY 10018 or info@skyhorsepublishing.com.

Skyhorse® and Skyhorse Publishing® are registered trademarks of Skyhorse Publishing, Inc.®, a Delaware corporation.

Visit our website at www.skyhorsepublishing.com.

10 9 8 7 6 5 4 3 2 1

Library of Congress Cataloging-in-Publication Data is available on file.

Cover design by Tom Lau
Cover illustration courtesy of Rebecca McCannell

Interior illustrations courtesy of Richard Bunse

Paperback ISBN: 978-1-5107-5896-4
Ebook ISBN: 978-1-51070-372-8

Printed in the United States of America

For Chloë

Illustrations by Richard Bunse

Contents

Give him a place by the fire,
pour whisky and cold beer,
for he is a far casting angler
who's put a hook in my ear

—*Inscription found in longhand on a Long Island bar,
long washed away*

A Note on Truth

Truth can be a slippery notion for anglers who have traditionally been exempt from precise accuracy. The very word, "angling," appearing in possibly the first English language text on the subject, *Treatise of Fishing with an Angle*, possibly written by the nun Dame Juliana Berners in 1496, refers to the shape of the hook and those angled relationships between fish, line, rod, and agent. The author also tells us to "take good heed that in going about your disports ye open no man's gates but that ye shut them again." So I've adjusted a few names and details to set the neighbors at ease. Dame Berners further enjoins that in fishing we avoid vices and the pursuit of wealth and fame and angle "principally for your solace, and to cause the health of your body, and especially of your soul." Much to aspire to, but I'm willing to grant the good nun her passions and secrets if she and you would grant me mine.

Fishdate

Ａt the age of thirty-seven, I had no lover, and my only fish was a chipped plaster striped bass that my brother picked up at a yard sale and put on my backseat to keep me company. In the summer of 2002, I drove my beat-up Buick from Long Island, New York, where I grew up, to Monmouth, Oregon, for a position as an English professor. During the job interview they did not tell me that Monmouth was dry. In the neighboring town of Independence, I found a tavern called Leonora's Ghost and watched the New York Mets lose to the San Diego Padres, wondering if my father was also tuned in. Two women sat at the end of the bar. I tried to make conversation, but they weren't interested. I finished my beer and walked across the street to the Willamette River. A couple Latino kids plunked worms from the bank, boats dripped from trailers, and an osprey tore something gold from the current. *Fishing*, I thought and smiled.

Fishing new geographies can be challenging until you get to know the waters and the people. At eighteen, I left Long Island and the Atlantic Seaboard to live in South Dakota, Indiana, Japan, and China with trips around the Pacific, always fishing and meeting people, angling new environments and customs, connecting at all

1

depths in every kind of weather, landing lifelong relationships, and losing what might have been.

After a couple hot days of unpacking and orientation, I walked back into Leonora's Ghost and saw a rotund man inking fish and women on bar napkins. "That's my kind of art," I said. The man turned, a pink smile creasing through his thick white beard. "Pull up a stool," he said. Richard Bunse and I talked, while sipping a couple Mirror Ponds, about Oregon trout, steelhead, salmon, rivers, lakes, bays, boats, and techniques. His words illustrated by quick-sketched maps and fly patterns. When the shapely bartender leaned back against the glass door of the beer cooler, purring "This feels nice," Richard drew her, but instead of long-necked bottles, he penned trout swimming up beneath her as if she were floating over a placid river teaming with rainbows. "There's something about the smooth lines of women," Richard mused, "that remind me of fish."

A week later I joined Richard's drawing group, stepping into his River Gallery studio a few doors down from Leonora's, smiling at the men and women setting up their pads and charcoal. Richard waved me over and pulled out a drawing horse. "Just relax," he said and patted me on the shoulder. I looked forward and nodded respectfully to the voluptuous model undressing and sitting on a velvet-draped table. After an hour of pushing pastel, my hand stiff and sweaty, we took a break. The model put on her robe, Richard poured a round of homemade wine, and we all talked in soft tones about the session. The windowless old studio was like a cobwebbed grotto cluttered with art supplies, fishing tackle, statues, and walls of women and fish. "It's a temple," I declared. Richard smiled, rose, and called the congregants back to prayer. But prayer is nothing without action. Richard and I fly fished together a few times, and he gave me boxes of his hand-tied nymphs and dries and chartered shadowy streams, where we caught and released small cutthroat trout of spectacular speckled beauty. I met other anglers, like Jefferson, a lean, bearded rock climber who would smoke a bowl and then guide me along slick canyon ledges and across swift runs of mountain water, waiting patiently for me to catch up and always offering a hand and the first cast into a sweet spot where a steelhead sometimes lay. Steelhead, a race of rainbow trout, have evolved like salmon to leave their natal rivers for the sea and return after two or three years. They are wary and gorgeous—an olive back, spotted, and shading to cherry-blushed silver sides—and every bit as powerful as their name. I kept a clear head on these rushing adventures, but when the waders came off I'd join Jefferson in a beer and a smoke, listening to his colorful stories of people and fish. "Fishing is life," he'd say without an ounce of pretense or affected philosophy. "Life is fishing," I'd say, exhale, and smile.

Then there was Reverend Bob, the husband of our department secretary, who took me on his wooden drift boat down coastal rivers where we hooked, lost, and landed several salmon. Bob loved to talk about church, family, and fishing. "Right there," he lifted a hand off the oar and pointed to a bend in the river, "twenty years ago after service on a freezing-cold Sunday, my father tossed a pink corkie behind that rock and hooked a thirty-inch coho with a seal bite on its belly." I cast my bobber and pink jig in the same spot, mending the slack line and watching intently as Bob delivered a detailed reverential history spanning three decades of every fish hooked behind that rock. My bobber spun in the eddy but never winked.

"He can't remember to pick up milk," Bob's wife shook the empty jug one morning when we were heading out, "but he can tell you the weather, the lure, the time, and the place, spot, hole—is that what you say?—*the hole* where he caught every fish. It's uncanny."

And so it is, the focus and intensity of catching fish sharpens the hooks of memory and brings a net under the past.

That very morning twelve years ago, Bob and I drank bitter black coffee and cast pink-bellied spinners with chrome blades into the tidal surge three miles from the ocean on the Salmon River north of Lincoln City, Oregon. I told him that my father disliked fishing but took me often when I was young. "That's a good dad," Bob said. I was using fifteen-pound test and making long casts, recounting distant details from a fishing trip with my father on Long Island some thirty years ago. Bob smiled, closed his tackle box decorated with the intersecting arcs of a Jesus fish, and then pointed to an eagle sweeping down over a swirl in the river. The tide rolled in, sea lions barked, and around ten o'clock I hooked a fish that torpedoed a creamy wake upstream, taking line and sounding with the smack of its wide spotted tail. Bob hallelujahed—"Fish on!"

Landing a large fish on light line is realizing high hopes on modest means, and it always thrills me. You must stay firm to what you want—no slack—and crank in when you can, but also let the wildness run or it will break away for good. All living connections demand a little give and take.

Bob pulled the anchor and we followed the powerful salmon, working its energy away from a logjam and back toward our boat— its long silver suddenly glowing in the marbled water.

"What a blessed creature," Bob intoned. The fish raced around the boat, taking and surrendering line, finally tilting flank-up in exhaustion. Bob leaned over with the landing net, but the water exploded in scales and fur as a brown hump breached and rolled in a sucking swirl. "Damn sea lion!" Bob yelled. The revived and terrified fish shot a few feet from the boat, and I reeled and arched back on the rod, hoping the line would hold, finally horsing the

salmon's head toward the net, the sea lion chomping at its tail. Bob dropped the twisting salmon at our feet, pulled off his hat, and looked to the gray skies, "Dear God, thank you." When Bob, a born-again Christian, finished his prayer—Father, Son, and Holy Ghost—I hugged him, tipped my hat to the sea lion, and bowed to the thirty-six-pound Chinook salmon that we shared with Bob's family, a couple of my colleagues, and Richard.

"The Lord works in mysterious ways," Richard said after hearing my story. We were sitting at a long table in the River Gallery, sampling some of the salmon, which had been smoked by Jefferson using a bourbon-molasses brine and local alder. "*Mmh-mmh*," Richard said as he licked his lips. A couple visiting the gallery from California came to the table, and I offered them some fish. The woman puckered and said, "No thanks," but the man took a piece, chewed, and nodded approvingly. "So you catch these around here?" he asked. I told him about Oregon salmon and mentioned that California still had some runs. "We just buy fish at the supermarket," the man said. "I have no idea where it's coming from."

After the couple left, Richard and I talked about how little most people know about their food. Although the fish I catch make up only a small portion of my diet, it feels good to get out on the water and pursue, hook, and land some of my own food. Most meat eaters never do more than pick up a shiny wrapped package from the cold market, and perhaps that comfortably widens the distance between the necessity of killing to eat and the necessity of eating to live. Fishing shortens the distance, bringing us a little closer to our positive primitive vitalities. Our very language reminds us that fish are wild in our hearts. French-Norman conquests brought to Anglo-Saxon sophisticated words such as beef, pork, and poultry that attempt to fence us from creatures we know and eat. Fish remains fish. When I landed that Chinook, cut its gills to bleed out in the river, patted her hard bright sides, gazed into the black pupiled eye, and later sliced off deep pink fillets, taking a clean, raw hunk into my mouth, I felt close to my animal joy.

Centuries from now, if humans survive, they may look back on fishing as a barbaric blood sport gone the way of bear baiting and fox hunting. It may be perfectly acceptable to raise fish, chickens, and cattle on industrial farms, perhaps genetically engineered without pain-feeling nerve centers, or better, to synthesize their nutritious and delicious proteins in food factories. But to enjoy hooking and fighting a struggling fish—maybe even to let it go, so the torture could be repeated?—my God, what savagery!

Richard smiled and ate another piece of salmon. "There's no way we could exist without doing some harm. Even the vegetarian is a killer."

"What about vegan?" I asked.

"I'm not going there." Richard folded his arms tightly, as if refusing to eat his vegetables.

"Well, it's true," I said. "Agriculture does its damage." I told Richard about helping with the harvests in South Dakota, where I'd also seen rabbits, birds, and snakes chopped up by the combine. There's erosion and the deadly effects of fertilizers, pesticides, and herbicides. Worse yet, our fruits and vegetables are flown and trucked across the world on toxic fossil fuels that countless people fight and die over.

"Damn," Richard shook his head. But we also knew that even careful sportfishing led to some waste and destruction. "Ah, you do the best you can," Richard said and raised his hands like a referee. "We're all killers. At least with fishing you own up to it."

Our conversation moved from relationships with food to relationships with women. Richard had just turned sixty and he still enjoyed a good marriage with Carol, his wife of thirty years. At first Carol was frustrated with all the time he spent angling. So they started taking camping and fishing trips together.

"On those trips, fishing isn't the priority," Richard explained. "It's all about give and take and sharing time in a beautiful place." Richard's wisdom allowed that serious anglers would always want and need some time alone, but learning to balance fishing with the rest of life was important. "Maybe you'll find a woman that's as crazy about fishing as you are, but I doubt it," he said. "You just need to find a woman that likes fishing—or at least is okay with it."

"What about that new bank teller across the street?" I asked.

Richard laughed. "Does she like fishing?"

I withdrew cash the old-fashioned way and chatted with Haley, a perky bank teller with blue eyes and a frosted swirl of short blonde hair. She liked the outdoors, especially running, and we stepped out on a jogging date that ended nicely with a glass of chilled pinot gris and a brief kiss. She and I jogged together, ran a few road races, and even started the Portland Marathon together, but Haley steamed ahead and finished a half hour before I collapsed over the line. Haley was high energy. She loved to exercise, work extra days at the bank, shop, clean, and have occasional sex—her tan shoulders, small chest, and narrow muscled hips moving in rapid, almost convulsive spasms. And we had to keep it tidy, showering before and after, the drier always tumbling with a fresh set of sheets. Her Salem apartment was immaculate, her kitchen counters and stovetop gleamed like showroom store models. "I make a lot of salads," she said, slicing a tomato on a polished granite slab.

Haley said she also ate fish, so I planned to cook us a healthy dinner one Friday at my apartment in Monmouth. I caught a few trout at Detroit Lake that afternoon and had just set the cooler down on my kitchen floor when she pulled up. "Smells fishy in here," she said as her nose twitched.

"Probably my waders and jacket. I'll take them out back."

"So, did you catch anything?" she asked, kissing me lightly on the lips.

"Of course," I answered and smiled, popping the cooler and showing her five pretty ten-inch rainbows. Her face tightened.

"Bloody," she looked away.

Sensing Haley was put off by all the fishiness, I poured her a glass of pinot gris and set to chopping leaks and parsley, dropping them into a pan with bay leaves, peppercorns, salt, and an inch of water. As the paisley broth simmered, she went on to tell me about a manipulative supervisor, her coworker's wedding plans, and some policy changes at the bank. I listened then set the cleaned trout into the steamy pan and covered it, quickly turning to a marinated cucumber salad. "I can help with that," she said. And when I started to tell her about my day on the lake, she frowned, "It must be nice to have a day off."

When the fish came out of the pan, Haley asked, "Does it still have bones?" I showed her how the flesh easily slid off the spine and suggested she dapple it with a little mayonnaise and dill. She didn't like touching the trout but managed to fork up a translucent wedge, chewing and swallowing with a crooked smile. Haley ate her salad and some of her fish, but she clearly didn't savor it. When I held up my skeletal trout by the tail, her eyes went wide and then she screamed.

"It's okay. It's just Dash." The neighbor's cat peered in through the dark window. I pushed up the sash and Dash jumped in—the friendly gray tabby often stopped by for a bit of fish or turkey—and I set down my plate. Haley shuddered and went to the bathroom. When she came back to the couch, I could see she was tense.

"This place really does smell like fish," she said again. "So I have to ask you—why do you like fishing so much? I mean, isn't it boring just sitting there with your pole?"

"A jerk at one end of the line waiting for a jerk on the other end?" I tried to joke.

"I didn't mean that," she said. "I know it's your hobby."

"Well, I wasn't just sitting there. I walked around the lake casting spinners."

"And?" she arched her eyebrows in another question.

"I saw loons and eagles. The snow on the mountains—you know Detroit Lake—it's beautiful. And I did a lot of thinking."

"About me?" she interrupted.

"Sure. Of course. Hey, why don't I take you fishing up there on Sunday."

"I thought we were going shopping for wedding clothes. Don't you want to get some new pants?"

It was clear that Haley and I were different. She was squeamish around waders, fish, and cats, and she showed no interest in
angling. We listened to some music, and then she said she had to
go. When I returned from walking her to her car, Dash was on the
kitchen counter eating the rest of her fish.

"Not fishy enough," Richard said and chuckled when I told him
about Haley. It was true that every one of my serious girlfriends
liked fishing. Rain lummed down on the leaky roof of the studio,
and Richard set out a few pails to catch the drips. "What about
Morgan?" he asked. Morgan, one of the life-drawing models, had
just broken up with her boyfriend. I liked her. "But be careful,"
Richard added. "She's got a lotta drama in her life."

Morgan worked at a supermarket and took psychology classes
at Chemeketa Community College. She wanted to be a counselor.
Fleshy and wide-hipped with large breasts and wild brown hair that
sometimes smelled of cooking oil and cigarettes, Morgan liked to
eat, drink, smoke, cook, and play with her three cats. She rented a
house with another guy and girl and said they once got drunk and
had a threesome. "How do I apply?" I smiled. And when I told her
that I liked to fish she said, "Let's go."

Avoiding her family over Thanksgiving break—"I'm not going
near that mad house," she hissed—we fished and frolicked, starting on a drizzly afternoon catching stocked rainbows from Foster
Reservoir and cooking them at Morgan's house. Her place smelled
a little sour with dirty dishes glued to the counters and a mountain
of old mail spilling off the kitchen table. The cats eyed me warily
then slunk into the dark bedroom. Morgan wiped out a pan and

dropped in a stick of butter, telling me to chop some garlic. She put up brown rice, handed me a beer, and we cooked, drank, laughed, and ate fried trout down through the crispy fins and tails, moving to her bedroom for dessert.

We woke slowly with cats and coffee and then drove an hour west out of the foggy Willamette Valley over hilly pastures and rusty logging towns through a dense corridor of Douglas fir that opened to the sunny Pacific Ocean. At Depoe Bay we boarded a party boat, motored a couple miles off shore, and bounced tail-twisting jigs for rockfish and lingcod, the blue satin swells buttoned with small dark birds and the thrilling geyser of a gray whale. Morgan had been fishing with her father—"When he wasn't a goddamn drunk"—and she knew how to use a spinning rod and how to grab the four-pound black rockfish she swung over the rail onto the deck. "Nice job," I cheered. Morgan dropped the bleeding fish into the white pail, wiped her hands on her jeans, and touched my face. "Mmm, fishy," she sung softly, pulling me into a kiss.

We spent the night at a cheap inn over the water. Her round body moved slow and steady and wanted me everywhere. After, we lay back, smoking a couple of her cigarettes and drinking cheap bourbon from plastic cups as we watched *South Park* on TV. The next morning came even later, but by early afternoon we were below a campground on the Siletz River, casting bobbers and jigs for steelhead. Morgan was into it at first, targeting the green bubbly pools and dark ledges, but she soon grew tired and wanted to smoke a bowl to kill her hangover. I didn't like getting high and wading swift water, but I sat with her on a rock and we talked. Morgan asked about my mother. "My mother?" I smiled, hesitated, then told her how she once helped me release a shark I'd caught, and how she praised me when I carried home a few flounder for dinner. But my mother died when I was thirteen.

"I'm sorry," Morgan said.

"It was a long time ago," I said and shrugged. Morgan asked about my time in Japan and China, and I told her a few more stories.

"Wow. It's always fish, water, and women with you. That's weird."

"I never thought of it that way." I laughed.

"Do you drop women because you're afraid they are going to leave you or die or something?"

"I don't drop women. Things just change and we move on."

"You move on."

"I'm not possessive," I said, trying to explain myself. I'd heard these things before from girlfriends.

"You like the chase. You like to catch fish and eat them. And *then* let them go!" she laughed. "Then move on downriver, right?"

I didn't like the way this was going. "And what about you? You seem pretty free," I asked.

"Yeah. I'm free of charge," she answered with a smirk. Morgan had known a lot of lovers, men and women, but rather than letting go and moving on, her stories ended in cut lines, overturned boats, and drownings. "Shit," she said. "The last guy borrowed a ton of money from me, totaled his fucking car, spent two months in a hospital—of course, I was like there almost every day—then he gets out and moves in with his ex-wife." I listened. She told me about her alcoholic father, enabling mother, sister's dreams of becoming an actress, and a brother who was doing okay. "He likes to fish," she pulled her wool hat down over her ears. "You'd dig him. Fishing keeps him sane."

"I can understand that," I said. "Maybe we can all fish together."

"I'm cold," she said with a shiver, and we walked back to the car. I started the old Buick and cranked the heater. As we pulled off our waders and jackets, Morgan grinned: "Look at that big back seat.

But what's that stupid fish doing in there?" My brother's gift of the plaster striped bass was lying on the floor. I jammed it in the trunk, breaking off part of its tail. The car stereo no longer worked, but in ten minutes Morgan and I were naked on the blanketed vinyl, spinning our own music as a rivery, fishy steam filled the air and fogged the windows.

"Fish and Sex," I wrote on my notepad. Recovering after the long holiday, I sat at my desk and jotted down notes for an essay. I had always enjoyed literature where fishing became a metaphor for some great salvation or revelation earned through patient and mindful practice. There was the possibility of emotional healing in Hemingway's "Big Two-Hearted River" or the victory of respect and love for a fellow creature that fills Elizabeth Bishop's poem "The Fish." Norman Maclean's *A River Runs Through It* offered the beautiful story of fly fishing as way into nature and human understanding that ultimately expresses itself as spiritual grace. But at that moment I was angling more primitive currents.

Junior high boys joked about their "trouser trout" and a salty old Long Island fisherman once advised me, "Head before tail, boy," as he set another snapper on the cutting board, chuckling and winking at his double entendre, completely lost on me at fourteen. I would soon learn, however, that there was something inherently fishy about the sexual encounter.

In Aristophanes' *Lysistrata*, the war-weary women exclaim that they could suffer the loss of men but not the eels—"Surely you'd spare the eels?" With this in mind, Plutarch tells the mournful story of Isis searching for the remains of her slain Osiris. When she learns that his penis has been thrown in the Nile and eaten by eels, she makes those long and slippery fish sacred. In "L'anguilla," The Eel, Italian poet Eugenio Montale praises that "torch, lash, arrow of Love upon earth" that points "back to paradises of fertility." Shakespeare abounds with fishy vulgarisms, including Iago's implication that some ladies may "change the cod's head for the salmon's tail," that is, give up men for women, and Cleopatra likens seducing Antony to angling for "Tawny-finned fishes."

Collected in a stained file from years of reading were Yu Xuanji's ninth-century Chinese love poem to her man gone fishing, John Donne's "The Bait," Edmund Waller's "Ladies Angling," and Lorca's "brunette of Granada . . . who will not bite." I pushed through a sprawl of books to Herman Melville's *Typee*, lingering over chapter twenty-eight and the eroticized descriptions of the young American sailor, Tommo, and his island beauty, Fayaway, eating raw fish. With a reluctance known to many unversed lovers, Tommo admits something "disagreeable" about his first taste of raw fish, and I recalled teenage jokes about fishy smells and confessions from *Vagina Monologues*. But Tommo opens the fish, exposing the smooth, slippery pink walls, and finds them "remarkably tender," telling us that "after a few trials I positively began to relish them. . . ."

I considered the "Nurse Duckett" chapter in *Catch-22* when Yossarian claims, "My fish dream is a sex dream," disappointing the truly disturbed Army psychiatrist who tells him to find a "good hobby . . . Like fishing." And there was the trolling scene off the Oregon coast in Ken Kesey's *One Flew Over the Cuckoo's Nest*, where the topless Candy battles a salmon with the rod between her legs. Freud and Jung identify fish as phallic, but Richard Bunse draws women as salmon-curved mermaids, Yeats catches a "little silver trout" that becomes "a glimmering girl," Sandra

Alcosser offers a beautiful woman as "A Fish to Feed All Hunger," and Roseann Lloyd spreads it right out there with "Song of the Fisherman's Lover":

> Dip me from the water.
> Bite the gash. Say fish.
> Say woman.

Fish were phallic, yonic, beautiful, seductive, messy, delicious, full of sex, and all over my desk. I took a break and called Morgan, who sounded stoned and said my angle on fish and women was funny. We hung up, and I made myself a tuna salad sandwich.

Humans are pumped with salt water, but we can't live very long under the sea. Morgan and I dated off and on for a year, her drinking and smoking turning more and more reckless. We'd meet after work and she'd already smell of booze, her eyes red and tired. Lines deepened in her face and she coughed constantly. Reverend Bob said we should try to do healthy things together. I'd get Morgan out on a walk and she'd march right to a bar.

I didn't hear from her for a month, then she lost her job and called to ask if she could move in with me for a while. "That won't work," I said. "I'm sorry."

"Too fishy?" Richard scratched his shaggy white beard when I talked about Morgan. Women and fish could be a hard match. There's Magritte's somber, washed-up attempt at a fish and woman fusion in "Collective Invention," Dalí's cold elongation of a languid lady and a sail-finned mackerel in "Forgotten Horizon," and the surreal concentration of Picasso's "Seated Woman with Fish," where the lady's hat, breasts, and interlocked fingers all swim absurdly around her serious terrestrial gaze. I took more comfort in Ray Troll's zany illustration, "Embrace

Your Inner Fish," and Richard's simple renderings of happy women and their finny friends.

That night in life drawing I was happy to sit next to Chloë, a professor at the university, about my age, with whom I shared a committee. Chloë had straight coppery brown hair that swayed around her tan freckled shoulders. Her bright hazel eyes were flecked with green. She had just joined the drawing group and said she found it relaxing after a long day of teaching. "Me, too," I said, and we worked charcoal into thighs, backs, necks, and breasts. I had real trouble with faces and hands, and Chloë, a much better artist, helped me. At break we talked about books—she loved reading—and I even risked telling her about my essay connecting fish and human sexuality. "Fascinating," she said, describing a late night Japanese restaurant in Seattle that serves sushi on a reclining nude woman covered in plastic wrap. I made notes above the wonky figure on my sketch pad.

At the university honors-committee meeting that week I looked at and listened closely to Chloë. Her slender figure bloomed into a full bosom, and I loved her soft British accent and the way she deftly turned over a problem and solved it. After the meeting we had a cup of coffee and talked about her life growing up in England, and of course, I angled for fish. She remembered catching pollock as a little girl on a seaside holiday. "The sea is everywhere," she reminded me, describing fish and chips wrapped in newspaper, kippers, fried white bait, and smoked eels. "Really, eels?" My eyes widened.

Chloë described other fishy dishes like baked gray mullet with oranges and skate in black butter—"the capers and vinegar darken the butter, and you pour it right over the sautéed skate wings." Her favorite dish was kedgeree, marrying lightly smoked haddock and hard-boiled eggs with an Indian dance of coriander, red peppers, and curry folded into basmati rice. "My mother loved to make it," she said with a smile. "She'd cook up a huge batch that would last for days." Chloë talked about her family. Her mother had died young from alcoholism. "Such a waste," she said. When we stood up to leave I gave her a hug.

Later that week Chloë came by my office in the English department and gave me a tin of Fortnum & Mason's trout pâté.

"Thank you. But really, what's this for?"

"Just having someone to talk to. You were kind to ask all those questions and listen to me go on about home. I don't have much family here. And it's been hard to make friends with taking care of my kids and the job and all."

Chloë lived in the States for a decade, but there were problems. She and her London husband were getting a divorce, and she had just moved to the university town with her two boys, aged five and seven.

I felt closer to Chloë with every shared conversation. And when we hugged there was that unmistakable charge of an electric eel. The mind-body connection was there. Everything was there. When Reverend Bob saw us walking together in the park, he smiled, "You let me know if you need my services." I nodded, and Chloë blushed. "Let your hook always be cast," Ovid tells us in *The Art of Love*. "In a pool where you least expect it, there will be a fish."

Chloë and her sons stopped by my apartment one afternoon and were immediately smitten with the neighbor's cat, Dash, stroking his dark back and rubbing his white chin. Using an ultralight spinning rod and a rubber frog bass lure with the hooks removed, I sent Dash bounding and clawing madly down the hall and over the couch and table. The back door was open, and when Dash, frog in fangs, saw his chance, he dashed. I stepped out after the cat, adjusted the drag, and let him run across the empty parking lot—the boys squealing in delight. I was able to turn Dash and gain a couple yards, but his next run was too powerful and he broke free, slipping under the fence with the rubber frog. Everyone laughed.

"It's getting warmer now. Maybe I could take these boys for some real fishing?" I asked. And they cheered.

On a sunny June day after the school term ended, we packed gear and lunches, and the older boy, Zach, tried to help me lift the plaster striped bass from the trunk, but he dropped it into a dozen chalky pieces. Zach burst into tears. "Don't worry about it," I said, hugging him. "It's nothing. It's not real. We'll get some real bass today."

I drove to a little known pond out in the country. When the boys groaned over the quarter mile walk through the pasture I told them we were "fish walking," and they giggled, suddenly flopping on the ground like mudskippers. As we stepped over the grassy berm to the water, a family of glossy brown muskrats swam for the bank and disappeared into a burrow. The boys had no experience fishing, and I rigged up spinning rods with bobbers and small hooks, showing them how to bait with a worm and make a cast. The lesson proved challenging, but I took my time, remembering my father's patience. When Gethin, the youngest, launched his bobber a few feet from the bank it instantly disappeared. He felt the tug and resistance, yelled for his mother to look, and reeled in a hand-sized sunfish with a bright orange breast. There were many tangles, snags, complaints, snack breaks, and a few more satisfying sunfish until the boys had enough and walked down through the flower-studded meadow, picking up spent shotgun shells. Chloë and I sat close and watched them.

"Is that safe?" She grew concerned.

"Sure, the shells are empty. I used to collect them when I was a kid."

"You Americans and your guns," she frowned.

But we were, indeed, safe in this secluded meadow beside this little pond. "Make another cast and set the rod down on that stick. We'll have a beer," I urged.

"I think I might've caught something already."

"What?" I jumped up. She put her hand around my leg and laughed.

"Oh no, I'm supposed to say that. Women think I'm fish crazy. Too many fishing metaphors. Weird, right?"

"No," she said. "It's how you think."

The teeming waters of a summer pond, the lessons, frustrations, casts, hopes, and a hooked sunfish flopping on the grassy bank raise a child's delight and a man and woman's growing interest in each other. How wonderfully simple. If fishing brings us closer to the earth's essentials, can it also help us transcend that realm? Is angling an art that can actually lead to enlightenment, salvation, grace, and even love, as promised by some writers?

Chloë and I leaned back on the warm grass. "This is marvelous," she said, and I bent over to kiss her. Her lips returned the soft, warm gesture with something more, and we looked at each other and smiled. "This is a nice fishdate," she said.

Redwing blackbirds called from the cattails, a dragonfly alighted on the tip of my finger, then Chloë's rod bounced off the stick and slid toward the water. "Fish!" I yelled. She chased the rod down the bank, picked it up, and reeled. A big bass thrashed and swam.

"Fantastic," she cried. The boys saw the splashing and came running. The foggy green water burned gold as the bass flashed clear before us.

"I can really feel it," Chloë said and smiled back at me, reeling in her fish.

"Me, too," I said, even before I did.

Casting Off

"It's clear," my father said as we looked out over the water then turned into the potholed yard of Ralph's Fishing Station on Long Island's Mount Sinai Harbor. There were dinghies flipped over on cement blocks, runabouts, cabin cruisers, and barnacle-bottomed game boats on trailers and wooden racks. A speed boat spilled corroded parts out of its transom while an old sailboat, partly draped like a flapper after too much champagne, flashed bare oak above her waterline.

Spring 1973. People talked about Vietnam, Watergate, George Steinbrenner buying the New York Yankees, the amazing red azaleas outside our house, and a new TV show *Sanford and Son*, whose junkyard set reminded me of Ralph's. My father parked his yellow Chevy pickup near two men in greasy sweatshirts poking into an Evinrude outboard tilted in a water-filled barrel. A tall man walked up, handed one guy a spark plug, then yelled, "Damnit, Charley. What-da-hell you think ya' doing?" I jumped. It was my father's name. But he walked right past us and stood below a guy pulling some wires out of the wheelhouse of a propped-up lobster boat.

"Either get me dat six months or get dis piece-a-shit outta here."

"How'my gonna get your money if I can't fish? For Chrissakes, Ralph!"

21

"Well, get in the goddamn water then."

I was seven, and my father turned me away from the dispute. Rancid fish wafted from blue barrels on a flatbed truck stacked with wooden lobster pots. Men were drinking canned beer and smoking cigarettes. Among them stood a short, stocky guy in khaki trousers and a flannel shirt.

"Hey Herbie," my father greeted him. "What's going on?"

"Getting my skiff outta hock. Didn't catch many muskrats this winter."

"No, hah? You working?"

"Here and there," Herbie said. "I'd rather be fishing."

My father introduced me to Herbie Clark, a union laborer he knew from work. The man was older than my father, with a high-tide hairline, reddish face, and bulbous nose, but his eyes were warm, and he asked if I liked fishing. "Yes," I said, though I'd never really been.

The men talked construction. My father was a crane operator, and Long Island was building, but there were highs and lows, good jobs and bad. Such things bored me and I wandered behind a wind-torn blue building, admiring a quiver of rods leaning against a fence. Squatting to touch the reels, I looked up and screamed. A huge pig bore down on me, his snout and jaws smeared red. My father and Herbie were right there. "That's Arnold," Herbie laughed. The boar sniffed me, snorted, and trotted off.

"He killed something," I gasped.

"No," Herbie laughed some more. "They gave 'im some spaghetti and meatballs. He loves Italian food."

Ralph finished chewing out the lobsterman and walked over to us, his face softening in concern. "Everything okay?"

"Arnold scared the boy, that's all," Herbie said.

"He's a big pig," Ralph nodded. "Ate a whole bucket of flounda d'udder day." Ralph offered the men cigarettes and lit one for himself.

"The boy wants to do some fishing," my father said. "Can you help us out? I don't know nothin' about it."

"Yeah, d'er gettin some flounda." Ralph smiled at me. "Fishing's a lotta fun. You wanna ren a boat, Charley?"

"Sure. It'll be me, the boy, and his friend."

"Okay," Ralph said. "High tide's at nine tomorrow. Come over round six-thirty. We'll set you up."

"From fish-shape Paumanok where I was born," wrote the Long Island bard Walt Whitman. But I was born into an Island family that did not fish. My father grew up in Port Jefferson, near where we lived, and he knew a bit about boats and motors but never had any interest in catching a fish. My mother grew up in Queens. "Your grandfather liked to fish," she told me. Aunt Lillian, my mother's older sister, wrung a dish rag and smirked, "Yeah, he caught things all right." I would later learn that my late grandfather was a philanderer, but the daughters had made peace with him in the last years. Lil lived with us in our cedar shingled Cape Cod on Central Avenue and did a lot of the cooking.

"Yes, yes. He liked to fish," Lil said and surrendered a smile. "He'd dump 'em in the sink. What a mess. But he cleaned 'em and I cooked 'em." I was too young to remember my grandfather as anything more than a red sweater rowing off into the fog. A couple of his varnished wooden rods and corroded Penn reels hung in the garage.

We ate fish at least once a week, almost always on Fridays, and I liked going with my mother and Aunt Lil to Wally Brown's Fish Market on East Main Street in Port Jefferson. Wally and his wife, Gladys, smiled and nodded when I named the characters on ice.

They let me walk behind the counter and peer into the bubbling lobster tank or examine the whole cod and striped bass before they were filleted. Wally had no right hand, but his flippered forearm pointed encouragingly. I poked eyeballs, touched skin, stroked fins, and smelled on my hands a salty, mucusy something that was both familiar and strange. I asked Wally questions then just listened to the iced silence of the fish, dreaming into their watery world.

I loved fish, dead and alive, managed a few home aquariums, sat glued to every episode of *Jacques Cousteau*, and poured over books about fish, beginning with *Fish Do the Strangest Things*, which my aunt read to me over and over. I had been to the New York Aquarium and The American Museum of Natural History in Manhattan, where my mother put a time limit on how long we could stay in the Hall of Ocean Life—the ninety-four-foot blue whale breaching above the dazzling walls of life-size full color fish. But aside from my father's half-hearted attempt at letting me soak a worm in a fuzzy duck pond while he listened to the Mets on his truck radio, no one had really taken me fishing.

The next morning we woke in the chilly dark, picked up my friend Joey, then drove the four miles to Mount Sinai Harbor. There were very few cars, raccoons crossed in our headlights, and it felt—as it still does, driving early to fish—like having more of the world to yourself.

The flounder were waking up in the shallow April waters, and good weekend weather meant fish and fishermen would be on the move. People milled around Ralph's Fishing Station drinking coffee from white Styrofoam cups, listening to radio weather, smoking cigarettes, and talking quietly. There was the clang of buckets and rods and snarly boat engines starting. Standing alone smoking a pipe was a wildly bearded old man with a strange mole centered on his forehead under a dirty white yachtsman's cap. "Good morning, Captain," my father greeted, holding open the rattley door as I pushed through with my grandfather's fishing pole, spearing Joey in the back. Ralph was busy taking orders for sandworms, filling out rental cards, making change. It was all cash over the counter. Rigs, sinkers, line, bait, gas. Ralph scratched his head and poked the cash register while another puffy faced man counted sandworms into rectangular white boxes.

In no rush to get started, my father carried a cup of coffee out to Captain, had a smoke with him, and then came back in the store. "Old Captain was in World War I," my father said. "On a ship made right in Port Jefferson." I looked out the window and saw the grizzled man standing alone. We shuffled forward to the counter. "Okay, Charley. We got ya boat," Ralph said. "A few of dese spreader rigs heer, some two-ounce sinkas. A couple dozen wirms should do. Barbara'll set you up on the dock. Just anchor outside the channel. Fish right on the bottom through the tide, okay?" My father nodded.

Down on the dock, Ralph's wife, Barbara, was arguing with a group talking in Spanish. "Six is duh limit," she commanded in a loud voice. "Three, four, five, six. Dat's it. You'll need another boat." She saw us and walked up the dock followed by two large dogs. "Hi Charley. Is dis your crew? Gonna get some flounda, boys?" She tipped her chin toward the people rocking the green skiff. "Puerto Ricans. What are ya gonna do? Dey love to fish."

Even early in the morning, Barbara had a bright, smooth face, her movements swift and strong like a Diana of the docks as she handed us three life jackets and then bent to pet one of her dogs.

She looked at my old blistered fishing pole and shook her head, "Sorry, honey. These'll work betta for you." Three white fiberglass rods stood against the red sign for gas. "You want me to start it, Charley?"

"I got it, Barb. Thanks." My father smiled. She pointed down the dock. "Boat numbah five. Have fun."

My father held the boat steady while Joey and I stepped in and sat down on the wooden seats. I was a plump child, but I felt magically light in the boat, like the world was suddenly more supportive. The rental was a fourteen-foot green lapstreak skiff with a six-horse Johnson outboard. My father was good with engines. He vented the gas tank, squeezed the ball on the fuel line, opened the choke, and pulled the starter rope twice. It popped. He pushed the choke halfway in, pulled again, and it started. After letting it warm up for a few minutes, he reached over and untied the bow line from the cleat. "Cast off," he urged with a gesture, and Joey and I pushed the boat from the dock.

Like any beginner, my father just followed the others. About half a mile from Ralph's in the vicinity of a couple small boats, he asked Joey and me, "Well, you wanna try it here?" What did we know? He turned off the engine and told me to drop anchor. But by the time I had untangled the mess of rope and heaved the heavy iron over the bow, we had drifted deep into the channel. My father began rigging the rods, Joey's first, tying on a double-hooked spreader rig with square knot and burning off the excess with his lit cigarette.

Poking through the seaweed-packed bait box, my father recoiled with an, "Ouch." Then, like a snake wrangler on Mutual of Omaha's *Wild Kingdom*, a favorite Sunday evening television program, he grasped a sandworm firmly behind the head and held it up, fangs flashing. "Damn," he said. "This worm means business." But this was bait, so he pushed a hook through its skin. Blue blood squirted and the worm writhed and twisted. Right from the beginning I would recognize that there was pain connected to fishing. A medic attached to an aid station during the Korean War, my father was not squeamish, but I could see he was not enjoying himself.

"You crucified him," Joey wailed.

"Take it easy, Joey," my father said and frowned, always skeptical of high drama. "You wanna catch a fish, right?"

My father knew enough about reels to understand the clutch and drag and how to avoid backlash—some of the same principles applied to crane operating—and he gave us simple instructions. Joey flipped the clutch and sent the clumsy rig down to the bottom, the reel spooling on into a bird's nest of green line. "You gotta keep your thumb on the spool," my father repeated. "Stop when you feel it hit bottom."

"How do I know it's the bottom?"

"You feel it, I guess. Okay, just hold on. Let me get this other one going."

Just as my father started helping me, Joey's rod jumped. "I got one! I got one," he shouted, cranking the reel to a tangled halt. "It's stuck."

"Okay, relax." My father grabbed the line and started hand hauling. "Oh yeah, you got something on here." Up from the dark water came a bizarre creature, about a foot long, with bright calico wings, leggy forefins, and a horned and armored face—a sea robin. My father grabbed it, punching a spine through his palm. "Goddamn it," he yelled. More pain. "Hand me that rag." The big-headed fish emitted a rather sweet bark, like a distressed underwater puppy, its green eyes shining. Getting a hook out of the fish's mouth was another challenge. Not thinking to bring one of his fifty pairs of pliers, my father wriggled and twisted the hook around the barking mouth until it wore a hole big enough to back out the barb. "Can we keep him?" I asked. "He's not a flounder," my father said and threw him over.

By the time we got Joey's line untangled, which required cutting and completely rerigging, the tide flooded and several boats anchored just outside the channel were catching fish. "They caught one," I reported. "She's got one," Joey noted. "He's got another one," I complained. Then my rod bent and I yelled, "Got one!" But it was just the bottom. Another strong pull and the line broke. I reeled in and my father studied the pigtails where his square knot easily snapped. "What the hell?" he puzzled.

Joey caught a second sea robin, and my father raised two small crabs. A couple boats went by, and one guy shouted, "You're in the channel." We all looked at each other, figured something must be wrong, undertook the laborious task of pulling up the anchor, and re-established ourselves in shallower water.

"It feels mushy down there," Joey said. Almost immediately I felt the tap of life. Something was down there. The thrill of fishing is charged by the knowledge that something desirable lies unseen in the darkness below. But it's not enough to know it's there. You've got to hold it. My father and Joey also had bites but couldn't hook anything. We were, of course, using whole, delicately pierced sandworms—an expensive and relatively safe form of feeding marine fauna. Retrieving our bare hooks and mud smeared sinkers, we exclaimed, "Stole the bait," and, "He cleaned me," having at least mastered the parlance of bait fishing failure.

Finally, my father hooked one. "Here we go." His rod bent and pulsed, he put his cigarette in his mouth and reeled in a genuine winter flounder, slapping it down on the floorboards of the skiff. My father grabbed the fish with the rag, its back a dark brown and its creamy white belly shining beneath a haze of fine mud, unhooked it, and dropped it into a galvanized bucket I had filled with seawater.

Why are they called flounder? They are the steadiest of fish: wide-beamed and well-grounded. This fellow mellowed on the bottom of the bucket, frowning through a thick-lipped sideways mouth, his topside frog eyes seemingly unperturbed.

"Look at those weird eyes," Joey said.

"They evolved to live on the bottom," I told him. My books, museum exhibits, and Channel Thirteen's programming on science and nature convinced me at a young age that evolution was the way creatures came to be, despite my mother's cocked eyebrow, "You don't believe we came from monkeys, do you?" or my father's, "What about Adam and Eve and Noah's Ark?"

My father handed around bananas, poured hot chocolate, monkeyed with a transistor radio, looked at his watch—"Ah, what the hell"—and cracked a beer. "You're missing Sunday school today," he smiled at me.

"I have to go to mass later," Joey groaned.

"Do you like church?" my father asked Joey.

"It's okay." Joey slumped.

"I hate Sunday school," I declared.

"Well, you're back next week," my father turned serious.

Sunday school was boring and tedious. I believed in God, though seeing Charlton Heston in *The Ten Commandments* was more awe inspiring than anything experienced or heard in the basement of our church. The greatest miracles were those of ever-changing, ever-surprising nature. Sometimes I brought my worn copy of *Fish Do the Strangest Things* to Sunday school and tried to explain that flounders are born with eyes on each side of their heads, and their left eye migrates around to help the other see up from the bottom. I wanted people to know about the little male angler fish that attaches itself to the big female, becoming part of her body and bloodstream. "And the two will become one flesh," the classroom helper quoted some scripture, and the head teacher cut her off, saying, "That's something different." But it wasn't. Nor could any Bible story top the miraculous journey of the salmon, wagging the wide ocean for five years and returning to the little pebbly stream of its birth, or Long Island eels zigzaging down to the Sargasso Sea to join other eels from all over the Atlantic in a slimy love fest. And there were amazing living fossils, such as sturgeon, sharks, rays, and the famous coelacanth, thought to be extinct until one came up in a net off South Africa. Long before animals walked the earth, the seas teemed with fish. And when I evangelized that the "whale" in the Jonah story must have been a great white shark and that Jonah was definitely not okay after the three days in its belly, the Sunday school teacher told me to "Pay attention!" and "Be brown!" while we crayoned a huge banner depicting Noah's ridiculous ark.

The church service upstairs was worse with dull directions and grand promises. The world outside promised plenty, I thought, breaching the sanctuary doors and graduating into the firm conviction that true worship was a morning of fishing. Sometimes I even kept the money my mother gave me for the offering plate. A dollar sealed in a blue envelope had better boats to build.

We had more bites, seaweed, tangles, hooks in our clothing, smears of sandworm blood mixed with ham and cheese sandwiches, cookies, more cookies—"I think you've had enough," my father said as he pinched his brows and flicked his cigarette over the side where it hissed and floated on the gray surface. Joey swung a hand-sized flatfish in my face. He and my father each caught a couple more, but I didn't land a thing. "I don't know what's wrong with me," I said. The tide began to ebb, our boat swung in the opposite direction, and the action diminished. My father and Joey talked on and on about the Mets—they had a great bullpen—while I gazed down into the dark stadium below, deep in my desire for another game.

Snappers

By midsummer, the New York Mets were in last place in the National League East, Joey had moved to Brooklyn with his family, our garden tomatoes were ripening, and I received a Zebco spinning outfit for my eighth birthday, practicing on the lawn and driveway with a chewed-up sinker the cats loved to chase. Zebco was originally the Zero Hour Bomb Company, which held a patent on an electrical time bomb but found making simple spinning reels more profitable. The company advertised the reel's easy use at sporting shows by having a trained chimpanzee execute near perfect casts, one after another. I put sinkers in the trees, on our roof, and through the tool shed window. "Evolution, hah?" my father said and rubbed the top of my head.

"The paper says the snappers are running," my mother looked up from the kitchen table, her soft blonde curls pulled back in a blue hair band, an icy cocktail on a paper napkin beside her. She smiled, tilting her head toward my father drinking a beer and watching the Mets. She would sometimes tussle my father's neatly parted short brown hair, telling him, "Don't be such a square." Today she made a kissing gesture across the room. "Okay, okay," his eyes left the screen for a moment. "The Mets are traveling tomorrow. We'll try for some snappers."

Although many more men than women enjoy fishing, and the angling tradition favors fathers and sons, it was my mother who made me a complete angler. In a way completely different from any boy or man, she would ask me questions about my passion. "What is your favorite fish? What do you use for bait? Do those fish fight hard?" And when I answered with bursting enthusiasm, she looked into my eyes and smiled.

The great Russian angler and author Sergei Aksakov lamented that his mother hated fishing and, worrying over her son's obsession with the sport, often forbade him from angling. My mother never fished with me, but she always encouraged me to go. Over the years she inquired earnestly about new rods and reels or the lures and hooks I fondled on the kitchen table; and she stiffened in humorous mock alarm when Aunt Lil scolded, "Get those damn hooks off the dinner table. You wanna choke us to death?" Once my mother carefully picked a Rooster Tail spinner from the top shelf of my tackle box, asking, "What would you catch with this?" And when I told her trout, she nodded, holding the lure up to the light, her soft, rounded face squeezing gently in reflection. "It's so pretty." She swung it to her ear. "I need some earrings like this." She knew little about fishing but registered my discourse as significant and open to creative association. She bought me the wrong hooks and impossible lures for tarpon and trevally that did not exist in our waters and suggested grapes for flounder bait—"They might really like grapes," her eyes wide open to the various fruits of temptation. I rudely corrected her and stomped off in frustration, but my taste for the holistic, aesthetic, and quirky was taking shape on the vine; my flinty boy knowledge and brutal energies for the chase would soften and ripen under the warm, sensitive gaze of this woman.

"Saw a few nice snappers at the pub last night," Herbie said as he lifted his amber tilted glass. "But they didn't seem interested." He and my father sat on chairs in the garage.

"Maybe your bait's no good," my father said, popping another beer.

"Too soft to stay on the hook," Herbie shook his head and laughed. I didn't know what they were talking about. The word "snapper" has many meanings in our language, and it names many fish around the world. For most Long Islanders, snappers are young bluefish, but I had never caught one. "Sweet young blues," Herbie sang, opening his hands to an estimated size of nine inches. "And damn tasty," he grinned once more, winking at my father.

Long Island reached right into a summer swarm of blues. Adult bluefish up to eighteen pounds—voracious, stout-toothed predators, long and narrow, that travel in schools of like-size thousands—followed the East Coast from Nova Scotia to Argentina, migrating south in winter and entering Long Island Sound in early summer. Bluefish lay eggs in the ocean, near the edge of the continental shelf, and even the larvae have well-developed teeth. It's a fish born to bite, and the maturing snappers chomp their way into the harbors and bays, feasting on smaller fish, baby lobsters, shrimp, and anything else they can swallow.

My father did not like fishing, but he was usually willing to take me. Herbie told us to meet him over at Ralph's Fishing Station the next evening. The long summer had thinned out the boatyard, but the store and docks were in steady swing. Sunburned and dark tanned men carried coolers full of steel gray bluefish and coppery porgies. Occasionally a huge striped bass was brought up to the scale, its gaping mouth and golden eye entrancing the crowd.

The air was hot and sticky. Herbie and Ralph sat on a bench, drinking beer, red-faced and loud. "Half in the bag," my father would later say. Ralph grumbled over a health inspector who wrote a citation after finding Arnold the pig sleeping in the kitchen. Arnold had a splash of blue paint across his back from another mis-adventure and had reportedly rummaged through a woman's purse and eaten her makeup. "You missed the tide," Ralph said. "Try over at Stony Brook tomorrow. It's better there."

"Sorry, Charley," Herbie said and rubbed his face, looking a bit embarrassed for being drunk and of no help. Quick to hook a dis-traction, Herbie pointed his flushed nose at a large boat still racked in the yard. "Look at that shit." A woman wearing only a long base-ball shirt emerged from the cabin, and I followed the length of her chocolaty legs and the bounce of her breasts. "I told you she was shacked-up with him in there," Herbie shook his head.

"How 'bout some rent, sweetie?" Ralph yelled out, and the woman flipped him off.

My father steered me into the store.

Fish photos, some cracked and faded, decorated the walls like cave paintings. Umbrella rigs for bluefish, crab traps, and killie pots hung from the ceiling; wall racks glowed with big red bass plugs, bright yellow and green bucktail jigs, and an array of hooks, swivels, sinkers, and lines. A pimply teenage girl working the counter and eating fries sold us long-shanked snelled hooks, mooring-sized bobbers, and a package of frozen silvery minnows called "shiners." The girl handed us a tide calendar and pointed to the times for low and high tide. From a briny back room humming with refrigerator compressors emerged Old Captain. "Fried snapper, fried snapper," he muttered. "You gotta get those snappers and fry 'em up, right Ralph?"

"Right, Captain," she answered, rolling her eyes. "Ralph's outside."

"Fried snapper, boys," he kept saying, leaning to port and shuffling out the front door.

"Why doesn't someone take him fishing?" my father asked.

"All his fishing friends are dead," the girl said.

"Or drunk," my father glowered, and we walked out.

On Friday night, my father came home from work in his greasy overalls, set his lunch box and a ninety-nine-cent six pack of Schmitz beer on the kitchen table, kissed my mother, pressed a cold beer bottle to the back of my neck, and said, "Okay, so we're going fishing tonight."

"But the Mets are playing the Cardinals," I said.

"That's okay," he said and smiled. "Let's get those snappers." He twisted the cap off the bottle and gave me a sip.

My mother and Aunt Lil had arranged an early and simple supper of salad topped with hardboiled eggs and tuna fish. We always ate at an oval wooden table in the kitchen, always covered in a plastic tablecloth printed in some bright geometric pattern. I hurried my father along, and he drove us to Stony Brook Harbor, parking the Chevy pickup head-on toward the narrows, where many people were casting from the bulkhead railing. We set up my Zebco with a long hook and a big red-and-white bobber. The shiners had thawed in the fridge, and my father hooked one through the tail.

"They'll pull it right off like that," a woman next to us barked. "Hook it through the eyes."

My father smiled and drove the barbed point right though the sockets.

"Come on, Dad," I urged.

"Relax. They ain't here yet," the woman leaned over and spat.

I was fired up. Pushing the button on the reel, I whipped it forward and cast right across the woman's line. "Sorry," my father said, squashing out his cigarette, taking my Zebco, lifting the line over her rod, and retrieving. The woman frowned, perhaps fearing a long night of fishing next to us. My next cast was straight, but the shiner flew off the hook and into the pink mouth of a herring gull. My third cast was okay, though within seconds the bobber drifted into the pilings below. "Cast up-current," advised a man to our right. He had long sideburns, smoked a pipe, and wore a button-down blue shirt and dungaree shorts. "If you cast up with the current, your bait will have more time in the strike zone."

"Thanks a lot," my father touched his blue Mets cap, leaning in close to me and whispering, "I think I dug this guy's cesspool."

The tide rolled in, and I watched my bobber with devotion. Then from down the dock, we heard, "Hey, nice one. Okay. Here we go." People at the east end were swinging snappers over the railing, and the action was heading our way. Gulls gathered, crying and dipping, voices grew louder and happier, and then the little bobber of the man next to us went down. Pipe in mouth, he reeled in a dime-bright ten-inch snapper. The woman to our left also had one, and people all down the rail were into fish. It was as if the fish had passed over me completely. "Pay attention," my father coached. "You'll get one." I beamed on my bobber until it knocked against the barnacled piling. When I reeled it in, the bait was gone. "Damnit, Dad," I said accusatively.

"Hey, watch your mouth," he scolded, threading on another big shiner. I cast, watched, and when the bobber blinked underwater, I yelled, "Got one," reeling frantically to find another bare hook. "Damn shit," I cried.

"I'm warning you," my father said. "If you can't behave yourself we're going home."

The man to our right had caught a couple more, slipping them into a red lunch cooler. He came over and looked at my hook. "I'd try a smaller hook," he said.

"They're snapper hooks," my father shrugged. "That's all we got."

"May I?" His eyebrows fluttered, and he produced a pair of clippers, snipped off the long shanked impaler and its heavy snell, pulled out a little packet of hooks—Eagle Claw, size six—and tied one on with a knot I had never seen. He pushed the hook right through the gill plates of a small shiner. "I find it holds better there." He also snapped off my huge bobber and put on one of his smaller floats. "It might be a little harder to cast, but the fish won't feel it. Just flip it up-current. I'll stay out of your way."

"How much do I owe you?" my father asked.

"Nothing," the man smiled. "You did a nice job on that cesspool."

"Aha, okay. You're the professor, right? I remember." The two men laughed. "How about a beer then?" my father offered.

"Okay. Sounds good," the professor said.

My father got two beers from the truck, and the men began talking about drainage and sand. Conversation over a beer about construction, sports, or fishing seemed to bring together men from very different backgrounds. I made my best cast of the evening, and in seconds the bobber went down. I started reeling, the rod dancing with a fighting fish I could really feel. Wild with excitement, I swung the snapper over the railing and into the grill of the woman's car. The men were laughing, the woman smiled. I leapt on the fish like a cat. My father brought the galvanized bucket from the truck and filled it with water. I picked up the snapper—smooth and soft—and dropped it into the bucket, watching it circle frantically.

It was a beautiful silvery fish with a slate back and aquamarines shimmering through its milky flanks. I would add four more to the bucket that night, constantly looking at them, inspecting their toothy mouths, each fish stiffening in death with flat or flared red gills. They were so different than the flounder that clung to the bottom of the bucket and lived for hours. Snappers swam madly and expired quickly. "Like some people," my father psychologized when I shared my observation.

I felt a strange blend of sadness and delight—sad that these fish were dying and delighted that they were mine—and this would remain an emotional paradox throughout my life as an angler who kills and eats and, in that sense, fully possesses the fish he loves. As Santiago vows in *The Old Man and the Sea*: "Fish, I love you and respect you very much. But I will kill you . . . ." Rather than a kind of cognitive dissonance, though some animal-rights moralists may see it that way, I came to understand this paradox as a truth about what it means to be human and a predator. The killing of fish both upsets and thrills me. When the bobber went down again, I thrilled beyond the moon, which had just risen in the east.

On the far side of the narrows something ripped and splashed across the surface. "Bunker," the professor said. "They're being chased." People looked and pointed at the rusty colored school, and one man pulled out a surfcasting rod and tried to reach them. The bunker, an Atlantic menhaden of the herring and shad clan, teemed in our coastal waters, feeding on plankton and relentlessly being pursued and eaten by bluefish and striped bass. Too oily and bony for most American palates, bunker are not sought by anglers except as bait and indicators of feeding gamefish. The big bluefish had returned ravenous from their ocean breeding grounds, flashing like underwater lightning, attacking and biting the juicy bunker as they leapt into the unsustaining air.

The bunker and blues quickly vanished, the snappers stopped biting, and the woman next to us packed up and went home, leaving a small bag of trash that my father threw into a bin twenty feet away. The professor stowed his gear in the back of his Honda. "Japanese, hah?" My father noted the car and asked about the gas mileage.

"I think that's the direction we're heading, Charley."

"I'm afraid so," said my father, glancing back at his beloved gas-guzzling Chevy.

The professor showed me the fisherman's knot. "Okay, you try it," he handed me the line. After a couple times, I got it. My father and I studied the neat barrels stacked in the fastening. "That won't weaken your line like a square knot," the professor said, and my father nodded, thinking crane cables and splices. A teacher's lesson had never felt so enjoyable. The professor shook our hands, told me I was "a real angler," and hoped we'd see each other again soon.

As we loaded the pickup under the dock lights, teenagers were parking, Rolling Stones blaring from open doors and windows. I heard the clink of beer bottles and girls' voices. It was still very warm. Some of the girls wore revealing tops. I stared and felt the strange desire to see more. A girl in cutoff jeans and a halter top walked up to a couple of guys near the rail. "Catch anything?" she asked.

"Lotta snappers, honey," one man said, pulling a towel off his bucket.

"Wow," she smiled.

These early fishing experiences shaped and intensified my sense of what it meant to be alive. There was Old Captain and his fading, confused desire to fry a few more snappers; the vitality of the men and women, talking and laughing, catching joy and supper from the teeming July waters; and the fish, so wild with eating and being eaten. I thought of the professor's kind and wise administrations and the sexy girl walking through the music to the water's edge with her, "Wow." I don't know how many of those people are still alive. Like the snappers and blues, we were all just living up our summer.

As we drove home, my father caught the end of the game on the radio. Tom Seaver pitched the Mets to a win. When we pulled into our driveway, my mother and Aunt Lil came outside. They had been to the movies and wore bright summer dresses that seemed to bloom into open petals across their chests.

"Well?" they asked.

"We caught some nice fish," I said, showing them the bucket of little snappers.

"That's wonderful," my mother said. "We'll have them tomorrow. You boys gonna clean them?" My father reached an arm around my mother, but she giggled and spun away—"Not with those fishy hands"—then swung back for a kiss anyway.

Worn out but happy, my father and I cleaned my five snappers on the picnic table under the buggy flood light, running the garden hose, swatting mosquitoes, talking about the evening. Our cat, Tommy, joined us, and we tossed him some of the leftover shiners.

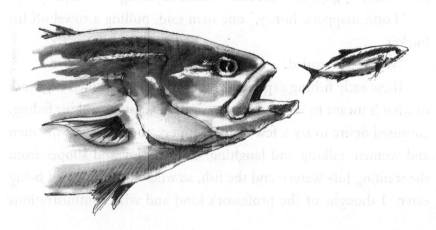

The moon was as bright as the pale flanks of the little fish, slipped into a square Tupperware to be fried in butter at noon the next day, the small sparkle of heads and guts turned into the garden with a spade.

the moon was as bright as the pail. Hunks of the little bait, slipped into a square Tupperware to be fried in butter at noon the next day, the small sparkle of beads and guts turned into the garden with a

Tickle Trout

"**H**e's desperate to fish on Saturday," my mother said to my father as he dug through the newspaper for game times.

My father showered after work and put on a pair of plaid polyester shorts and a clean white T-shirt, the tattoo on his forearm now the blurred blue phantom of a drunken night after basic training in the Army. School started in September, and the Mets were three games out of first place. "Come on, Marion. Just a few more games. 'Ya gotta believe,'" he'd plead, echoing relief pitcher Tug McGraw's rallying cry.

Still, he took me fishing, listening to games on the truck radio while I landed more snappers. One night at dinner he asked if we should take Old Captain fishing. "Okay," I hesitated, not sure how much fun that would be. But when my father stopped by Ralph's, where Captain kept a small room, they said he had passed away. "He's dead?" I asked in disbelief, and my father nodded. I remembered Old Captain lunting around the boatyard, muttering about fish and storms. That fall I drew a picture of him—yachtsman's cap, forehead mole, beard, and pipe—for my second grade memory project. But instead of legs, I crayoned the smooth gray body of a fish with a tail, something like the first vertebrates that came ashore in the Devonian period. One boy laughed and said he was a mermaid and I wanted to kiss him. I punched the kid in the face, and my mother had to come up to school. "It's hard for him," I heard her say to my teacher. "He misses his fishing."

The Mets made it to the World Series but lost to the Oakland A's, my parents worried over rocketing fuel prices, and I survived winter by devouring catalogs and more fishing books. In the spring of 1974, my father rented another boat at Ralph's, and we hooked flounder after flounder, as if the whole harbor were paved with fish. That summer, when I turned nine, we also started catching sea robins, bergalls, porgies, seabass, and blackfish off the local beaches, jetties, and docks. My father knew the crane crews unloading gravel barges at Gotham Stone in Port Jefferson, and they'd let me drop baited lines off their gravely bulkhead, where I'd pull in small fish and eels, wiping my hands on a pair of cut-off corduroy shorts that Aunt Lil said stunk up the wash. Herbie introduced me to the abundance of sunfish in local ponds, and my eccentric Uncle Jack, who knew even less about fishing than my father, took me to Lake Ronkonkoma, insisting that bacon and dough balls on red spray-painted hooks were the way to go. I served this neon deli special to the edge of a weed bed and miraculously hooked a chunky largemouth bass, its powerful black-belted body and belladonna eyes coming out of the water like a celebrity. Fishing books, catalogs, calendars, and ads for beer and whisky paid great attention to bass and trout. They were the freshwater stars I wanted to catch.

"We catch trout," my third grade friend Arthur Wakoski told me. "Maybe you can come with us." Arthur came from a fishing and hunting family. His father was a plumber, his mother a high-school teacher. Their house was dank and odorous with a huge algae-veiled 80-gallon aquarium stocked with sunfish, bass, and a young pickerel that was eating his way toward solitude. Splotchy English setters had the run of the place; guns, antlers, and mounted gamebirds sprung from the walls. And walking into Arthur's garage was like wading into a ransacked sporting-goods store—rods and tackle in wild profusion, stacks of decoys, coolers, nets, boots, boxes of ammunition. Through Arthur, I was introduced to the open-faced spinning reel, the importance of light line, split-shot sinkers, and seductive lures. There were fly rods in Arthur's garage, but those were his father's, and we were not to touch.

The trout season in New York State opened on April first. Mr. Wakoski was taking Arthur and me fishing at Lower Yapank Lake, a millpond on Long Island's Carmans River. I was nine years old on opening day in 1975. It was a Tuesday, and Mr. Wakoski took a day off work. My mother gave me permission to skip school.

The Wakoskis picked me up before dawn in their Chevy Blazer with a ten-foot square-bowed jon boat sticking out the back. Mr. W was a big man prone to flatulence, Arthur was chubby, and I was fat, and we all sat up close in the front seat. "Do you think trout is the most important fish in America?" I asked Mr. W.

"That's a stupid question," he said.

"I thought maybe the bass is the most famous. I don't know if that would include the striped bass. I was talking about the largemouth bass. But everyone seems to love the trout. We don't have salmon. What kind of trout will we catch today?"

"Tickle trout," Mr. W said, staring into the headlit morning.

"I've never heard of it."

"Oh, yeah. They raise them in special hatcheries. And if you hook one and get it alongside the boat, you need to reach down and tickle it."

We arrived at Yapank Lake just as it was getting light, parking below a creepy Victorian mansion with one cracked window aglow.

A man and a boy my age were casting from the bank, and I walked over and asked if they had caught any tickle trout. "What?" the boy laughed. The man just ignored me and kept casting.

Arthur and I helped pull the jon boat from the back of the Blazer and slide it partway into the lake. Jon boats were popular with fishermen and waterfowlers on Long Island. Flat bottomed, square ended, and low to the water, they were convenient and stable in calm lakes and bays. "Cast off," I cried, our awkward weight suspended like a magic carpet over the dark water. I started asking questions about the depth and temperature of the lake, and Mr. W shushed me. He handled boats much more quietly and gently than my father. Rowing a couple hundred feet, he eased down the mushroom anchor and silently handed us rods that had already been set up with small snap swivels and Mepp's spinners.

Many people had lined the bank and the culvert around the spillway. Mr. W whispered, "The fish like to hold here. It reminds them of the hatchery." Folks were casting lures and baited hooks hanging from bobbers. Arthur said little, he just started casting. Cars with people going to work whizzed toward the expressway on Yapank Road. One boy swung back to cast and hooked a passing sedan. The rod shot out of his hands and bounced down the pavement, parts flying off before we saw the deep red brake lights and heard angry voices. I recognized that the boat gave us an advantage over those people on the bank. We could approach from the deeper water and had much more space to cast. There were no branches above, no sunken shopping carts below. I heard some splashes and then started seeing fish rise. Mr. W lit a cigarette, opened his Thermos, poured a cup of coffee, farted, and started casting. Someone on the shore caught a fish, then someone else was into one. Long silvery trout were swung up on the bank or steered into landing nets. Then Arthur was on. The fish jumped. "That's a nice one," I said. The fish splashed again, ran a bit, then slowly surrendered to Mr. W and the landing net. "Is it a tickle trout?" I asked.

"Just a rainbow. But a good one," Mr. W chuckled, snapping the fish on an aluminum chain and dropping it over the side. We fished on. I could hear Arthur's trout rattle the chain alongside our boat, and I thought of prisoners in medieval dungeons. As it got lighter, I could see the fettered fish, its greenish spotted back and flashing pink sides, and I felt sorry for him.

Then I got one. My nerves tingled when the fish ran, taking line. But I kept good tension and reeled when possible. When it skied in a silver shiver, someone from the bank yelled, "Nice one!"

"That's a tickle trout," Mr. W said. "You can't net him. Bring him alongside and just tickle his belly."

Even more anxious, having never caught a trout, I wanted to land it and show it to my family. Its long resplendent beams glowed in the green water. I wanted it. My heart raced faster. "Oh, wow," Arthur spoke up.

As the fish tired and lay on its side, I put my hand underneath it—maybe sixteen inches of trembling brilliance—and did just as Mr. W said. But when I tickled the fish it flipped wildly and was gone. *No, no,* my heart dropped. Arthur had his hand on the handle of the net, but he let it go and wouldn't look at me. There were voices from the bank: "Sorry, dude," "Bummer, man." "Why the hell didn't you use the net?" one guy shouted.

"It was a tickle trout, you idiot," I yelled back, choked with tears. "You can't net them!"

"Wakoski's an asshole," Herbie Clark said as we sat in our garage. My father had the woodstove going and we were helping Herbie bend wire mesh into muskrat traps.

"Easy, Herbie," my father dampened him and handed him a long block of wood that he used as a form, pushing the mesh around its corners and tamping it with a rubber mallet.

"Well that's just damn cruel," Herbie shook his head and started telling a story about a charter-boat captain out of Montauk. "This rich guy calls him up wantin' to catch a big tuna. There were no tuna around at that time, but the captain needs the money and knows this guy doesn't know shit about fishing or the ocean. So he takes the guy out to where a lot of porpoises gather. He hooks up some mackerel on a light leader, figuring maybe a porpoise will bite, the guy will feel like he's fighting the fish of a lifetime and then the porpoise—a strong fucking animal—will break off, and a good time's had by all."

"Except the porpoise," my father looked alarmed.

"Well that's right, Charley. The plan works and the porpoise takes the bait. The rod's down and the reel's going, and before the captain can get off the bridge, the fucking guy picks up the pole, tightens the drag—he's doesn't know shit—and *zing* the rod flies out of his hands."

"Get outta here," my father sat up in his chair, squinting at Herb.

"It happened, Charley. The porpoise washes up on the beach a few days later with this line trailing out his mouth. They pull in the captain's rod and reel—the guy puts his damn name on everything—and call the cops. People are going crazy. The whole town is in an uproar. I think that whole marine mammals deal— you know the thing to save the whales and all that shit—started right there. That jerk never worked again."

I learned from a teacher in school that trout tickling was a real practice, often associated with poaching and deceit, though young

Abe Lincoln is said to have tickled trout for his hungry family's supper, and in Shakespeare's *Twelfth Night* Maria marks the despised Malvolio as a "trout that must be caught with tickling." Still, it was no way to teach a boy how to land his first rainbow.

I was wounded by the lost trout and Mr. Wakoski's joke, but I found relief in retelling the story. In school on Monday, I enthralled friends with splashing accounts of trout caught and lost. There were boys interested, of course, but I watched the eyes of Denise Cavalo as I relived in words the big trout coming alongside the boat. Denise and I talked more and more in third grade. She wasn't just cute, she was smart. You might say I wanted to catch her, but I dreaded what a girl might think should I expose my methods in terms of lures, hooks, nets, and the possibility of being eaten. I did tell her that fishing was my hobby; she said hers was cats, and that did it. The next day at recess I asked Denise to be my girlfriend. She was very pretty, and I wanted to kiss her. She said she just wanted to be friends. "Why?" I pressed. "My mother thinks I'm too young to date," she said. But her friend told me it was because I was fat.

I always knew I was a fat kid. "Chubby," my mother would say. "Too heavy," my father shook his head. My family vowed to work together and restrict my diet. Aunt Lil gave me a bag of grapes for the movies—"Instead of that greasy popcorn"—and my buddy and I threw them at other kids sitting below. "Can we get a slice of pizza?" I'd ask my father on the way home from fishing. "Okay, but don't tell your mother." And after a few hours of painful shopping, my mother would suggest a reward, "Let's get some ice cream, but don't tell your father." They were also concerned that my favorite activity was too sedentary. "He's got to lose some weight, get some exercise," Dr. Greco admonished during my yearly physical. "What sports do you like?" he asked me.

"Fishing."

"Fishing? What, you just sit on a rock all day drinking soda? You gotta be moving. Maybe like Hemingway you can walk a river. Or row a boat. But you can't just sit around."

My mother nodded. She had never read Hemingway, but she understood the idea of a vigorous sporting life and encouraged me with books about Teddy Roosevelt and Zane Grey. In the car ride home, when I put my head down in shame, she snugged her arm around my shoulders. We didn't wear seatbelts then, and she could pull me close. She was pregnant, her body big and warm. "Oh, sweetie. It's gonna be all right. We just want you to be healthy. You've got to start taking care of yourself."

So I started fish-walking. I walked, sometimes with a friend, sometimes alone, miles down the beach, throwing lures to nothing or snappers or snags. The strand line along the beach was heaped with dead reeds and garbage: cans, shotgun shells, plastic wrappers, cigarette butts, soggy rats, you name it. I learned about tampons and poked my stick at what I first thought were eel skins, describing them to Herbie, who laughed and said they were "rubbers." But there were also the treasures of snapped lures, lobster buoys, seashells, crispy crab carapaces, and notable dead fish: a dinosauric Atlantic sturgeon; a giant angler, known as a goosefish, with its crescent mouth of curved teeth; and a sun-pleated shark nearly eight feet long with a propeller gash across its head. I was fascinated and terrified by the idea of sharks close to home.

Much more dangerous than swimming with sharks, however, was pedaling my bicycle across two highways and down a narrow winding road to dig clams or help Herbie catch eels around Ralph's Fishing Station. I'd smell the brewy fumes of low tide as the trees opened to reeds, gulls, and miles of shining silt cut with silvery streams where sandpipers needled and dipped. Sometimes Ralph's wife, Barbara, would invite me in for a cookie. The old house smelled damp and marshy, their big television raised on cement blocks above the boggy carpet. Even the cookies were redolent of salty tides that often flooded the back rooms. But no one in their family seemed to mind. Herbie told me their house was built too low and close to the water and that the Town of Brookhaven wanted the place condemned to make a park. Living so close to and even *in* the water seemed wonderful to me.

Walking out on the mud flats I'd often join a group of black men in high boots, chopping away with flat-tined bent pitchforks, picking steamer clams from the mud and dropping them into wire baskets. The salt shallows shimmered with all sorts of creatures: snails, clams, crabs, killifish, an array of birds, curious dogs, and even Arnold the pig, who would happily eat a steamer clam, crunching it in his mouth, shell and all like a half cooked egg.

Every spring, dark brown horseshoe crabs, sometimes more than two feet long, shoveled in for small clams, worms, and shrimp. Closely related to extinct sea scorpions and resembling the trilobites that once covered the earth's shallow seas, horseshoe crabs also look a bit like '54 Hudsons, Darth Vaders, or medieval knights— the rounded front helmet martially ridged and arching into meshed eyes, the triangular lower plate fiercely spiked and hinged to a dagger tail that helps the chevalier pivot and change direction. After four hundred million years of evolutionary success among the brutal armies of the sea, their toughest joust is certainly with humans. Men loaded pickup trucks with spawning horseshoe crabs to use for eel bait, calling for my help. I'd reach down and lift them by their tails, revealing clusters of BB-sized blue eggs, small clutching claws, and leathery book gills rhythmically flapping the damp glissando of changing times.

However conservationally unsound, the best bait for eels, Herbie confirmed, was a female horseshoe crab with eggs. He devised a guillotine, chopping the crabs into blue-blooded quarters that we stuffed into eel pots fashioned with funneled entrances and back doors hinged with squares of old inner tube. American eels wriggled all over Long Island's muddy harbors, and we dropped the baited pots on the bottom for an overnight high tide, singing "Pay day" when they came up heavy and writhing with dark brown custard-bellied eels. Coated with a heavy slime, they were hard to grab, but I tried, suffering a couple nasty bites that healed slowly. "This is how you do it," Herbie said, tipping the open traps into a cooler and putting the shiny maze to sleep on ice. Fresh or smoked, they fetched a good price at market. Once Herbie cleaned and skinned a bundle for our dinner, and as Aunt Lil dropped them into the hot oil they twitched noticeably. "God help me," she prayed, turning them with a fork. Knowing eels could live in fresh water, I introduced a pair into one of our twenty-gallon home aquariums. The eels remained quiet during the day, but turning on an evening lamp revealed their serpentine soirées. They glided like ribbons around the tank, frisking each other and gobbling up the remaining mollies and tetras. One night an eel escaped and was found in a semidry state on the kitchen floor, first by our early rising cat Tommy and then by my pregnant mother. Eels were no longer welcome in our home.

But almost every other creature and person was welcome. We had five dogs, two cats, a rabbit, a pen of ducks and chickens, a small turtle, a garter snake, and a few aquariums bubbling with various species of fish. And then we got my brother.

In December of my tenth year, 1975, ten days before Christmas, my brother, David, was born. It didn't mean all that much to me, but everyone seemed happy. Presents under the tree, roast turkey, eggnog, John Denver's *Rocky Mountain Christmas Special.* I peeked at my mother breast feeding in the bedroom. Her boobs were huge,

and I wanted to see more but knew I shouldn't. My father handed
out cigars and bought a bottle of Johnny Walker. Herbie came over,
got very drunk, went to the bathroom, and fell backward into the
tub. "Tickle him," I suggested, and my father laughed. Passed out
and immovable, we put a pillow under his head, covered him with
a wool blanket, and let him sleep it off. Waking in the early hours,
the battered, homebound reveler alarmed our German shepherd,
Heidi, and the dog bit and ripped the back pocket of Herbie's holiday trousers. Aunt Lil later repaired the pants, but said, "The drunk
fool deserved it."

The Shark and the Fox

One late afternoon in the summer of 1977, my father dropped off my friend Tony and me at the docks in Port Jefferson. Dad was meeting a buddy and driving to Shea Stadium for a Mets game. "Behave yourselves and be careful," he'd always say.

"Thanks, Mr. Hughes," Tony waved, pulling a *Playboy* out of his bag.

A few months earlier, Tony had caught me in a joke. "You're good at fishing, right?" he asked me in front of some other boys in our sixth grade class.

"Yeah, I am," I lifted my head with pride.

"Are you good at putting on the bait?"

"Yeah, sure," I said.

"Then you must be a master baiter." Tony and the other boys cracked up laughing and made jerking off gestures. First I felt angry, then I smiled.

Tony and I became good friends and proficient dock anglers, using bait and hooking a variety of delights—flounder, porgy, bergall, blackfish, late summer snappers, and an occasional girly magazine snagged from a dumpster.

But most of the fish we caught were light—"How you gonna clean this?" my father asked, looking at a postcard-sized flounder, shaking his head and telling me to bury it in the garden. Sometimes these corpses would be exhumed by a dog or raccoon. I remember a rank breeze across the yard one hot day, the pallid, maggot seething heads writhing above ground. Sickening and wasteful but for a little fertilizer. Still it was hard for me to let things go. Possession can be empowering, and understanding and controlling my desires for things—toys, fish, and even people—were lessons slow in coming. As a boy I wanted to come home with a prize, something of value—boasting rights, dinner, eel bait, even fertilizer, anything. "Just let 'em go next time," my father repeated, handing me the shovel.

Tony and I were determined, therefore, to catch larger fish—a ten-pound bluefish, a doormat fluke, a lunker weakfish, or perhaps even the coveted striped bass. Mr. Caraftis kept a tackle shop on Barnum Avenue, named after P. T. Barnum, who bought property in Port Jefferson with plans for headquartering his bizarre circus. Barnum's scheme failed, but Mr. C's showmanship under a mounted striped bass played on. "Sometimes at night the big fish come." He leaned over the counter and whispered, "Very, very big fish." We were riveted. "They smell the bait," he tapped his nose. "They circle slowly, then move in." I looked at the shining bass above him. "You'll feel a tug," he paused, staring into our eyes. "But let 'em take it and count to five—okay?—then *Yah!*" he gestured a dramatic hook set.

We spent ten dollars—a lot of money—on whole bunker, large hooks, and slide sinker rigs, and then deployed our baits and waited, reeling in small sandy colored rock crabs that often dropped off as we winched them from the water. Gulls and herons flew by; pigeons picked grit from the parking lot. We looked at the *Playboy,* quickly stuffing it in Tony's bag when anyone approached. Tony's rod tip twitched, and he leapt up, reeled, and declared, "I got one," bringing up a horseshoe crab as big as a sink. I lifted it by the tail.

"Should we save it for Herbie's eel pots?" I asked. "Ah, throw it back," Tony said.

It was dusk, and my mother was going to pick us up in an hour. Tony and I sat on our huge cooler, disturbing each other constantly to grab another cookie or a can of R.C. Cola. Some other men came down and started casting their baits. Tony said they were Italian. "You speak Italian?" I asked. "A little," he said. The men were loud and swigged from bottles wrapped in brown bags.

"Aye, you catcha anything?" one man asked.

"Crabs," I said.

"They catcha da crabs," he repeated to the others, and they all laughed.

My rod tip began to twitch. I picked it up and felt life—then a smart strike. This was no crab. I waited a few moments like Mr. C. advised, then set the hook and felt everything come alive. "I got one! Oh, yeah." Tony reeled in and coached me. "Take it easy. Do the drag. That's it. Easy."

The fish took line and I stayed with him, finally reeling in a bit when it circled back. "He's big," I said. The men started cheering. It took ten minutes to bring the fish in close. Never had I experienced such a contest. Then we saw a long brown form in the dock-lit water—head and tail unmistakable. "Oh my god," I yelled. "It's a shark."

I had never really recovered from seeing the film *Jaws* in 1975 when I was ten. My parents took me to the Coram Drive-In where the great white lunged from the screen like an immense nightmare. I loved the movie—titillated by the naked girl and shocked by her ill-fated swim, fascinated by Hooper's marine biology, and absolutely enamored with Quint and the fishing scenes, line ticking off the big reel as he buckles himself in the fighting chair. The film was set in a southern New England town not unlike my own. And I learned that Peter Benchley's original story was inspired by shark fishing off Long Island's Montauk Point with the famous Captain Frank Mundus, as well as the history of the 1916 Jersey Shore attacks, including the case of a shark entering Matawan Creek and killing two boys. This made me anxious about swimming in any water connected to the ocean. Although the chance was infinitesimally small, it was possible, I thought, always possible, that I could be attacked by a shark—the pointed head, eyes rolled back as the white skin wrinkled behind the widening, tooth-filled mouth. I even contemplated my karma: after all my predations on fish, would I justly be eaten by one? Through delight and fear, the film *Jaws* ignited in me, as in many people, a fascination with sharks and shark attacks. I borrowed every book on the subject from the school and public libraries, did fifth grade reports on shark biology, and gave the class a chilling recitation of the *USS Indianapolis* disaster in World War II, during which more than 200 sailors were killed by sharks after their ship—which had successfully delivered components for the atomic bomb—was torpedoed by the Japanese. I collected shark teeth. I wanted to catch a shark.

"Dogfish," one of the Italian men waved his hand dismissively as the great fish thrashed on the surface. "We gotta get it," I screamed at Tony, eyeing the twelve-foot drop to the water. But not far from where we stood there was a ladder down to a floating dock. I started moving the fish in that direction, its floppy dorsal slicing the water like a shark, a real shark. "Go down the ladder," I ordered Tony, and he started down the old barnacled rungs. He looked uncertain. "Ouch. Shit," he yelled. "I cut myself."

"It's okay. My mom's coming. She's got bandages."

"Are you crazy? Sharks can smell blood. No way." He was back up on the gravel sucking his hand.

"We gotta get this shark!" I screamed and just started cranking up the fish, my fiberglass pole bent double, my drag conceding until I screwed it down, the two-foot shark splashing out of the water. After about four feet of craning, the rod snapped and the fish plunged back into the harbor. But he was still on. I cranked him up on the short splintered boom and swung him onto the gravel.

"I don't know what you're going to do with him," my mother said, driving up Port Hill toward Tony's house. She had reluctantly let me put the cooler, filled with seawater and shark, next to me on the towel-covered back seat of her Buick. I held it steady, listening to the soft splashes. At our house, my mother helped me lift the cooler onto the lawn and then went in to check on my baby brother and Aunt Lil. I opened the cooler and stared at the shark, touching its sandpapery skin, marveling over its yellow cat eyes narrowing in the lamplight. Running inside to the upstairs bathroom, where my mother wouldn't see, I drew a cold bath—too excited to think about the difference between fresh and salt water. I ran back outside, pulled on a pair of garden gloves, grabbed the shark, twisting like crazy, and carried it through the house into the bathtub. In the bright water every shark line was clear: the famous fins, the dashing checkmark of a tail, the sharp nose against the porcelain as it made tight turns and pulsed forward into another white curve of nowhere. Then I thought of the fresh water.

Running downstairs, already sobbing, I cried, "Mom, mom!" and opened her bedroom door to find her standing in bra and panties listening to Nat King Cole.

"Yes," she said, a little annoyed.

"I'm sorry, I'm sorry. The shark. We gotta let him go."

"What?"

"He's going to die. Please, Mom. Drive me back to the harbor. Please!"

"It's ten o'clock at night. I'm getting ready for bed. Why did you keep him?"

But the shark went back in the cooler of salt water, back on the towel next to me in the backseat of the Buick, and my mother drove us back to the dock. The Italian men were still fishing, and when they saw my mother in her denim shorts and the low cut top she would only wear around the house on summer evenings, they whistled and whooped, lifting their bottles. Together my mother and I carried the cooler to the edge of the dock and tipped out the fish, watching him fall through the blue light into the dark water, swimming smoothly away. There was a moment of silence, and then my mother said, "He'll see his friends now and tell them quite a story," hugging me with one arm and kissing the top of my head.

In the fall of 1977, when I was twelve, my mother began experiencing terrible migraines. She took afternoons off and lay in her shaded room. She was irritable and impatient, then apologized and hugged me and sometimes cried. After several visits to the doctor and hospital, she was diagnosed with a large brain tumor. Just after Christmas, surgery confirmed a malignancy. I remember my father bringing her home. Her trembling smile, the kerchief slipping to reveal a rectangular panel, like an attic door, cut and stitched in the side of her head. Aunt Lil made her comfortable on the couch and brought her a cup of tea. Our shepherd, Heidi, nosed up, and my mother rubbed her ears. My brother, David, was two. My father carried him in, and my mother held him tightly. There was an awkward silence between us, then my mother told me that one of her doctors had taken his family to a cabin on a lake in New Hampshire where they caught loads of trout.

"He'd showed me the pictures," my mother said. "Maybe we should go there next summer."

"I'd love it," I said, snuggling into her.

That November I started trapping with Herbie. He'd pick me up in his rusty tan Oldsmobile, and we'd drive to Setauket to set and check muskrat traps. Wading through the marshes and tidal creeks at low tide, we pulled swing-door cage traps from muddy burrows with drowned muskrats. When skinned and dried, their glossy brown pelts fetched six dollars apiece. With my father's work unsteady, trapping gave me the only extra money I'd have before Christmas. Herbie was also a licensed nuisance trapper, and his reputation for success and courteous professionalism landed him many jobs in the affluent neighborhoods of Belle Terre, Setauket, and Old Field. We pulled up to a big house, and a stately, silver-haired woman directed us to the stables. "Mr. Clark, just let me know if there's anything you need," she'd say and leave us to our work. Herbie set a couple of Tomahawk live traps for raccoons and explored the shelves and cabinets of the tack room. "Looking for pest signs," he'd say as he pulled out a bottle of Scotch. "Don't mind if I do, Mrs. Wright," taking a long pull and smiling at me. "Now if she'd just give me a blow job, we'd call this quite a day."

Herbie removed unwanted squirrels, possums, and raccoons, accepting a check and assuring his clients that the animals were going to a better place. He released the squirrels and possums far away, but it was mid winter in New York, and a prime raccoon skin could be sold for thirty dollars. My father did not like trapping, but he supported my interests and enjoyed the project spirit. With the woodstove cranking in our garage-gone-shop, my father and I fashioned wire traps, dyed and waxed Conibear traps, welded stakes, and cut and planed wooden stretching boards for fleshing and drying skins. Herbie taught us how to skin, hanging the muskrat or raccoon by one foot, then the other, pulling and cutting the pelt off the carcass like a great glove. It was greasy, sometimes stinky work, especially if I slipped and cut open the belly of a muskrat, its sour green undigested dinner bulging out. In school we did a lesson on the Hudson Bay Company and the fur trade. I raised my hand and told the class that I trapped and sold furs. "On Long Island?" the surprised teacher asked, her raccoon collared coat hanging at the back of the room. "Sure," I said. "Just down the street."

"There are fox on the beach," Herbie told my father and me one winter evening as we sat on folding chairs in the garage. "I saw them digging in the sand."

"Oh yea?" my father raised an eyebrow and tipped his beer. "How do you catch those guys?"

"Fox is smart. Gotta use leg holds. Double coil spring. I got some."

"I don't like those traps," my father grimaced.

"Fox is bringing seventy-five dollars, Charley." Herbie drank from a coffee cup half filled with Old Crow.

"Well, you guys do what you want," my father stood up, lit a cigarette, and tapped the shiny, sweating raccoon skin on the stretching board. My father's words, *Do what you want*, stayed with me. He would allow me to participate, and even support me, in endeavors that he did not like but could not oppose on any rational or moral grounds. "I eat veal, and look at the way those poor things are treated," he'd confess. "I think leg hold traps are cruel. But if you can live with it, go ahead."

My father rescued a badly dented twelve-foot aluminum jon boat from a scrap yard and bought a used Sears outboard to set me up with my first watercraft. I loved it. After a test run in the harbor, he said that I could use it for trapping. One early February afternoon, he helped Herbie and me load the jon boat in his pickup, wished us luck, and Herbie drove us down to Port Jefferson's East Beach. The north shore harbors could be brutally cold, windy, and rough in winter, but on this cloudy Saturday, a mild south breeze merely rippled the surface. Clammers dropped their long rakes from wooden scows and dug hardshell clams. "Damn hard work," Herbie shouted over the engine noise. Flocks of broadbill ducks congregated in long rafts, sometimes lifting in flight before our bow. Herbie kept pointing and smiling. He had his beat-up, double barrel 12 gauge—a gun he claimed to have ditched in the reeds a few times when the game wardens were after him—and when a few broadbill flew toward us, he swung up and fake fired two shots. We landed at Seaboard Hole, often just called The Cove, a five acre gouge created by the dredging of the Seaboard Sand and Gravel Corporation, where my father's father—who died long before I was born—worked as a marine mechanic for twenty years. Herbie and I pulled the boat up on the sand beside the rotted remains of an old wooden barge and walked the barrier beach toward the east breakwater, noting the droppings and long prints of rabbits. Then Herbie kneeled down and showed me the tracks and diggings of a fox.

Fox trapping was not easy. I carried long iron stakes my father helped us cut and weld, my mother's garden trowel, and wax paper. Herbie hammered down a stake anchoring a trap and then dug an angled hole, just as a fox might. He unscrewed a dirty jar and, with a stick, skewered out some of his special marinated chicken bait and dropped it into the hollow. After troweling out the soil before the hole, he set the trap and delicately placed it in the depression. I handed him the precut square of wax paper, and he gingerly covered the pan and trigger, sifting small leaves and dirt over the wax paper and exposed jaws. "Dirthole set," he instructed, spraying fox urine and brushing over our boot trail as we walked out. We made half a dozen sets, finishing at dusk as dark flocks of waterfowl swept the sky and settled in the cove.

Returning at dawn, I burned with something like the possibility and expectation of a first cast. We flushed a couple cottontail rabbits from the bushes above the beach then crested a hill and saw that our first set was empty. The first five sets were empty, one sprung and turned over. "Damn clever devils," Herbie grumbled. We came up on the last set and I was breathing heavy and sweating under my coat. Then I saw the fox, like a flame in the gray brush. The animal quickly pulled back against the chain, whining and leaping in different directions. As we got closer, an excited fear came over me. Herbie approached slowly, the fox strained in one direction, and Herbie slipped a dogcatcher's noose around its neck and pulled tight. "All right, hold this," he ordered me. I hesitated. "Come on, dammit," he said. I walked up and could hardly believe I was so close to a wild fox. Although we knew there were foxes around, I had never seen one. Now I was inches away.

I held the fox and felt it struggle in the noose. "Hold it still now," Herbie commanded. The animal was breathing rapidly, its sides rising and falling. I can still see its plush orangey fur, the sharp ears, long snout, the black nose, and whiskers. Herbie pulled a .22 pistol from his pocket, put it between the eyes of the fox and pulled the trigger. There was frantic kicking and twisting. I held it so tight, my arms and shoulders ached for days. Then the animal was quiet.

"Okay, boy. We got ourselves a beauty," Herbie patted me on the back.

When we got home I ran into the house, shouting, "A fox, we caught a fox." Aunt Lil was giving my brother breakfast at the kitchen table. "Wow," she said. "That's great."

"Where's Dad?" I asked.

"He's with Mom," Lil said. "She had a bad night."

"Oh. Okay." I stood silent for a moment, frustrated by the suspension of excitement. Herbie hung the fox in the garage. He said it was a vixen. Again, I studied the stunning rusty red body, black paws, and black-lined ears. Hanging from its hind foot, the thick, coal-tipped tail arced down over its back, the pink tongue and a bit of red foam dripped from its mouth.

I called Arthur, and he and his father came over to admire the fox and ask where and how we caught it. "Snared it in Montauk," Herbie growled, having never warmed to Arthur's father after the tickle trout incident. My friend Tony rode his bike over. He stared, stroked the fox's fur and asked if we were going to make a coat for my mother. "That's a good idea," I said. My father came into the garage and congratulated us. I watched him go up to the fox and touch the paw where the trap had held her. There was a ring of raw skin and a bit of dried blood. Herbie said he'd be back later and we could skin it.

That afternoon, when I was up in my room doing homework, I heard yelling downstairs. Our shepherd, Heidi, was lying on my bed. Her ears perked up, she lifted her head, then jumped off and ran downstairs. I followed.

The door to the garage was open, and my mother was standing baldheaded in her bathrobe on the landing. "What is this!? What is going on here!?" she screamed. "How could you do this?" She started crying hysterically and my father put his arms around her. "It's okay, Marion. Come inside. Herbie and Henry are trapping now. You know that." My father guided my mother back into our family room and onto the couch. "Oh, that poor fox," she cried. She looked at me with tears and what seemed like a crazed expression of confusion and horror. "Henry, no. Please." Aunt Lil brought her a pill and a glass of milk. I walked outside.

My father came up to me later that afternoon. "No more trapping this season."

"Why?" I asked.

"Why do you think? It upsets your mother."

"She's acting crazy."

"You heard what I said."

Herbie came and took away the fox. "Your mother's very sick," he said. "You gotta understand that."

The night's dinner might have been painfully quiet were it not for the antics of my two-year-old brother. "Mushrooms, mushrooms," he loved the word. "Stinky mushrooms in Daddy's shoes." And we all laughed. But right before my mother left the table, she put her arm around me. "Please, dear," she said. "Please, for the fox, okay?"

There was chemotherapy, radiation, mega doses of expensive vitamins purchased from a quacky relative, but my mother's condition deteriorated. There were days when she was lucid and loving, asking me about school or to help her in the garden pulling a few weeds. She laughed, watching television with us, and came into the garage to admire a cooler full of icy mackerel. "These would be great on the barbecue," she'd say. "Fish are so healthy." But there were more and more days when her mind was lost. She rambled on nonsensically, looked at me as if I were a stranger, ordered friends out of the house, and told me no one would care if she died. One evening while my father and I were watching television, my mother came into the shadows of the kitchen, pulled a carving knife from the drawer, raised it above her chest, and screamed, "I'm going to kill myself," bringing the knife down gently into the folds of her robe and sobbing as my father leapt up to hold her.

The summer I turned thirteen, 1978, is hard to recall. I remember praying, asking God to heal my mother. "God has a plan for all of us," our pastor counseled. I wanted God to change his plans.

There were kind friends. Mr. Wakoski and Arthur picked me up at four in the morning, always asked how my mother was feeling, and we drove to Montauk and Captree, where we boarded huge party boats and felt the great swells of the ocean, sometimes getting sick, usually feeling good, training our black binoculars on knobby nosed humpback whales and catching doormat fluke and big bluefish. Mr. Wakoski once reeled in a thirty-inch bluefish with a normal head and an emaciated body. Thorned deep in the throat, the remains of a hook and a lump of scar tissue prevented the poor fish from swallowing. The head clear and sharp, the body wasting away. "Save him," I begged. Mr. Wakoski twisted his lips, then reached in with his needle nose pliers and extracted the hook, opening a space in the scar tissue. He slipped the bluefish below the boat rails into the ocean. "He might make it," he smiled.

After fishing at Montauk, we'd sometimes go over to Captain Frank Mundus' boat and see if he'd caught any sharks. Captain Mundus hammed it up for the crowd, wearing a safari hat and hoop earrings, his toenails painted red and green for port and starboard. A couple blue sharks hung from gin poles one afternoon above the dock, their stomachs bulging out through their mouths. One of the sharks was still alive, and its rippling gills made me uneasy and sick.

"Are you okay?" Mr. Wakoski looked at me with concern.

"What are they going to do with those sharks?" I asked.

"Nothing. Maybe cut out the jaws. Cruel, isn't it?" he said.

Mr. Wakoski seemed kinder and more patient with my endless questions, but when I asked him if he believed there was a benevolent god in the universe, he just farted and rolled down the window.

Tony's parents invited me over often, brought trays of lasagna and ziti to our house, and dropped Tony and me off at the docks or a pond to fish the day away. Tony's grandmother told me in Italian—Tony interpreted—that she lit candles in church for my mother.

Herbie was also a good friend. When frost covered Long Island, he would sit and talk with my father and me around the woodstove in the garage, drinking his cheap whisky and smoking a Camel. Sometimes we'd just stare at the garage floor, by now a Modernist collage from all the projects we spray-painted over the years—duck decoys, fishing lures, buoys, model airplanes, and tanks. Herbie talked about World War II when his tank crew landed in France after the invasion. "It was the first time I saw a lot of dead people," he said, and we stared at him. "In a truck. Germans. Young, most of them."

My father rubbed his face and lit a cigarette. "There were some dead in Korea."

"Never know what the world's gonna throw at you, Charley—there, here, anywhere." Herbie stood and warmed his hands over the stove. "You just gotta get through it."

That November, Herbie and I launched the jon boat into Port Jefferson Harbor looking for big blues on their fall feeding binges.

We had medium spinning rods loaded with twelve-pound test, and a box of hand-turned cedar plugs about the size of half-smoked cigars lit with bright red concave mouths and trailing treble hooks wrapped in local deer hair. Birds were working outside Seaboard Hole, and I moved the boat in slowly then cut the engine, and we drifted close to the thrashing shoal of feeding fish. Herbie made the first cast, and after two chugs, a fish attacked his plug, missed, and then was on. I took up the oars and eased us off the shoal while Herbie fought the fish, his face composed in familiar pleasure. "Good fish," I said. Then there was a gray leap as the bluefish broke the surface and got free. "Damn," he said. "Well, go on. Get in there." I cast and retrieved as he showed me, jerking the rod back to chug, splash, and dance the lure like a wounded baitfish. But the blues had gone down and disappeared. We did not see another rise all morning. Clouds rolled in with the wind, dropping the temperature, forcing us to zip up and turn for home. Canada geese filled the sky with their honking, flying over the headland where we set our traps the winter before.

I thought of the fox. Had she been alive, would she have tilted her ears to the sound of those birds? And though I believed there was nothing morally wrong with killing that fox, I regretted doing it. The wind brought up a nasty chop, and we slapped back to the takeout with frozen hands and faces, glad to be in the warm cab of the truck.

Two weeks later in the middle of a cold night, my mother died at home in bed next to my father.

Holy Mackerel

In the spring of 1979, following my mother's death, our azaleas were as bright as ever, but my father and aunt never mentioned them. The country was in a recession, again people waited in lines for gas, and my father was out of work for weeks at a time. The residual bills from my mother's illness, despite insurance, strained our family, and Aunt Lil stayed up late cutting coupons from the paper and sewing my torn pants. Then there was my brother, a three-year-old who needed daycare so Lil could return to work. My father sold some of our antiques and split firewood, hustling an odd job here and there. He never turned angry or dangerously despondent, he just stilled. I was thirteen. He let me do what I wanted, never checking on my homework or chores, and I could come and go pretty much as I pleased. I was running and lifting weights, my body slowly changing. I tried out for the junior high basketball team and got cut. My father didn't say anything. In the evening he drank beer, watched a game on television, and occasionally went out to the local gin mill with a friend.

"Come on, Dad," I shook him from his sleep on the couch.

"Okay, okay," he raised a hand in surrender.

He had been out late but promised to take me fishing in the morning. I got him up. Lil cooked breakfast, but he hardly ate. His truck was full of scrap metal, so we loaded the jon boat in the back of the family station wagon. It was May, and I was keen to jig for mackerel, which entered the spring Sound in vast numbers, readily biting anything twinkled before their pointed mouths.

We drove past old Ralph's Fishing Station, condemned by the Town of Brookhaven and deserted. When we last saw Ralph he looked miserable. "Dey wanna make a park," he said, egg-shaped pouches under his eyes. Ralph and Barbara fought hard against eviction, lost their lease, but were offered new property above Mt. Sinai's east inlet. "Ralph works hard and drinks hard," my father said. "We'll see what happens."

"Barbara's a really hard worker, too," I said.

My father looked at me, then turned back to the road, and there was long silence in his foggy head. "Yeah," he finally spoke. "They're a good team. They'll make it."

We followed the winding road around Mount Sinai Harbor and pulled into the parking lot facing the sound at Cedar Beach. A nor'wester was pushing swells and whitecaps. "We're not getting out there today," my father said.

"It's not that bad," I countered.

"You wanna drown for a damn mackerel? Don't be silly."

We drove to the harbor side, and it was relatively calm, although a stiff breeze clanked lines against the aluminum masts of sailboats.

"This looks okay," he said. "Why don't you try for some flounder?"

"I don't have any bait."

"Pull some mussels off those pilings."

I rolled my eyes in frustration. "That stinks," I said.

"Well then, we're going home." And as he put the car in gear, I relented. We backed down the ramp, launched the boat, and my father helped me pick some mussels, then told me he was staying in the car. He needed more sleep. "Stay in the harbor," he said. "I'll be right here. Okay?"

It was okay. I headed out, waving to him over the noise of the outboard, into the channel past a sailboat named *Sanity*. Fishing alone was fine with me. The air was chilly, but spring was greening the marsh and leafing the high wooded hills to the west. Anchoring near Crystal Brook, I rigged for flounder, pulled out the stained plywood cutting board, cracked a mussel, baited up, and dropped. The tide was rising, black ducks flew overhead, and a mute swan parted the cord grass. I thought of those times my father and I brought home a bucket of flounder that Mom admired. Sometimes the fillets were thin, but she dipped them in egg and breadcrumbs, shook on Old Bay Seasoning, fried them in butter, and set them on the table with tartar sauce and ketchup. Secretly she would buy more flounder fillets at Wally Brown's fish market to supplement our meager harvest, the impossibly thick pieces heavy on the fork and satisfying in our mouths. "You guys did a nice job catching these flounder," she'd say. I would mention Jesus multiplying loaves and fishes, and my mother would laugh, "So, you did learn something in Sunday school." Aunt Lil reminded me that Jesus's disciples were fishermen and that I should follow their example.

I thought of my beer-drinking father listening to the Mets while his neglected pole slumped against the side of the boat, and me, eating two sandwiches and a bag of chips washed down with orange soda, worshipping a ten-inch flounder like some old Cananite kneeling before scaly-suited Dagon, the fish god who promised a bountiful catch and more religious holidays in the school calendar. Even the apostles started out as wayward goofballs, so maybe we did have a chance at respectable discipleship. I thought of the grief the disciples felt when Jesus died, their amazement when he appeared after the resurrection and gobbled down a piece of broiled fish, and then their elation and transformation over his proven promise of eternal life. But even as a child I knew the resurrection was no different than the fantastic stories of the Setauket Indians who sent their dead drifting into a glorious, torch-lit, fish-filled afterlife.

Anchored alone in Mt. Sinai Harbor, soft lapping under the hull, my hand holding a rod at attention for the slightest sign of life, a single gull hovering above, I just started crying. I didn't cry at my mother's funeral. It all seemed confusing, her death impossible, worse, an intrusion into my life. How could she have changed so much? How could she have grown so weird, sick, distant, and ugly? My once beautiful mother, bald and bloated, wandering madly through the house or screaming at me. Then I felt a wave of guilt. *I'm sorry, Mom. I'm so sorry*—and I wept on.

Maybe we have souls, I thought, but really we are just animals with brains and hearts, and when they are destroyed and fail, we disappear. Mussels smashed on the cutting board. Our seventh-grade science teacher explained that a salt deficiency in our brains could render us idiots, could make happy people depressed and suicidal. We are fragile estuaries with billions of neurons flashing like shiners. I prayed to God to heal my mother. I prayed with utter sincerity. Now it seemed silly. It was just nature. She got sick and died. Like fish, we would all die in the bucket or in the dark tide, lost to sickness, age, or bigger fish. I could die right now, tie the anchor around my neck, and roll over the side.

I got a bite—a tentative tapping, then a tug—so I set the hook, reeling in a hand-sized flounder. I carefully unhooked the fish and let it go. "Not today," I said aloud. Five minutes later I caught an even smaller one. Flounder made a weak showing that year. No one else was fishing for them. *Mackerel.* I had to get out and get the mackerel.

I started the outboard, pulled up the anchor, and shot across the harbor toward the inlet. Cormorants came up black and shimmering with sand eels in their bills. A returning cruiser rose and fell as it entered the breakwater. It was still rough. With the engine in neutral, I changed out my flounder rig for a Christmas tree, a line of red and green two-inch tubes on long hooks weighted with a two-ounce diamond jig, ready for mackerel.

The inlet was a horse market of confused water. Back in gear and surging forward into a large swell, a wall of water came over the bow and soaked me. Other waves came in from the side. Scared but not sure how to turn around, I pointed the boat's square face toward the biggest waves and pressed on, salt water drenching my body and stinging my eyes. A couple inches of water sloshed around my feet, so I picked up the little bucket that held the mussels and bailed with one hand, keeping my other on the tiller throttle. Beyond the jetty, the waves became more regular, and I could see a line of boats about a half mile from shore. That's where I needed to be. My father was sleeping. He'd never know.

Fortunately mackerel are fished on a drift, not by anchoring. I approached the line of boats, most of them twenty feet or longer, put the engine in neutral, and dropped my line. My father and I had jigged for mackerel the year before on a calm day from a friend's runabout. I knew how to do it, but this tossing made things tough. Head down and picking a bit of backlash out of my reel, the boat suddenly lurched to the side and I smashed my hand on the oarlock. I put the engine back in gear, got aligned in the waves, and started jigging, my hand throbbing and swelling. Instantly there were fish.

The Atlantic mackerel is a two-pound torpedo that fights like hell. Get three or four on the line, and it's a rod-bending thrill that

rewards in astonishing color—an iridescent blue-green back ver-
miculated in dark stripes. Mackerel are easy to grab, and I quickly
unhooked the first fish and was back in the water.

Boats drifted by pulling up dozens of fish. *Mackerel-crowded
seas*, indeed, I would think back years later reading Yeats, amazed
that my own young heart was so "sick with desire." One cruiser got
close, and a man yelled, "You shouldn't be out here, kid. It's way too
rough." A woman in yellow raingear fishing sturdily off the stern of
a forty-foot gameboat shouted, "Hey, do your parents know you're
out here?" The way she cocked her head and studied me, I wondered if she knew them. "Put on your life jacket," she told me. We
never wore life jackets. Mine floated next to the gas tank.

Over fifty mackerel flopped and drummed on the wet floor of
my boat. *Holy mackerel*—I suddenly understood the expression as
a blessing. Our line of boats drifted closer to Cedar Beach, and I
could see people jogging and walking dogs. A boy was flying a kite.
Not thinking anything of it at first, I heard a persistent car horn.
And when I looked over I saw headlights flashing. It was our station
wagon. It was my father. He got out of the car and waved his arms.
I waved back. He pumped his pointed hand toward the inlet.

"What the hell is wrong with you?" he said when I cut the
engine, gliding the boat onto the ramp. "Didn't you hear what I
said? Are you deaf?"

"No," I said. "I'm fine."

"You're not using this boat for the rest of the summer."

"Why?" I yelled back. "'Cause you're too scared? 'Cause you'd
rather get drunk and sleep all day?"

"Let's go," he said. "Get that engine off."

My hand swollen and bruised, I unscrewed the outboard, lifted
it off the transom, and set it on the ramp. We tried lifting the boat,
but it was too heavy with all the fish and water, so we unloaded the

gear, pulled the drain plug, and stuffed the fish into burlap bags. My father was silent.

At home I washed and put away equipment, and my father brought out the Castro Oil can. "You know what to do," he said. I filled the can with water, set the engine inside, and ran it to flush out the corrosive salt. At the sound of the engine the neighbors came over, as they often did, to see what we caught. "Mackerel," my father said. "Take all you want." Grouchy old Mr. Stanley from next door wrapped a couple in newspaper and muttered, "Thanks." My three-year-old brother, David, came out with Aunt Lil. "You catched fishes," the little boy chirped, picking one up with both hands and bringing it to his lips for a kiss. Herbie drove up and looked at the heap of mackerel. "Holy mackerel! How the hell did you get these? There was small craft warnings this morning." My father just shook his head and said nothing. I smiled at Herbie and watched him light a cigarette. "You wouldn't be smiling," he said and paused to take a drag and exhale, "if you went swimming in that cold water. I known a few that's done it, and they ain't around to tell the story."

But here I am, telling you the story, reminding you to wear life jackets and know the water that your craft can handle. *Don't drown for a damn mackerel!* I say. But going out that morning also saved me from drowning.

China Cat

Later in the week of our mackerel, at the end of dinner, my father pushed aside his plate, lit a cigarette, and echoed one of our favorite lines from *Jaws*, "Well, I think you're gonna be needin' a bigger boat." There was no money, so I asked, "How?"

"Nicky's got one he wants out of his yard. It needs a lot of work. We'll start with that and then figure out an engine."

I was throwing a baseball with a new friend, Tim, when my father pulled up towing a boat. It was a sixteen-foot wooden runabout with a sports car windshield and a red scripted brand plate, Eltro, dangling from one screw on the plywood side. Keel splintered, floorboards and bow deck rotted, it also needed caulking, paint, and an engine, but it had solid ribs and gunnels and beautiful chrome running lights.

We stripped the deck hardware, removed the windshield and plastic steering wheel, and, with the help of a couple neighbors, turned the boat over on blocks, nearly crushing Mr. Stanley's gouty foot. He growled that "a boat was a hole in the water where you threw your money." The image of a hole in the ocean enraptured me for a long time. A deep windowed well or a glass elevator down into the fish haunted depths. "A hole in the water," I repeated to

75

my focused father as we sized up the hull. "Hole? Where?" he asked.

I had worked with my father before, unenthusiastically repairing the porch and building a shed, but the boat project brought us close, and I learned from him. We took measurements for a new keel, scraped, patched, and caulked, finally painting the boat's belly red. In a month we were ready to turn the Eltro back onto the trailer and roll it into the garage. Rotten decking tore off easily, and we stripped old paint with a torch and scraper. My father had heavy pneumatic sanders, and on my first go I lost control of the wheel and chewed a moon out of the mahogany. Then I got the hang of it.

Arthur came by and said, "Wood boats are a lot of work," and that he and his dad were "fiberglass men." Tony said it was "great," and hoped we could get out soon because his grandmother had been sick and fish made her feel better.

My new friend, Tim, who had moved to the neighborhood a few months before, helped me with the boat after school. Tim's father died when he was just a baby, and he lived with his mother and sister in a small house one street over. He was a good looking boy with smooth dark skin and deep brown eyes. And though he was a year younger than I was, a lot more girls hung around him. We both played lacrosse—he excelled and I struggled—and I'd see him after practice in the locker room, his lean muscular body so different from my pink hamminess. I thought him as beautiful as any girl and once said he had "nice eyes." He snapped his head back and sneered, "Are you queer?"

"No," I said and never talked about his body again. Tim was athletic and could handle any game, routinely beating me in everything from horseshoes to one-on-one basketball—my motor skills still warming up in my mid-teens. My father took us to his union picnic, and during the softball game I misjudged a pop fly that hit me in the head. He and Tim joked about it later. "The only thing he can throw is a hook," my father quipped. "The only thing he can catch is a fish," Tim rejoined, and they laughed, pleased with their teamwork.

But I was strong enough for my age to handle heavy tools and materials, patient enough to measure, remeasure, cut wood, and drive screws. On nice days I'd pull the boat out of the garage into the sun. "Did you move this yourself?" my father would ask when he got home.

Herbie came by to check on the job and give advice. "Put a foot a water in it and let it sit for a few hours before you launch."

"What are you talking about?" I said. "It's all caulked and painted."

"It's an old wooden boat. It's gonna leak until that wood swells up."

Herbie would sit and watch us work, sipping whisky, and recounting small boats that had bashed rocks and sunk, run aground, or gotten swept away by wind and tide. When Aunt Lil wasn't around, he would also tell Tim and me about women he laid in boats. "We were suckin' and lickin' and stickin' and—Oh, God, this woman couldn't get enough. I tried to get up, but she had me like an octopus." I shook my head and laughed, becoming used to his sordid tales. Tim blushed but listened.

By my fourteenth birthday in the summer of 1979, the Eltro was ready for her maiden voyage, powered by a rebuilt Evinrude 25 that my father financed through a friend at the local marine shop. For a final touch, an old ship's wheel came off our living room wall. My mother had bought it at an antique shop and hung it next to a tacky print of a sailboat. I took the wheel apart, sanded and re-varnished the rim and spokes, and, with the help of my father, refastened everything with stainless steel bolts. From here I'd steer the

China Cat, christened after a beloved Grateful Dead song, Garcia's guitar and voice dancing high like a crazy junk on the cosmic tides.

We launched *China Cat* on a sunny Saturday afternoon. The ramp at Port Jefferson was a madhouse—amateurs and professionals putting in and pulling out vessels of various sizes with varying degrees of patience and politeness for their fellow boaters. My father was skilled at backing up trailers, and he zipped us down between two rigs, pushed off our boat, and handed me the bow line. Tim stood next to me and asked, "Do we get in?" I didn't know. There was a slight breeze and the boat started drifting toward an adjacent trailer. Someone else was backing down, and he yelled, "Are you guys going out or what?" Other boats were stacking up on the floating dock and idling in wait. We were getting squeezed, so I climbed in the boat and Tim followed. We bumped the trailer next to us and spun slowly around. I dropped the engine in position, pumped the gas bulb, opened the choke, and pulled it to a roaring start. I had no idea what to do next, but I saw my father quicken his pace in the parking lot, flick his cigarette, jump over the railing, and run down the ramp onto the floating dock. He leaped into our boat, idled down the engine, and put it in gear. "Good job, boys," he said, maneuvering us through the traffic. Something felt squishy, and we looked down at a few inches of water rising in the bottom of the boat. "That's all right," my father said, and we laughed, bailed, and toured the harbor.

Aunt Lil didn't find leaky boats so funny. That summer, like every summer on Long Island, there were drownings. A young boy fell off his Sunfish sailboat and drowned in Long Island Sound; a girl slipped from a dock and perished in the Great South Bay. Lil stuck the *Newsday* articles on the fridge. She made me promise to wear my life jacket and not go out so far. I promised but did whatever I pleased.

The *China Cat* was leaky until she swelled, underpowered but cheap on gas, sluggish on the turn but steady in the waves, and she brought us to the fish. My father let me take the boat out with friends, launching us in the early hours before work. "Be careful," is all he'd say.

Herbie showed me how to troll for bluefish with color-coded nylon-sheathed leaded line, a six foot leader of thirty-pound test monofilament, and an umbrella rig. The umbrella was a cross of heavy wire, each arm trailing a foot of mono and a large hook jacketed in colored tubing. It looked like a ceiling mobile mimicking a school of sand eels. Some old-timers said to tip the hooks with pork rind, but it didn't seem to make much difference.

Tony, Tim, and I would take the boat through Port Jefferson's breakwater, heading northeast toward Buoy 11, a large green can buoy marking Mount Misery Shoal. "Troll the can," people would chant. Throttling down as slow as possible, we'd carefully lay the umbrella rigs out behind us, making sure each tube was spinning properly, and then drop back four to six colors of line (each color marked ten yards) depending on the depth and speed variances due to wind and tide. The schooling blues were typically on the shoal inside Buoy 11 in fifteen to twenty feet of water. Some mornings the rods would come alive immediately. I'd hit neutral, and we'd take turns reeling in the fish, sometimes doubles, rarely triples, once a bluefish on every one of the four hooks. We celebrated with cigarettes pilfered from my father's pack, feeling woozy but triumphant.

Trolling too close to a cluster of lobster buoys on a foggy Friday morning, our umbrella rig snagged one of the pots below. Tim and

I pulled up the heavy trap to free our hooks, and we saw that it held a large dark lobster. We took it. Thrilled by the idea of bringing home some delicious and valuable lobsters for the weekend, we pulled a couple more pots and grabbed three more lobsters, hiding them at the bottom of our plastic Coleman cooler. That afternoon when we got home and unpacked, my father saw the big antennae waving up from the ice. "Where did you get these lobsters?" he asked.

"We caught them," I said. "They took our clam bait on the bottom. Can you believe it?"

"I don't ever want to see that again," my father turned serious. "You understand me?"

"Yes," I dropped my eyes. We ate the lobsters, but my father offered none of his usual appreciation. "They hang pirates," he said, leaving the table and never mentioning it again.

On most summer days, we'd catch a couple dozen bluefish of two and three pounds each, tossing them in our coolers packed with ice made from milk cartons in our home freezers. Blues were easy to fillet, and if kept cold, the meat would stay firm. "A bonanza!" Tony's grandmother clapped her hands in delight when we lifted the dripping plastic bags of gray and red fillets.

Some people didn't like the taste of bluefish—"Too gamey, too fishy," they'd say. Aunt Lil picked up a recipe from the owner of the Stony Brook appliance store where we bought a new range. We soaked the fillets in milk for an hour, then frosted them with mayonnaise mixed with pepper, garlic, cilantro, and dill. Wrapped skin-side down loosely in foil and placed in the oven at 350 or on a hot closed grill for about fifteen or twenty minutes, they cooked into a creamy cadeau. For the last five minutes on the grill, my father would open the foil and punch holes through the bottom, the ignited drippings smoking the fish to an even finer finish.

My friends and I loved to catch blues, but we also found that fighting fish on trolled leaded line and wire umbrella rigs was losing its luster, the power of the fish drained by the heavy tackle. With no knowledge of or access to downriggers, we tried to jig or spin cast with lighter gear whenever possible. It was often at daybreak that we'd spot a whirl of white birds or a writhing school of rusty bunker and motor in for a closer look. *Blues!* Anticipating the direction of our drift, I'd cut the engine, and we'd slide silently toward the pack—gull cries, wild splashing, oil, and blood in a haze across the water. We'd cast to the edge of the boil and feel the attack.

Even after a thousand times, even now after the millionth time—from the hook, through the line and rod, into the body and mind—fish thrill. There's a thrill in the chase. Tackle and boat preparations the day before, early rising and stalking, setting or casting lines, the hopeful repetition and careful adjustment, the waiting—and then the big thrill of the hit, the rod bent and jumping with the living power of the fish. Fish thrill us with their struggle to survive. It's a human pleasure that doesn't translate into anything else except animal wildness—like cats and killer whales that toy with their living food—and the worst forms of human cruelty where someone enjoys the long struggle and suffering of his victim. Even in hunting, one hopes for a fast, clean kill. In fishing, the greater the fight, the greater the thrill. "Nice," Tim would say with a grin when the hooked bluefish made a panicked dash. It may be barbaric, but anyone who loves to fish loves the sensation of a struggling creature. The blues jumped and ran and eventually came to the boat, snap-jawed and yellow eyed.

One morning my father helped me launch the boat then drove off to work in Middle Island. I had arranged to meet Tony, but he never showed. I waited more than an hour, finally motoring out alone, crossing the rough breakwater into the choppy sound. Birds were working off a large tumble of rocks on the sound side of Seaboard Hole, near where we had caught the fox that February morning. I moved in close to the boiling fish and cast a stainless steel Hopkins lure that I had buffed up with Aunt Lil's silver polish. Something powerful struck. My rod bent double and pulsed wildly as line sang off the spool. *Yes, yes,* I thanked the heavens, adjusting my drag and gaining line when I could. For fifteen minutes I stayed with its long runs and broad dodges, keeping the line clear of the prop when it got close and shot under the hull. Finally, in the sweating thrill of an instant, my flimsy blue net at the ready, there was a huge swirl and tail splash, then a glowing bronze flank just below the surface. *Oh, my God,* I said aloud. *Striped bass!* Stripers were scarce in those days around Port Jefferson, caught only by pros with live eels under the moon. But I was into a huge one—how big I'll never know. Suddenly it was gone, the snapped line sagging between the guides of my rod. Another boat had pulled close to watch the battle, and the man behind the wheel just shook his head and sped away. The late morning sun suddenly felt hot, a ferry horn groaned in the distance, and herring gulls hovered above. I would later learn that Tony's grandmother, a great old Italian lady who loved to hear about our adventures, had died in the night. "You boys bring home some nice fish, okay?" she would always tell us. All I brought home that day was a story.

"The story doesn't really explain insanity, it just dramatizes it," I heard this tough-looking guy tell a cute girl in the hallway of our high school. It was my sophomore year, 1980, and I was playing junior varsity football. I recognized the guy from the locker room. He kissed the girl goodbye and waved me over. "I hear you're into fishing," he said. Eugene Jones moved with his family from Valley Stream, where his father had an appliance store. He was a year older, played varsity football, wore an earring, and had the street cred of a guy who had grown up close to the action of New York City. Tough but artistic, he painted the back of his denim jacket with the skeleton and roses of the Grateful Dead. I liked him.

It was mid-October and getting colder, but I suggested we take my jon boat to Lake Ronkonkoma, joking with him about my uncle's delicatessen special of bacon and dough that nailed my first bass. "Hey, whatever. We'll try that shit." He told me about a deadly chum for snappers—canned mackerel mixed with oatmeal—and I made a note.

"Where'd you fish for snappers?" I asked.

"Stony Brook."

"Me, too." We shared a history of snapper fishing not far from where his grandmother lived and where his father had set up a new store. "We bought a stove from your dad. And got that recipe for bluefish. It's good," I told him.

"No fucking way?" he said, picking up his books when the bell rang. "I'll tell my dad you like it."

I was fifteen, without a driver's license, but my father said that on Sunday Eugene could drive our station wagon, loaded with the jon boat, to Lake Ronkonkoma. We both had football games on Saturday—we both won—and Eugene came over to talk to my dad before heading out to a party. "Nice ta meet ya, Mr. Hughes," Eugene said, though it sounded like "Mista Yooze." I could tell that my father was circumspect. Eugene had a city accent, scarred face, and, at that hour, somewhat glassy eyes. But my father admired the great blocks and tackles he made that afternoon, and they shook hands. "Don't worry," Eugene said, "I'll take care a dis guy."

On the drive to the lake the next morning, Eugene said he was a little hungover, and we stopped at 7-Eleven to get some coffee and bagels. He told me about the post game party and how he pulled off Bonnie Gambini's shirt and she gave him head in his car. "She's got great tits and great lips, man." I had kissed a couple girls and squeezed Tracy Bromberg's breasts over her sweater in the woods behind our house, but she pushed me away. It seemed girls were not physically—sexually—attracted to me. "You're alright, man," Eugene assured me. "There's a lot of fish in da sea. It'll happen." But he had been laid. "With the right girl, it's fuckin' awesome," he said. "Look into her eyes when you're hanging out. After a while, man, you can tell if she wants it." I made a note.

Eugene also liked school and reading, and we talked about our favorite stories and poems.

"You know that one about catching the big fish?" he asked.

"Sure," I said. Elizabeth Bishop's "The Fish" was a high school standard.

"Good poem, but if I catch a sonofabitch like that—fuck it, man—I'm keeping it."

A gorgeous day dawned over the kettlehole of Lake Ronkonkoma—cool but clear and windless. Having moved beyond the deli special, I showed Eugene how to cast and twitch rubber worms around the lake's submerged timber. It was snaggy, and we got hung up a few times, but that's where the fish were. Good things don't often come easy, we agreed. Eugene was skilled with a spinning rod and soon caught a chunky largemouth bass, clipping it on the stringer. "My father's gonna love that," he said. We each caught a couple smaller bass, then Eugene hooked a huge fish that crashed the surface and was gone. "Jesus, man," I said. "That might'a been a five-pounder." Eugene didn't swear or complain, he just smiled and said, "That was so cool." As the sun got higher and the bite subsided, I rowed to the Islip side of the lake and recommended anchoring up and still-fishing with worms. "Might catch a catfish."

"Sounds good," Eugene said.

The anchor set and the lines down, Eugene pulled two Heinekens from his lunch cooler. He popped the caps with his lighter and handed me one. "Nice," I said. Red and orange maples glowed back at us from the still lake, and a pair of wood ducks flew by. "Beautiful ducks," Eugene smiled.

We talked about birds, football, the Iran hostage crisis, boycotting the Olympics, grain embargoes, the upcoming election, the Grateful Dead, fish, and girls. I told him the Ronkonkoma story of the Indian princess who drowned heartbroken in the lake and now lures young men to their watery graves. "Shit, man. I'm putting on my life jacket," he acted a bit of panic. Getting into our second beer, I felt wonderful. Then Eugene reached into his pocket and pulled out a joint. "You up for a smoke?"

"I only tried it once. Don't know if I felt anything," I said. "But sure. Yeah."

Eugene admitted to being busted for weed and sent to a counseling center in Valley Stream. "What a joke," he said and puffed. "I learned more from those fuck-ups about drugs and shoplifting." With that confession out of the way and the day so fine, I smoked with my friend and felt the world become even more beautiful. Our conversation ranged from global politics to vast cosmological inquiries. If ice existed on other planets, certainly there must be more water in the universe, certainly more life, more fish. What would angling be like in other worlds? Does the moon affect tides in a lake of this size? Do fish understand time or just move to the rhythms of light and dark, warm and cold? Did that bass feel pain when the hook went through his mouth? "It certainly tried hard to get away," I observed. Did the other fish feel good when we released them? "Shit yeah," Eugene said. My rod tip fluttered and I reeled in a yellow perch. "Maybe you should thank the Indian princess," Eugene said and smiled. I held the golden, black-barred perch up to the sun. "These are good eating," I said.

"Put 'im on the stringer," he said and nodded approvingly.

I looked at the perch, its gills rising and falling. "Do you think fishing is wrong?" I asked.

"Are you stoned, man?" Eugene laughed but began working over the question.

"You could become a vegetarian," he opened his hands before some invisible salad. "But if you're gonna eat meat, this is the way to do it. We're predators."

Long Island Sound rippled with predation and offered good bottom fishing for blackfish and porgies feeding on worms and small shellfish. Starting in the spring and summer of 1981, Eugene and I took the *China Cat* on many trips off Old Field Point, west of Port Jefferson. The point's original lighthouse was built in 1823, and from 1830 to 1856 it was tended by a single woman. I imagined her out in her craggy garden, picking flowers for her table, as I rowed by in my wool suit, waving and coming ashore with a basket of fish and a bottle of wine. "You like older women?" Eugene asked. He had slept with a friend's mother and said it was wild. "They really want it. And they know what they're doing." Eugene often spoke in clichés about women unless pressed for more detail. "Confidence," he said. "When a woman—I mean a guy, too—is confident and comfortable with themselves, then they're better in bed. Active, you know. Not just lay there like a fish."

"A fish?" I took offense.

"A fish outta water. You know what I mean. Just flopping there."

Without depth recorders or sonar, we drew on experience, past scuba diving missions, recommendations, and the observed success of other anglers to locate fishy spots. On this June day there was a northwest wind and considerable swell, but the *China Cat*'s deep vee cut nicely, and I told Eugene about my high-seas adventure mackerel fishing with the jon boat. "That's crazy, man," he shook his head. There were two other boats around the point. Four black men were out in one of Ralph's new rental skiffs fishing for porgies, and when we anchored and turned off our engine we could hear a man singing, "My baby loves porgies, so I bring her some." Another boat with a ghostly pale figure behind the wheel motored near, a child hunkered below the windshield. "Anything?" I raised my open hands.

"No," he shouted. "We're not feeling so good. Weather report's really bad. I'm heading in."

"Take it easy," we said. We never thought too much about weather reports—except hurricane warnings—we just looked at the sky, at the tree tops, maybe the barometer, and said, "Let's go!"

Owning to past success, we tied on double golden hooks, size four, accented with red beads and weighted with two-ounce bank sinkers. Our bait was fresh hardshell clams. I shucked the live cold clams and cut the dense feet into one-inch strips, tossing the shells and soft bellies into a bucket. Sandworms worked well, but they were expensive and hard to find on the flats. We could dig our own big hardshells or buy them cheap off young clammers along with a bag of weed, coded "chowder." I'd be on the phone tethered to our kitchen wall, Aunt Lil sitting there cutting coupons, and could safely ask Eugene, "Hey, did you get some chowder?"

We dropped our baits and felt little bites. "Bergalls," Eugene grumbled, finally hooking a bluish three-inch fish, wrenching it off the hook and tossing it to a gull that swallowed it whole. Bergalls, also known as cunners, are small wrasses common to the rocky coast. I told Eugene that my kid brother had a pet bergall. In our cool basement, I set up a thirty-gallon marine tank and let my six-year-old brother bring home clams, starfish, rock crabs, and finally a bergall that lived a few years, dining on old bait and bits of turkey and roast beef. "They're sweet fish once you get to know them," I said. Eugene gently unhooked and released the next bergall, cooing, "Sorry little fella."

After twenty minutes and two frustrating snags that forced break offs, we reeled up, let out another twenty feet of anchor line, and dropped again. Both Eugene and I immediately felt strong porgy hits, then nothing, retrieving bare, shining hooks. The guys in the skiff were laughing, singing, and pulling in porgies. "They're down there," I said. Hooking porgies requires a feel. I rebaited, dropped to the bottom, lifted the rod slowly, eased it down, then lifted again, feeling the firm rap and gently setting the hook into a solid fish.

Varieties of porgie, also called scup, bream, tai, and snapper, are known in temperate coastal waters around the world. Deep and broad, like a freshwater sunfish, but at home in current-swept rocky bottoms and sandy shoals, the fish is an angler's delight, fighting well and flashing up to the light like brass bells layered in pearlescent turquoise and purple. They are also good eating.

After Eugene hooked and landed another nice porgy, I dumped the clam bellies, shells, and some crushed mussels into a paper bag plumbed with rocks and tethered to a cord. It was an old chumming trick Herbie taught me. Lowered into the water, the paper bag quickly softened; once on the bottom, a firm pull on the cord broke it open, releasing a cloud of appetizers.

The fishing got hot, and we were catching porgy after porgy, sometimes two at a time, letting go lots of small fish. Like the guys in the skiff, we also talked it up—"Oh, yeah, porgy time"—and started singing our own version of "My baby loves porgies." This was not serene, contemplative fishing; there were no analyses of the human condition or cosmological inquiries. Rather it was a picking party, and we just got silly. "Porgie time, brother!" I called, swinging another brassy bream into the *China Cat*; Eugene responded, "Here come another."

I have been on party boats where thirty men and women—white, black, Italian, Puerto Rican, Vietnamese, Brooklyn Jew, and born-again Christian—would chatter, swing, and sing, deliriously drunk on porgies. And on more than one occasion I've actually heard folks sing lines from the musical *Porgy and Bess*. Porgies electrify the rod, but they lack the sober gravity of the flounder and fluke or the fierce magnetism of the pelagic bluefish, who bolts through the water gnashing his teeth. Some fish make us predatorily serious; porgies make us goofy, their dorky, long sloped faces raise joviality and musical theatre.

I was rambling on about porgies when Eugene's rod jumped and bent deeply, pulsing down as he cranked on the reel. "Double?" I asked.

"Don't think so," he said. "Feels like a black."

He was definitely into a big fish that didn't sport the erratic flutter and juke of a porgy but pulled hard and steady toward the rocks. Sure enough, up came the marbled dark sides and beige belly of a big blackfish, also known as tautog. I grabbed the net, scooped head first, and boated the bull, easily eight pounds. The guys on the skiff cheered, and I noticed their boat pitching pretty high in the waves. Then they pulled anchor and waved goodbye.

Eugene and I talked about the blackfish's name. They weren't really black, more of a smoky dark marble.

"Like people. I mean, who's really white or black?" I pointed to my black Van Halen concert shirt leaping with a very white David Lee Roth.

"Mookie Wilson's pretty black," Eugene cited the Mets' center fielder.

"And I guess Cheryl Ladd's pretty white," I offered up one of *Charlie's Angels.* "Maybe we can get them to do a porn movie together." Both of us fell into crazy laughter.

I wondered aloud if the blackfish's big lips had contributed to its name. The names of the Florida jewfish and the American Northwest's squawfish have been found objectionable by some people. Sadly, there's even a Caribbean grouper that for years was called the niggerfish.

"Pretty racist, hah?" Eugene said.

"Old caricature," I shrugged, remembering a social studies lesson illustrated with racist depictions of black people as coons, monkeys, and distorted minstrel clowns. The teacher showed us a 1941 Universal Pictures cartoon where thick-lipped Southern blacks dozed away in "Lazy Town." A man asleep in a boat fished with lines tied to his toes, but even the fish were asleep in the river below. There were plenty of racist jokes still in the air when I grew up on Long Island, but I was white and didn't feel the sting. And though we jokingly tagged the fleet of rental skiffs, "The Puerto Rican Navy," and called the town pier crowded with Asians, "Dinky Dock," there was more diversity and amiable camaraderie in fishing than in any other activity I knew. Fishing stations, public piers, and party fishing boats were multicultural centers of contemporary recreation that often included more than a few women. Fishing also crossed Long Island's money lines. Laid-off laborers in leaky little skiffs fished the same waters as vacationing doctors on million-dollar game boats.

Around all our fishing and talking, the sound had grown raw with whitecaps. It became harder to stand, our thighs bruising against the gunnels, our bagels rolling off the dashboard. Eugene knelt on the bow deck and began weighing anchor, spray coming over us. The engine started on the first pull—always a relief—and I held the wheel and watched. "Goddamnit," Eugene growled. "The anchor's fucking stuck." As he pulled, we rolled into a deep trough and a wave soaked us.

"Wrap it on the cleat. I'll run over it," I shouted. Eugene was quick, and we gunned forward against the jammed anchor flukes and freed them. He pulled up the line and chain, dumped the anchor on deck, and jumped onto the bench with me. We climbed and rode the growing gray waves toward the Port Jeff inlet. *China Cat* would go deep into a trough and climb out, cresting and surfing down another wave, sometimes bow shoveling, sending a wall of water over us. Cresting one wave that was, itself, cresting, the whole boat vibrated as the prop spun out of the water. Then we plunged down and the anchor spilled off the bow. "Fuck!" I yelled. Eugene grabbed the rope and started pulling it back. We should've let the whole thing go because when I eased off the throttle, the boat yawed sideways, everything on board tipping over and rolling across the floor, water pouring in from the side. The anchor crashed into the hull, but Eugene got it in, and I throttled up and turned hard into the next crest. One of the spokes snapped off the steering wheel, but everything came up straight. Eugene bailed and I steered, and without another word between us, we strained and planed back through the inlet and into the safe harbor, turning east for the calm of Seaboard Hole. "That was fucking crazy, man," Eugene said. He dog-shook his wet head and handed me a Bud as a porgy swam over the floorboards between our feet.

Some days we took girls out fishing. A sunny, warm mid-afternoon high tide was ideal. We'd pick up our dates on the dock at noon and fish for about three hours. Sometimes Tim and his new girlfriend, Cindy, would join us. Cindy was thoughtful. "Are you okay?" she touched my hands, red and swollen from fish bites, hook pricks, and lines that had cut into the joints of my fingers.

"They're fine," I said, opening and closing them like a crab on its back. "But I'll probably never wear a wedding ring."

"I don't know about that," Cindy smiled. She and a couple of her friends really liked boating, and I often found them more patient and careful anglers than my guy friends with more experience. If it got hot, the girls would strip down to bikinis. The sight of their bodies excited me more than a leaping bluefish. I leaned into the gunnels to push down my shorts. My life's dreams definitely included women, but I never dreamed of being married.

After fishing, we'd sometimes dock at the flourishing new Ralph's Fishing Station at the mouth of Mt. Sinai Harbor, say hello to Ralph and Barbara, buy some beer (no ID required), and motor over to Crystal Brook for a bit of scuba diving. I had learned to scuba dive when I was fourteen, taking the course at Port Diver with three sets of couples on their way to Bermuda. One of the guys in the class asked the instructor if it was okay to dive after having a few drinks, and the instructor exclaimed, "No!" So I always got everyone to hold off on the beer until we finished our dive.

I loved everything about scuba diving—the way the wetsuit streamlined my chubby body into a smooth seal, the spacey magic of neutral buoyancy, and the ever-amazing view of underwater life. The visibility off Long Island's north shore was often poor, however, and our best dives were right along the bottom in shallow water on calm, bright days. Eugene, Tim, Cindy, and I went diving around Crystal Brook one Monday after the July Fourth weekend, and I found a little gold ring. When we climbed back on the boat I gave the ring to Cindy. I'm not sure why. Tim later told me that he'd be the one giving his girlfriend rings and that I should hang on to my junk.

If we were fishing around Port Jefferson, we'd often beach the *China Cat* at Seaboard Hole, stretch out on towels, drinking, smoking, talking, and swimming in the warm water. I loved swimming, but even with a bit of a buzz, I still felt self-conscious about my body. If I pulled off my T-shirt, I'd get right in the water or lie flat on a towel. Night was best, my body veiled in dark water or the swirling glow of phosphorescence.

In my junior year of high school, in 1981, I locked eyes with a girl at a festival sponsored by the Catholic Church with beer and wine where no one checked ID. Theresa was a voluptuous Italian-American with dark skin and thick black hair that smelled faintly of jasmine and garlic. We drank red wine and strolled down to the water for a long talk and a goodnight kiss. Theresa lived in Belle Terre, an affluent community overlooking Port Jefferson Harbor and the Sound, and I would learn that her family had money, spent vacations in Europe and the Caribbean, chatted about World Cup soccer, art, and continental philosophy. They were also nice to me, a construction worker's son from the other side of town. When I sat on their leather couch, Theresa's cat would climb on my lap and purr.

Theresa, a year older, was experienced with sex, and she gently led me into deeper, warmer water. On breezy beach evenings and nights around the campfire we kissed and touched each other, her olive skin smooth and lotioned in coconut, my scarred and calloused hands redolent of bait. One night sometime after my sixteenth birthday, we walked far down the beach, laid out our towels, slipped off our clothes, and Theresa guided me inside her.

Although driven hard by the flesh, I also felt something like love for this dark and mysterious girl, Theresa. How do we come to feel this way about a stranger? "Who are you?" I asked her one night while we made love in the dark. She laughed—maybe at my question or the impossibly of answering it—and I could feel the vibrations of her laughter pass through her diaphragm and into my body.

After sex, we rolled back on towels under the stars and talked about our families, the living and the dead, and she believed there were mystical connections between us all. Theresa felt she knew my mother, though they'd never met. She said that my mother asked her to care for me, to love me, and help me. I did not believe such communication was possible, but I did not deny Theresa her beliefs.

"Don't worry, your mother is watching," Aunt Lil said as I left the house for our playoff football game in November of 1982. For two seasons I started as right guard for our high school varsity team.

We ran a wing-T, reverse-rich offense, and nothing felt better than pulling and charging full speed at a confused defensive end, burying my shoulder into his hip, and folding him like a straw. In my senior year, we were undefeated league champs, losing that Saturday in the first round of the playoffs 7-0 to Deer Park. It was a long intense season, and for a while it consumed me more than fishing. And unlike fishing, my father absolutely loved football. I walked off the field, bruised and dirty, and saw him coming down from the stands. My father had been to every game but was always thrifty on praise. He walked up to me, smiled, and said, "You did good."

"We lost," I said.

"I watched. You did your job. Hey, I know there'll be a big party tonight. But maybe we should go fishing tomorrow."

"Me and you?"

"Sure, why not?" My father and I hadn't fished together in a long time. We didn't need to. He liked me—I knew that—but he didn't like to fish.

"That's all right, Dad. You watch the Jets. I'll take David with me."

"Well, that's a good idea. If it's not too cold. He'd love that."

I woke up hungover on Sunday and took my seven-year-old brother surfcasting off Cedar Beach. My brother loved fish and water and was easy company, casting clams and reeling in sea robins and small flounder. The sand- and shell-dotted shallows glowed gold, the deeper water beyond darkening to a bruised purple. "Why can't we see into that water?" my brother asked, and I explained about light and refraction and all the creatures living in the cold sound that make it thick and hazy. "So it's different than a swimming pool," he said. "Right," I nodded, wondering how much smarter we'd be if we could see more clearly through space and time. I thought about the game, what I did right and wrong. If I had beaten my guy on a couple more plays we might have scored and won. Correctible mistakes appeared clearly today, but so did my limitations. I played hard but lost, and that was it. We couldn't see into the deeper water where our sinkers landed, we could only see the fish we dragged from its realm.

Swimming

I got a job as the mate aboard a charter fishing boat, *Misty*, captained by Ron, a forty-something air traffic controller who got fired when President Reagan broke their strike in 1981. Ron cashed in his retirement and took a chance on a thirty-eight-foot game boat out of Port Jefferson. His wife screamed, his daughter cried, his friends thought it was great.

On a breezy morning in July, I was getting the boat ready and our clients came down, a young couple and their two boys who were maybe ten and seven. Things always felt a bit awkward when customers first came aboard. People were unsure where to put their things, what to do, or where to sit. I turned on a small brass lamp in the cabin and made coffee, started the engine, and told them Captain Ron was on his way and they should relax. The father's name was Bob, and we started talking. He was working as an air traffic controller. *Scab*, I shuddered, hoping it didn't get mentioned to Ron. Beth was Bob's wife. She looked at our *Blues* sign in the window and said she never cooked bluefish. Was it any good? I described our recipe where we soaked the fillets in milk before grilling them. "Delicious," I said. Bob asked if we'd fish for flounder. I said flounders ran in spring and fall, and we

97

wouldn't work the bottom unless the blues weren't biting. "I only eat flounder," Bob told me. I shrugged and went to work rigging for bluefish.

Captain Ron hopped aboard, said a quick hello, filled his coffee mug, and went up to the bridge. He was lean with a smooth, beardless face and dark hair cut above the ears. He wore a blue cap and a navy nylon jacket with *Misty* silk-screened on the back. At his signal I freed the ropes, and there was a blast of gray smoke, the prop churning roily flowers that bloomed across the surface. We turned from the dock and cut across the choppy harbor. The boys, Peter and Sid, were leaning against the sides, pointing to the high sandy bluffs of Belle Terre. "That's where my girlfriend lives," I told the boys and they made *yuck* faces. Theresa had spent the last year at college studying child development and education. When she came back our relationship wasn't the same. She talked about being a teacher and finding a nice house. I wanted to be an explorer and angle new waters. I wasn't sure if she took me seriously, and we had less and less to talk about.

Beth asked if I was in college, and I told her I'd be going this fall to a small school in South Dakota, studying biology.

"South Dakota, wow. Will you be near the Missouri River? That's an amazing system. Some different fish, that's for sure."

I was a little embarrassed telling some people about heading off to a no-name school on the prairie, but Beth made it sound cool.

"I went to a small college," she said. "You'll get a lot of attention from your profs."

"And I can play football," I added.

She looked right at me, smiled, and nodded. I felt an electric zing.

The breakwater was rough. *Misty* pitched high and the boys' Batman thermos rolled off the bench and broke. Another wave caught us and Beth lost her feet and slammed against the ladder. I asked if she was okay and told everyone to sit in the cabin. "It's the roughest part. We're in the breakwater." I corralled the boys toward the cabin door. "Just sit down. Are you alright, Beth? I'm sorry about that."

Misty plowed northeast toward Buoy 11. The waves softened, and I heard Beth singing John Denver's "Calypso" to Sid on her lap. She looked okay, and we smiled at each other. Bob, however, looked like shit.

Ron idled down, I lifted the first rod, swung the umbrella gently over side, flipped the reel clutch, and let the tubes swim slowly behind us. We used wire rather than leaded line, and each tag marked ten yards. After four tags, I yelled to Ron, and he put up six fingers. We were heading for the shoal's edge and going deep.

Peter came out on deck and kept his feet pretty well. "Are there sharks here?" he asked.

"Sure," I said. "But they're small and harmless." I told him about the one I caught and put in our bathtub.

"Are there great white sharks?" he interrupted.

"Hey, you know a lot about sharks. Have you seen *Jaws*?" His parents hadn't let him, and I nodded. "It's pretty scary," I said. "Great whites live out there in the ocean." I pointed east into the offing. "Threshers and blue sharks sometimes come in the sound. There's nothing stopping them. Fish swim where there's water."

In two hours we didn't get a bite. Purple jellyfish pulsed by. Sid said he saw a shark, but I didn't believe him. I climbed up to Ron on the bridge. He liked reports from the cockpit, Bob was sick and not really into fishing, I told him, but Beth and the kids were troopers. Another half-hour passed with only one strike—two quick pulls on Beth's line. When she lifted the rod it was gone.

"Sometimes sea robins, even sundials, leap at those tubes from the bottom," I said.

"Sundial?" she asked. When I described the translucent flatfish she looked in my eyes and asked more questions. I liked her. She was much more interested in fish than Theresa. Bob became irritated and asked me how long we'd go without a bite. "Beth had a bite," I said, getting a little short with him, which was unusual. Normally I just wanted smiles and tips from the clients. But Bob seemed like a schmuck who couldn't even rise to a day of fishing. Then he vomited over the side, retreated to the cabin, and curled up on the bench. I felt sorry for him. "I really don't like to fish," he said when I went in to get some coffee. "My wife planned this whole thing. Hell, I thought, for the boys and all, it'd be great. This is lousy."

"Beth fishes a lot?" I asked, surprised.

"Not with me. Oh, God, no. She spent a month down in the Caribbean with her sister on some Sierra Club nature trip. They fished and snorkeled with sharks."

I looked out the cabin door and saw Beth, drawing line from her clicking reel, checking the drag like I'd shown her. Maybe it was unfair to compare my girlfriend, Theresa, to Beth, but I liked Beth's attention to fishing. Theresa would go out on the water with me, but she never showed real interest in the technical and biological aspects of fishing. Beth was an angler.

We had some good tide left, and I climbed the bridge to ask Ron if I should shuck clams and try for porgies on the bottom. Ron rubbed his nose and pointed to the fish finder. "There are blues here," he said. He could have easily anchored up and put a few porgies in the cooler, but Ron thought big and took risks.

The Long Island Sound was calming and the air grew warm. Bob felt better and came on deck in his T-shirt, and the boys pulled off their pants to shorts underneath. Beth stripped down to a one-piece red bathing suit and cracked a beer. I don't know how old she was—probably thirty—but I liked her a lot. Her breasts curved like heavy dreams. Ron leaned over the bridge.

"My buddy's kids caught some snappers off the dock last night," Ron said. "They're in the fish box. Why don't ya clean them while there's nothing going on?"

I pulled the eight-inch snappers off the ice and set them on the board, slitting open their bellies and cutting off their heads as Beth and the boys watched. It struck me that the phallic-looking fish, once slit and rinsed, became positively vaginal. I ran two fingers past the drapes of skin and down through the glistening cavity, rinsing again. "These are good eating," I said to Beth, and she nodded.

The wind was dropping off. Bob sat quietly in the fighting chair, and I was about to ask Ron if he needed a beer—then noise like a mad tin clock. Both reels sounded and the poles were alive.

"Fish on! That's it, Beth. Keep the tip up."

But Bob was having a hard time. He had pulled the pole from the holder and somehow loosened the drag. Line peeled away while he cranked. I reached over, thumbed down the star drag, and he kept switching the now jumping rod from under one arm to the other until I planted the butt into his seat gimble. "That's it, Bob. Just sit down and reel."

Beth was standing as she reeled. I was impressed. Twenty yards from the boat, her fish broke the surface in a round splash. She brought the bright streak alongside us, and I gaffed it. A nice eight-pound blue. Ron gave a thumbs-up from the bridge. Sid got scared and ran under his father's legs; Peter reached down and grabbed the blue's flipping tail before I could get a rag on it. "Careful," I yelled.

"Its tail's warm," he said.

"They bite! See those teeth?" I squeezed the gills and the jaws unfolded, exposing a row of dental razors. I pliered the hook from the mouth and tossed it, bleeding, into our fish box, where it coughed up a glossy pink squid. Sid came over and both boys held the lid open and watched the twisting fish.

Bob was still cranking, but his rod lost action. He had let the wire run too high up one side of the reel, and it sounded like couple coils had slipped between the spool and the casing. The fish was off. "It's okay. It happens," I sighed, explaining about guiding the line evenly.

We got Bob's line straightened out and let the boys have a turn in the chairs. The fish were biting. Beth leaned over Sid and helped him reel. My eyes slipped into the deep cleavage of her chest.

We caught about six blues. The kids were laughing, smelling their hands, walking around the cockpit with sandwiches, throwing pieces of cheese and bread to the gulls. Captain Ron and Beth drank beer and talked warmly. There seemed to be some kind of vibe between them, almost as if they'd known each other before, and I started thinking maybe they had. Then Ron pointed to me. "He wants to give this all up for South Dakota."

"You told me to take some risks," I said, feeling more confident now that we had caught fish.

Ron shook his head and smiled. "But South Dakota?"

Before we called it a day we'd try one more thing, jigging on the ledge. Back on the bridge, Ron and I studied the sonar lines of the fish finder, then Ron turned to look down at Beth.

"She's hot, huh?" Ron said to me and smiled.

"Definitely," I nodded.

"And she can handle a rod, too," he laughed, slapping my back.

"God, Ron." I blushed with embarrassment. "I bet she can."

Like old Herbie Clark, Ron indulged in a bit of bawdy talk now and then, but I hadn't heard him get quite so steamy over a customer still aboard.

Back on deck I stowed the trolling equipment and passed out conventional jigging outfits—Ugly Sticks and red Penn Jigmaster reels loaded with smooth, twenty-pound test monofilament. "Okay, Bob, last chance." He looked funny—Yankees hat tilted over his eyes like an awning. Bob had a nice face and a good build that had been neglected for a few years. The engine stopped, and it got quiet. For a moment everyone hushed to the chuckle of water under the hull. Then there was the drone of a jet over the island.

"Take her in, Dad," Sid said.

"She's not mine today," Bob smiled at the boy.

"Are you a controller?" Ron asked.

"Yeah. I retired from the Air Force five years ago—bad experience, lost a friend, bounced around—I work at La Guardia."

"Nice job to walk into," Ron bristled.

"I needed it."

The tension was rising, so I just handed Bob a fishing rod rigged with a two-ounce diamond jig. "Let's jig. Here, Bob, let me show you. Keep the lure dancing." I couldn't understand why Ron didn't say he was sorry to hear about Bob's friend. That was ugly. Beth picked up on it, too, glared at Ron, and walked off toward the bathroom.

"Now what're we fishing for?" Bob asked.

"Anything," I said. "That's it. Give it a few cranks." And when he did his rod arced in a near semicircle, its tip underwater.

"Holy shit!" I sounded. The pole jerked repeatedly and line ran through the guides. "Now that's a fish. Give and take," I coached. "Keep the rod up. That-a-boy." Beth came out on deck—"What've you got, Bob?" The boys stared into the water.

"Okay. Let's get those lines down there," I ordered. "Might be a big school."

But Ron said, "No." He jumped on deck and lifted his hands like a symphony conductor, watching Bob's rod for a moment, then directing: "Keep those lines up. I don't want any tangles. This could be a huge bass."

Ron's words excited me. I leaned over the side, watching the line disappear into the green sunlit water. I looked back at Bob, and at that moment I wanted him to catch this fish more than I wanted anything in the world.

Beth saw it first. "Jesus, look at that thing." I pulled Sid off the gunnel and saw a magnificent striped bass—broad silvery-olive flanks streaked boldly in black. "Must be forty pounds," Ron said. As if the fish heard his voice, it dove.

Bob's shirt darkened with sweat, his cheeks muscled into a smile. I was anxious, remembering the great bass that snapped my line three years ago. Bob's fish started coming up again. Ron held the landing net. The fish rose, its mouth a round purse clasped by the shining jig. Beth pulled out her camera and began shooting photos, repeating, "What a fish, Bob. What a fish!"

The bass swam close and Ron scooped and missed. I gently pushed the kids out of the way and followed the line. Bob stepped left, and the fish dove for the blue shadow of the hull.

"Shit. I lost him." Then it pulled again but softer, and the line wouldn't come up.

"What the hell?" Ron leaned over the side. Beth stood holding the camera in one hand.

"What happened?" she asked.

"He's gone." "Where'd it go?" "He's stuck." Everybody was talking at once. "He's dead," Sid said. The boys were climbing over the sides and I had to yell at them to get down. Ron looked at me. "Must be hung-up on the boat." We both knew that with a straight pull the fish would break off.

I put my hand on the taut line and it still had some spring and pulse to it. "He's still there," I said.

Beth rubbed her husband's shoulders. "Hold on, hon. He's still there."

Ron looked at the rod tip and felt the line, and sure enough, the fish didn't have a straight pull but was fighting part of the boat, maybe a splinter in the keel. Ron tried to push the line off with the boat hook, but it wasn't long enough.

"Do you have a diving mask?" Beth asked. "I could go down there and push him off."

"No way," I said, suddenly anxious that I would have to do it. I was the mate. I was a diver. I was supposed to do those things—even crazy things. "Henry will do it," Ron said. We could hear the soft thump of the fish beneath us.

Beth kicked off her sneakers. "Really, I'm the best swimmer here. I know how to dive. I'll go."

Sid ran to his mother, yelling, "Nooh, no."

"Oh baby, it's okay," she said, hugging him.

"What about sharks?" Peter pitched.

"How many beers have you had?" Bob asked.

I rummaged around looking for a mask, thinking I might really have to do this, though I never would have offered. Beth was brave.

"I don't need a mask," she said and went over. Ron conducted what looked like a sudden allegro in the line, "Follow it down and just try to pull it off the keel."

Beth took a deep breath and disappeared, her hair dancing up like sea grass as she palmed *Misty*'s mossy hull. I imagined the bass's coppery tail flashing through the fuzzy blue-green shadows as it pulled against its own torn mouth. I thought of the fox pulling her bleeding paw against the dreadful steel jaws of the trap.

It all lasted a few seconds. We heard thumping and Bob's pole arced sharply then relaxed. Ron and Peter leaned to look. "Where is she?" I set Sid down and jumped to the other side, stretched over, and took both of Beth's hands as she broke the surface. "Incredible," she gasped. "I saw him." She put one foot on the wooden fin, and

I pulled her up. Something let go inside, and I hugged her, my lips grazing her cheek. Her shoulders were dripping warm. The fish was gone. It must've made one last bolt and tore the hook from its mouth.

At the end of that summer, walking the moonlit beach on the last date with my first love, Theresa, I felt change. "I can't believe you're going to South Dakota," she said for the hundredth time. "That's so far away. Do they even have water there?"

"The Missouri River," I said, a little annoyed.

The ferry sounded its deep horn and Theresa's eyes looked dark. "I'm sorry," she said.

"No, I'm sorry, Theresa."

There were feelings closing and opening between us. I kissed Theresa, but my mind turned to Beth, her hair streaming out in the sunlit water, her naked body rising up to mine. Theresa and I were falling out of love, and my erotic imagination was casting.

"I want to go swimming," Theresa said. She set down her cup of wine, slid out of her jeans, pulled off her T-shirt, and stood there in her bra and panties. I took off my shorts and shirt. A night heron flew close along the shore, veering and squawking when it saw us. I reached to hug Theresa, but she put her hands up. "Let's just swim," she said. We pulled off our underwear and slipped into the warm water.

Back Seat with Fish

As my father drove, I looked longingly at water—ponds and creeks, Lake Michigan, and the Mississippi. Even the muddy stock ponds stippled with coot and the low brown James River aroused my interest as we crossed eastern South Dakota, just outside our destination. But overall, the Great Plains looked flat and parched, and a hot wind—as if cranked from a truck heater—blew across our faces as we walked up to the crumbling athletic building, the door held open by a homemade barbell of pipe and two cement-filled coffee cans. I didn't know anyone at Dakota Wesleyan University, but the football coaches and players were welcoming. My father stayed with me a few days, helped me open a checking account, get phone service, and find the local sporting goods store. "There's a lake here," the man said, pulling out a map and showing us Lake Mitchell. We drove the reddish roads out to the sandy shore. The sun was high, grasshoppers snapped around our legs, and the water bubbled like green pudding. I dug out my spinning rod, made a few casts, dragged in weeds, snagged, and had to break off.

A freshman in the fall of 1983, I started at offensive guard for our football team. The season opened on a warm and bright September afternoon, but every week the prairies grew colder and darker. There were long bus rides to other small colleges in Nebraska, Iowa, and North Dakota, where, by the end of the season in November, sometimes only a handful of people bundled up in the gray stadiums. I got my ass kicked play after play. We won only one game that year—against the University of South Dakota at Springfield, soon closed and converted into a prison. I thought of our undefeated high school season, the marching band, the sunny stadiums packed with hundreds of fans, the plush grass, and short-skirted cheerleaders singing our names. On one bitterly cold, snowy day in Jamestown, North Dakota, we took the field against a team that outclassed us in every way. Our wool-zipped cheerleaders stayed on the bus—and I can't blame them—and when we got trampled by seven touchdowns, when their defensive end threw me to the frozen turf for the tenth time and then offered a polite hand to help me up, I let go of football.

But I held on to college like an exciting new friend. Even religion seemed interesting—a deep pool I had somehow missed on my first drift downriver. Dakota Wesleyan was a church-related liberal arts university, not a bible college; and though shadowed in some prairie parochialism, it was shepherded by a progressive campus minister, Duane Wilterdink, who exemplified an open-minded Christian light I could admire. In a public discussion on gay and lesbian rights in 1984, Reverend Wilterdink talked about friends who had loving, long-term relationships with their same-sex partners. "That love is as genuine and deep and long-lasting as my love for my wife, Mary," he said to an unsettled and aroused audience. One night over a beer, I talked with the reverend about the death of my mother and how our pastor and other Christians explained it as "God's plan," assuring me she was in a better place. Reverend Wilterdink told me that when Jesus lost his friend, Lazarus, he wept and brought the dead companion back to life. "I guess Jesus wasn't too happy with God's plan," the reverend said, and I smiled. "God didn't want your mother to die."

I asked Reverend Wilterdink what it meant to be a Christian. He told me that God's love, forgiveness, and mercy had come to him through Jesus of Nazareth. "Christ is my savior," he said. But I could see that he truly embraced people of other faiths and walks—the Native American students observing a sacred sweat, the Muslim students fasting for Ramadan, and wayfarers, like me, steering by the promises and deceits of Whitman's American Transcendentalism and the scripture of Melville's *Moby-Dick*. No other book had ever spoken to me like *Moby-Dick*—fishing, friendship, fanaticism, and all the big questions I'd been asking about God, man, and the universe rolled before me in words that felt warm and deep. I told Reverend Wilterdink that I must be an agnostic, and he reminded me that Thomas Henry Huxley, the popularizer of the term, declared that even he was "too much of a skeptic to deny the possibility of anything." That jibed with my journey, and I told the good reverend that I worshipped fish and sex. He closed his eyes and slapped a hand to his forehead, but I felt he really respected and liked me even though I was not a Christian.

Reverend Wilterdink taught a philosophy class called "Drugs, Alcohol and Altered States of Consciousness" that explored getting high through various cultural, literary, religious, and philosophical contexts. Were acid, mushrooms, marijuana, and alcohol possible means toward spiritual enlightenment? "Yes, of course," I answered, and the other students smiled—some in approval, some in condescension. Several of us argued that acid and mushrooms were in a different corral than marijuana and alcohol. "Weed and wine are easier to ride," one cowboy put it perfectly. In the end, the reverend helped me to see that drugs were at best a shortcut to what must properly be a long journey of meditation, prayer, practice, and study toward higher consciousness. "You can't just fish with dynamite," I concluded. "You'll ruin everything."

But the reverend and I also agreed that alcohol was a wonderful social lubricant and that peaceful sociability was at the heart of a happier universe. To assist in my pursuit of a happier universe, my old New York friend, Eugene, had set me up with fake ID, and I had no trouble buying beer and liquor and getting into South Dakota bars. There was also plenty of chowder available. "Iowa's fourth leading cash crop," a student-farmer told me, handing me a little bag outside the grain co-op where he worked.

With the harvest came South Dakota's hunting season. My father let me bring my 12-gauge shotgun from home. I kept it in my dorm room closet behind my only sport jacket. The campus was bristling with rifles and shotguns, but I knew of only one incident—discharged in the ceramic studio, where a shelf of wonky, unfired final exams were blasted to pieces, and the shaken teacher gave everyone an A.

"I had nothing to do with that," Birch Hilton chuckled, wiping down his old Winchester and putting it back in his closet. "Hey, you wanna do a little pheasant huntin' on Saturday?" he asked.

Birch was tall, muscular, and handsome with jet black hair, dark Persian eyes, and the five o'clock shadow of a rugged movie star. A linebacker and psychology major from White Lake, South Dakota, a very small town west of Mitchell, Birch carried the humble and generous plainsmen's spirit. After another Saturday home game trouncing, we eased our bruised bodies into his little Opel, a taped flashlight replacing one of the headlights where he'd hit a cow, and drove the 35 miles on Highway 90 to his house, a tired wooden three-story in need of a paint job. His sweet mother prepared a big dinner of roast chicken, peas, and mashed potatoes. There was fresh milk and government cheese, small provisions for rural communities devastated by the farm crisis. Birch's father, Clark, was also tall with a full head of salt-and-pepper hair and a finely chiseled face. Clark once owned a lumberyard but now worked part-time as a feed salesman. He dished out potatoes and asked me questions about my family and New York, while Birch's brothers and sister listened and giggled over my accent. There was no wine or beer on the table. We said grace and dug in. After dinner, his sister played piano.

In the morning we drove the family pickup out to a rundown farm where Clark had arranged for us to jump some ducks. A man in torn, stained coveralls came out and muttered about a tractor he "couldn't sell for shit."

"Bert's losing the place," Clark confided as we walked up to the first berm.

"All right," Birch coached. "We're gonna get low and come over that rise. If you see ducks, blast 'em."

Birch and I crouched and crept to the crest, peeking over at a half dozen puddle ducks and a couple coot swimming nervously away. We stood up, their wings opened, and we fired, dropping four birds. I ran down to the water's edge, tested the bottom with a stick, and then walked into the shallows and retrieved the ducks: two hen mallards and a pair of pintail, the drake's beautiful rusty head cradled by a crescent moon.

The same tactic on a larger pond dropped two birds that fell far from shore. I hated losing game and went waist deep into the cold water to get one duck, a small bufflehead Birch called a butterball, asking me if a mouthful of duck was worth a wet ass. The other bird drifted toward the middle of the pond. We walked back to the barn, and Clark found Bert and asked him if he had a dog. "Dead," Bert said. But he went into a shed and came back with a spinning outfit, the dented reel half loaded with heavy blue line tied to a melted rubber crayfish. "You know how to use one of these?" he asked me. "Yes, sir," I reached for the rod. Back at the pond, my first cast came up short. Clark had an old bolt in his pocket, and I tied it on, but I still came up short. Birch gave it a try and hooked a fish. Clark and I laughed, and Birch took his time playing gracefully, without any drag, a solid two-pound largemouth bass. He flipped the fish onto the dry grass, took another cast, and hooked the duck. We gave the bass and ducks to Bert, who showed not the least bit of surprise; he just nodded, took them into the back kitchen, and came out with a bottle of homemade wine, handing it to Clark. "Don't let your mother see that wine," Clark said, passing the bottle to Birch.

Church had let out, and we could see people hurrying home to change into their hunting clothes. We stopped for coffee and then drove on to meet a large party of hunters at the edge of a cornfield. There were introductions and curious exclamations that I'd come all the way from New York to hunt White Lake's fine pheasants. Marching across the field against four men stationed as blockers, Clark yelled, "Don't shoot the blockers." I laughed. "I'm serious," he repeated. "Happens every year." Wet pants chaffed my thighs, but I was happy to be walking the corn, the rustle of pheasants running ahead of us, suddenly flushing in wild bursts of cackling color. I was overeager and blasted one rooster just a few feet ahead of me. "Easy, New Yorker," someone said.

So I took it easy, waited for the pheasants to fly up and out, and dropped a couple long-tailed cocks that would make good eating. I thought of those British driven shoots where tweed-jacketed gentlemen and ladies swung Purdey shotguns, retiring to brandy-warmed talk on leather chairs in mahogany-paneled clubs. The White Lake hunt included the poorest of men in ripped coveralls, women of all ages, high school kids in Mötley Crüe sweatshirts, the town doctor, and a very old man in a forties-style orange cap and vest who bagged his limit of three male pheasants, drove the birds home, and came back for a second round. Limits were not strictly observed. Everything got eaten.

Birch and I were feeling achy from Saturday's game, so we crashed out in the pickup. I woke cold and prickly. Birch called over his father and drove us home. I needed some dry pants, but the only ones that fit my thick thighs belonged to his mother. While my jeans tumbled in the drier, I toured White Lake wearing Mrs. Hilton's turquoise stretch pants and Clark's mucking boots. After lunch, Birch said we should drive the back roads to Mitchell and do a little road hunting. We uncorked Bert's wine and, with our loaded shotguns resting between our seats, rolled slowly down gravel roads, watching for pheasants. Birch was great company, and we listened to Dylan and Hendrix and talked about the football season and Coach Bob Bozaid—how he had us pray after every practice and before every game, preaching that "God wanted us to win, that God would lead us to victory." Bozaid was a decent man, but he was a losing coach. Not that he could have done much with my body and soul, but the team had potential, and he could have tried harder to draw from realms outside the supernatural. "It takes more than God to win football games," Birch said. I agreed and handed him the wine. A coyote crossed the road and disappeared into the willows beside a slough.

Winters were long, cold, and snow-filled in South Dakota, and by April I was eager to fish. Without the demands of spring football, I could concentrate on studying and partying. One Friday playing eight ball at the Corner Pocket, a beer and pool joint downtown on

Eighth Street, I met Woody. With a father in the CIA, Woody had lived in Abu Dhabi, Cairo, and Rome; he knew languages and cuisines. He spent four years in the Marines and thought he might try some college. When Woody discovered new things he got excited. One icy night he blew into my room with a bottle of whisky, reciting Yeats' "Song of the Wandering Aengus." "They don't teach this shit in the Marines," he exclaimed, and I applauded.

Woody and I heard that northern pike and walleye were being caught on spoons in Firesteel Creek, so we stopped by the biology lab to talk with our professor, Bob Tatina, who confirmed the report. Tatina was setting up a lab, but he went to the board and drew a section of the creek down from the Lake Mitchell spillway, chalking in the bends and some downed trees, indicating spots where he caught fish. "Cast upriver and reel quickly enough to keep that spoon moving. Flutter and drop," Tatina said. "And be careful. Water's still cold and fast."

Woody and I jumped in his old car and swung by the courthouse to get fishing licenses, but they were closed. "Screw it," I said. We drove out to the Firesteel, parked along a barbed wire fence where some cows grazed, and walked through a stand of elm around heaps of crumbling bricks to the creek. The water was a little high and cloudy, but we were excited, hurrying down the trail to the spot Tatina recommended, casting red and white Dardevles and hoping. My well-worn green Penn spinning reel had a reliable drag, but the springs wore out periodically and the bail wouldn't snap over. This was happening today, and as I fumbled with the reel, my spoon found a snag. "Goddamn it!" I said, reeling up tight and jerking the rod. There is nothing worse than a snag to disrupt and frustrate the joy of fishing, and learning to physically and psychologically cope with snags in fishing and in life is necessary for long-term survival. Cursing really helps.

Down at the water's edge, trying to get a reverse angle on the hook, the mud greased my boots, and I slid into the cold creek. "Shit," I yelled and walrused up the bank. Woody laughed and scolded me for scaring the fish. I got my footing, tried to jerk loose my spoon, slipped again, and snarled my line in a spiky bush. I took a deep breath, untangled my line from the bush, tightened down my drag, and broke off from the snag. Then I recognized the distinctive tan uniform and badge of the game warden coming down the trail.

"How you fellows doing?"

Woody looked at me and squeezed his eyes shut.

"No fish, sir. But I just took a bath," I said.

"Creek's a little high," the warden replied. "Can I see your licenses, please?"

"I'm sorry, sir," I said. "We stopped by the courthouse, but they were closed. It's the first time out this year. We always get licenses."

"You can't fish without a license, son."

The game warden was cool and polite, but he confiscated our equipment and wrote us tickets for fishing without a license, one hundred dollars. We'd get our gear back when we paid the fine, but we'd lose our fishing privileges for a full year.

I didn't have an extra hundred dollars in my checking account, so I called Aunt Lil, and she gave me a hard time but wired the money. The warden visited the dorm and returned my spinning rod and tackle bag. I thanked him and asked if he wanted a drink. It was four o'clock on a Friday afternoon and the improvised bar in our Graham Hall room was in full swing. The warden laughed, "I thought this was a dry campus."

"How could a fisherman survive on a dry campus?" I said. He smiled and declined my offer. We parted on friendly terms.

The college officially prohibited alcohol, a ban that was not enforced in Graham Hall, an old granite building with large rooms reserved as a co-ed honors dorm. On most Fridays and Saturdays, not to mention many other nights of the week, the men and women of Graham partook in the honorable customs of drinking, smoking, and even bowling, using the third floor hallway as an alley with real balls and pins snatched from Village Bowl during the chaos of a power outage.

Woody did not pay his fine, and when he was absent from class on Monday, I explained to our beloved American literature professor, Joseph Ditta, that Woody had checked into prison. Professor Ditta questioned whether Woody, like Thoreau, who also loved to fish, was making a political statement against the government's infringement of inalienable rights, such as the right to catch a fish. "No," I said and smiled. "He just wants to save a hundred bucks." Woody's girlfriend, Xanti, a zaftig strawberry blonde partial to cigarettes and Led Zeppelin, shook her head in disgust. Another guy added, "Render unto Caesar." There was talk going every direction. "Okay, let's move on," Ditta raised his hands, calmed the class, and continued discussing *Walden*. Woody's time in the clean single cell with room service allowed him to study and read without interruption. He cleared his fine, retrieved his gear, and earned three A's that spring semester.

State law suspended my fishing privileges for the rest of the year, but with Thoreau in mind, I continued to angle without a license. I believed in fishing licenses and regulations. My fine was just. But that fine had been paid, and the extended suspension of fishing privileges seemed unfair. I felt morally entitled to fish and so became a renegade angler, taking long fish-walks, assembling my rod and screwing on my reel in the wooded backwaters, pulling essential gear from a pocket, and letting go everything I caught. Releasing fair-sized, edible game fish was good for me, and I began to appreciate catch-and-release, especially when I caught the same twenty-inch pike with an obvious nick out of his tail two days in a row. This sharply distinguished fishing from hunting, where the endgame is death. There was no releasing those pheasants we blasted. Legendary angler Lee Wulff said it well, "Game fish are too valuable to be caught only once."

Releasing fish keeps the game in play. And play it was, though still at the expense of the struggling fish. It was no longer emotionally necessary for me to bring home an actual fish and receive praise from my father and aunt or my brother's admiration—though I did show off a photo now and then. A photo of a big fish documented the specimen and helped quell the doubters. But more than ever I loved to fish for the sake of fishing. So was this a sport? Canadian outdoorsman, writer, and courtroom judge Roderick Haig-Brown explained that recreational angling started with "the first man who sneaked away to the creek when the tribe did not really need fish."

When Birch and our friend Ben Whitehorse started talking about the Missouri River and big walleye, I wanted to go. Birch was seeing a woman in Chamberlain, and he'd meet us on the water. Ben would drive me and Abe, a Methodist scholarship student from Zimbabwe, to the river, and I'd buy the beer. Ben was a heavyset Sioux Indian with neatly trimmed short hair and large glasses that always seemed smudged with something. He played football but had a gentle demeanor and spoke softly in a Lakota accent that reminded me, strangely enough, of the Yiddish-flavored voices of New York. Ben drove a dented, rough-running Plymouth Volaré with a good stereo and an overstuffed trunk tied down with baling twine.

We rode west, cranking the Scorpions and passing a flask of cheap whisky. Thinking a famous walleye spot on the Missouri might occasion a game warden, I decided to get a fishing license under a slightly different name with a new address—easily accomplished in the days before the Internet. Outside town, licenses were sold in mini-marts with fishing and hunting supplies. You could pull into M & H Mini-Mart and get a burrito, beer, whisky, a few boxes of shotgun shells, sinkers, hooks, and a fishing license. Reissued as Hal Hughes of White Lake, I bought us a case of beer and took the back seat for the long drive to Ben's brother's place.

"You're on the rez now, so watch your step, *wasi'chu*," Ben joked. I had fallen asleep and woke to rolling green hills and a wide horizon of bright water. I looked at Abe, a very black African with a shaved head and a beaded necklace. "What's who?" Abe squinted at me. "Wa-shee-chu," Ben sounded out the word. "You're a black *wasi'chu*," he pointed at Abe and laughed. *Wasi'chu*, roughly equivalent to honky, haole, gringo, or gaijin, refers, often contemptuously, to nonnatives, but Ben's teasing use of the term lightened up the whole issue of race when we were together.

We drove over cracked streets spouting grass, and what looked to be a squashed rattlesnake, into town where we were further instructed to keep the beer down and watch the blue dog. "I'll get him on his chain," Ben said as we pulled into the drive and a gray-blue heeler jumped on the hood, barking furiously. "Oh my god," yelled Abe, spilling beer on his pants.

Ben's brother lived in a trailer home reroofed in tin sheeting weighed down with tires. He and his girlfriend hardly looked up at us when we walked in. The place was overflowing with ashtrays, dishes, wrinkled magazines, and cassette tapes piled over a coffee table. Ben came out of a bedroom with two heavy spinning rods and a tin tackle box. He asked his brother if he wanted a beer. "You can leave some," the brother said and brought out a bong, setting it on the coffee table. Abe and I kneeled on the dirty rug and the others sat on the saggy couch, and we all had a good smoke. Abe loved to get high, and when I asked him if he smoked in Zimbabwe, he burst out in laughter and said, "Of course, Use." Abe always dropped the "H" off my name. The woman, Sandy, was quiet until she smoked, and then she kept talking and asking me questions about what I thought of "backward-ass South Dakota."

"You must be so bored here," she said.

"I like it here," I told her. She had a pretty brown face with some acne scars and shiny black hair to her shoulders.

"I'm sick of this place," she said. Ben's brother dropped a big Ziploc bag of deer jerky on the table. He said he shot the deer last fall, and when I asked him about it, he came alive with describing the mule deer buck and how it walked right up to him out of a draw.

"Nice job," I said. "This is good."

"Take the bag," he said. Sandy pulled out a big twist of jerky and bit into it. "Yum."

High and happy, we bumped and dipped down Tribal Highway 5 along the river, past endless rises of buffalo grass studded with scrubby cedar and juniper, turning north to Fort Thompson and Big Ben Dam. "This is my goddamn dam," Ben laughed. "So watch your step." From the back seat, using phrases learned in sociology class, I asked Ben about "the Native American community."

"Indian," he said.

"Indian?"

"Maybe you're native American, man. We're Indians. Indians. It's life on the rez, man. We scalped the last New Yorker who came here."

Ben Whitehorse was having some more fun with me, but I was interested in his life and asked more questions.

"Indians been fucked over for a long time, so we know how to do it," he said. "I'm just doing my thing. Live and let live, you know? Get a little business started and help my folks out. Maybe marry some big-titted Norwegian gal."

"That's cool, Ben."

"Fucking cool, Use," Abe said from the front seat, smiling and handing me a hunk of jerky. We parked below the dam and waited a while for Birch, then decided to head down to the water, climbing over big pink rocks that armored the banks. It was hard going over the rocks with poles and tackle and two sixes of beer; painful missteps killed my buzz. Abe said he was just gonna watch, but Ben rigged a rod for him and was teaching him to cast. I felt the need for a little space and climbed downriver a couple hundred feet, watched the high-shouldered pelicans swim and dip, and started throwing my crippled shad crank bait.

Before us was the Missouri River that once watered endless tall grasses, buffalo herds, and the Sioux high on their mustangs. The Missouri of Lewis and Clark, cattle ranching, depressed Indian reservations, eroding soil, riprap, five dams, and many cities. It was just getting dark, and there were lights and engine sounds from a few boats mixed with the steady hum of the dam's generators. People seemed to be partying around a fire on the Crow Creek Reservation across the river. The south bank where we fished was deserted. The river smelled flatter than the saltwater around Long Island, but the sound of gulls and lapping waves were familiar. Cast and cast, that's what you do, reeling fast, then slow, wondering if the next moment will connect you to a walleye. I stared at the darkening river, rubbed a bruise on my knee, and remembered my father giving me arrowheads that he found at construction sites. Long Island once had many flourishing tribes—Setauket, Shinnecock, Montauk—great fishing people wiped out in the early waves of European settlement. By the end of the nineteenth century, the plains Indians were also broken down. With land, water, and so many traditions lost, it was good to see the Sioux of Lower Brule still hunting and fishing.

After an hour of steadily increasing wind, I heard Ben Whitehorse whooping up a storm, and I scrambled over the rocks to see what was going on.

"It's big, Use. Like whale, man," Abe was standing and gesturing with his cigarette. Ben was fast to a fish. Birch showed up, honing in on our gusting voices and providing the only working flashlight. Something came into the beam. Was it a beaver? Its smooth black body spanned more than a yard, and it seemed to have the tail of a shark and the bill of a goose. "What the hell is that?"

"Spoonbill catfish," Ben yelled.

"Sure is," Birch confirmed. "Big paddlefish."

Here was another fish I had long read about but had never seen or touched. After three runs the exhausted creature, firmly snagged at the base of its rostrum, splashed beside the rocks. Abe held the light, and Birch reached down and grabbed its bill. The fish was easily four feet long, and we carried it under a light in the parking lot. Dark, small eyed, and flabby finned, it had smooth skin like a catfish and a large toothless mouth used for scooping plankton that it strained through gill rakers. "Ram-jet feeding," Professor Tatina would explain back at school. The paddlefish's amazing snout is loaded with electroreceptors for detecting schools of plankton that it swims through openmouthed. Responding to breeding cues triggered by the faster spring water, paddlefish congregate at the dam's tailrace each May. I imagined this fish finning like a right whale in the dark current until Ben's barbed hook struck home. "They're good eating," Ben said. "All but the red meat—I throw that stinking shit to the dogs."

We hadn't caught any walleye, but a strong wind was building, and this was enough for tonight. "Let's hit the bar in Reliance," Ben suggested, lifting the heavy fish into his already full trunk, setting it on top of a barbecue grill he never got around to assembling and some highway cones and raincoats. "Okay, Reliance. Let's go," I said. Birch followed in his car, and we sailed out, feeling quite pleased with our mighty catch, lighting and passing the pipe, smoke rolling out of the widows—the rusty, dented, taped, and twined old cars plowing through the prairie night. Ten minutes down the road, we heard screeching tires and a horn. Looking back, we saw Birch stopped on the shoulder. There were no other cars, so Ben backed up. Birch was standing over something on the pavement. It was the paddlefish, his snout and head ironed by the Opel's bald tire.

"That's some crazy roadkill, Birch," Ben said and laughed.

"Your fucking trunk started opening wider and wider, then shit, that fish jumped right out."

"My father used to get fresh rabbits this way," Ben laughed some more.

"Hell yeah, my old man brought home a pheasant he hit with his pickup," Birch added. "But never any fish."

We all started laughing, really laughing, and Abe told us about a bus that once hit a buffalo and the town celebrated with a feast. Not wanting to be outdone, I told the men about a raccoon Herbie picked off Route 112 with a prime pelt worth thirty dollars.

"Should've ate 'im, man," Ben said.

We wrapped the fish in some plastic from Ben's trunk, and I set it beside me on the backseat, patting it often.

I stayed up late in the dorm lounge watching a movie from the early sixties starring Rock Hudson as a tackle salesman and fishing pro who's never been fishing. A beautiful woman has to teach him to fish. The movie was terrible, but the opening song, "The favorite sport of a man is girls," and the photomontage of pointy-breasted women in sports attire stayed with me. There were parties where a girl from class and I would start talking, kissing, and if things felt right, we'd find a room or a bush or the backseat of a car. I had a lot to learn, and I paid attention.

One night after a few hours of steamy dancing, I hooked up with a girl and we had a wild time in the backseat of a friend's Chrysler. I noticed that the currents were saltier than usual, in fact, the aromas and flavors were downright fishy. Almost exactly like peeled shrimp at a summer picnic. People joke about this, but I was fascinated by the connection, the oceans within, some deep channel back to our marine origins. After a one-night stand or a couple random hook-ups in my first years of college, I found myself playfully objectifying sex in the language of fishing. "Got my limit last night," I grinned at Woody toweling off in the dorm bathroom.

"Oh yeah? Rod action any good?" he smiled.

"Not bad. But not quite a trophy for the wall."

Crude, sure, but such jokes allowed us to discuss those aspects of sex that swam below love.

Literature, I soon learned, took such crudities and turned them into art. A number of old poems compared courtship and seduction to fishing, but it was the women who were doing the casting, like Shakespeare's Cleopatra:

> Give me mine angle; we'll to th' river. There,
> My music playing far off, I will betray
> Tawny-finned fishes. My bended hook shall pierce
> Their slimy jaws, and as I draw them up
> I'll think them every one an Antony,
> And say, "Aha! You're caught."

Later in the seventeenth century, Edmund Waller talks of "Ladies Angling":

> At once victorious with their lines and eyes,
> They make the fishes and the men their prize.

And in "The Bait," John Donne describes "sleave-silk flies" that "Bewitch poor fishes' wand'ring eyes," but a comely woman:

> . . . need'st no such deceit
> For thou thyself art thine own bait;
> That fish that is not catched thereby,
> Alas, is wiser than I.

Wise or unwise, I was drawn to as many baited hooks as I myself did cast.

The Holiday Inn's Shipwreck Lounge in Mitchell, South Dakota, was a good place to hook up. There were older women eager to talk with college students, and I was taken home a couple times. In one instance, the woman's separated husband came to the house at seven in the morning to retrieve some tools. "Shit," she said and ordered me to "Stay." I waited like an anxious dog in the bedroom until he left, and she returned to free me. Having coffee together downstairs in her kitchen, I saw a number of photos of the man still taped to the fridge. In one photo he was holding a huge walleye. "Damn," I shook my head, "Where did he get that?"

In my junior year of college I started dating Janet, a perky, petite blonde who loved sex but also loved to think, talk, read, and even fish a bit. She was from Montana, and we launched a 1986 spring break trip into a blizzard. State police closed the interstate, directing cars into the town of Wall, where we bedded on the floor of a church and quietly consecrated the Lord's blessing of sensual affection when the lights went out. The next morning brought some stares from the congregation, more tire-spinning roads through western South Dakota and Wyoming, over the border into Montana where we slept in our car at a gas station in Garyowen. Just to the north was the Little Bighorn Battlefield. At first light, running the heater, Janet and I talked about Custer and his men, the terror they must have felt when they knew the battle was quickly turning against them. I imagined a man my age, twenty, clutching an arrow piercing his side. We talked about the Indians celebrating their well-deserved victory, the cries and singing, the women coming onto the field to cut the cocks and balls off the dead soldiers.

Janet's father met us outside Lewistown. Spending time with the father of a girl you're bedding can feel a little weird at first. But he introduced me to good trout water and liked the way I fished, coaching here and there, only admonishing if I did something stupid like leave my rod unattended on a rock ledge while I went to the car for beer. We fish-walked rivers, casting spinners and catching gorgeous rainbows. Janet joined us in Lewistown to fish Big Spring Creek. She was a good stream walker and spinnerette, making precise casts behind boulders and under logs, catching a nice brown trout that I killed with a rock and carried on a willow branch pushed through its gills. We also plunked spillways with trout eggs that Janet's father had saved from earlier catches. He wrapped dime-size clusters of eggs in small squares of stocking hose that stayed firmly on the hook while oozing the irresistible smell of spawn. Trout, like many fish, love to eat their own eggs. Janet and I hooked one- and two-pound cannibal rainbows, swinging them up and over the concrete. Retiring for drinks and lunch at the river-straddled Montana Bar, I stared down through the Plexiglas floor window at trout hovering safely in green light.

Janet's family had a camper that she and I used for another trip to the Black Hills and Lake Pactola with Woody and his girlfriend, Xanti. Woody and I poached a couple ducks with his Sears and Roebuck .22 and then unfolded chairs on the cold, rocky shore, plunking corn nibblets for trout. Like the old Montana poet, Dick Hugo, we set our poles on forked sticks, eased our bundled-up backs into folding chairs, drank blackberry brandy, smoked a few cigarettes, and waited for the rods to dance. When it warmed up a bit, the women joined us. We caught four or five nice trout, cleaned them by the lake, played cards in the camper, and started cooking. Woody breasted out the ducks and cut the meat into small chunks that we salted and fried in butter and garlic. Xanti baked the trout in foil with butter, mushrooms, and roasted almonds that Woody shoplifted from a mini-mart. The food was great, and as we finished, I leaned back, patted my belly, and forecasted, "More nice ones tomorrow." Janet looked at me in surprise. "We fished all day," she said. "I was freezing out there."

"We didn't fish all day. We fished a few hours," I retorted. I knew Janet found this kind of fishing boring—she was an active woman, and I admired that—but I had never been to a trout-filled mountain lake and was hoping to spend the next day working lures in deeper water. Woody and Xanti felt the tension and stepped out for a smoke.

"I didn't just come here to fish," she said.

"Well, what do you want to do?"

"Go for a hike, maybe some shopping in Rapid City."

"Shopping, are you kidding? With all this around us?"

"Well, a hike then."

Janet was, of course, making a reasonable request. For most normal people, six hours of fishing in thirty-degree weather was enough. We negotiated that I could have a morning of angling while she read. In the afternoon we would go for a hike near an old gold mine.

Early next morning, Woody and I fished-walked to the other side of the lake. With stinging fingers and freezing rod tips, we caught a few more rainbows. Back at the camper for lunch, we ate grilled cheese sandwiches and tomato soup and then set out on a hike through the spruce and ponderosa pine that proved perfect for getting the blood flowing, seeing the land, and bringing us together. This feels good, we agreed, warm in our strides. As we turned back, it started to snow. The women looked beautiful with crystals shining on their wool caps and in wisps of blonde hair. Three mule deer held dark against the whitening brush, and there were tracks of what might have been a cougar—big round prints as wide as my hand.

That night in the camper after another fish dinner, full, tired, and comfortably drunk, Woody and Xanti climbed in the bunk over the cab, and Janet and I got under the covers on the narrow foldout below. We started kissing and were moving into each other when I heard Woody and Xanti above.

"Do you hear that?" I whispered in Janet's ear.

"Yeah."

"Well, they'll hear us."

"It's okay," she said.

College life opened up many possibilities and made clear some limitations. Although I enjoyed my biology classes, dewy dreams of becoming a naturalist like John James Audubon, John Muir, or Aldo Leopold evaporated over the increasing heat of data crunching, statistical analysis, and the glowing promise of computers. I wanted to be in the field sketching and writing notes about spawning bass and migrating osprey. I wanted to describe the colors, sounds, and movements of animals in ways that would dazzle and excite readers. I wanted to use metaphor. "Then you want to be a writer," Professor Ditta advised. So I steered from biology to English, wrote poems and essays, worked on the school paper, edited the literary magazine, and put together *The Birch and Henry Show.*

Inspired by *Late Night with David Letterman*, Birch and I interviewed and roasted local personalities, featured live music, pet tricks, and our own parodic skits of campus life. In 1986 we hosted George McGovern, alumnus and former Dakota Wesleyan professor. McGovern grew up in the small town of Avon, South Dakota, and became a straight-talking populist plainsman. He had a progressive vision and a loyal following, but he lost big in the 1972 presidential election to Nixon. Cranking Van Halen's "Running with the Devil," we introduced McGovern—he was quick, funny, generous, and willing to roll with our irreverent interrogations. I asked him later if he liked to fish. "Yes," he said. "But the fish don't much like me."

Unlike McGovern, Birch had never ventured far out of South Dakota, so I invited him to Long Island for a few weeks of summer fun. A handsome dark tower with understated humor and gentle, polite manners, Birch was a huge hit with my family and friends. "Why can't you be more like Birch?" Aunt Lil said when he helped her clear the table and fold towels.

One calm morning in June, Eugene and I took Birch fishing aboard the *China Cat*. Port Jefferson Harbor and the Long Island

Sound lay like glass, and we cruised smoothly to our favorite spots off Old Field Point, telling Birch about the time we almost lost the ship. "That's crazy, man," he said. Birch had never been on salt water, and after a swig of rum from Eugene's flask and big smiles from two shapely women on the deck of a passing sailboat, he said, "I feel like a pirate." We caught some small porgies and a blackfish pup, but bottom fishing on the north shore wasn't what it used to be, and we decided to make the nine mile run out to Middle Grounds, a tiny island between Port Jefferson and Bridgeport, Connecticut. The bird-splashed island holds little more than an old boarded-up lighthouse electronically sounding and flashing for Stratford Shoal. Calm water allowed us to dock, step out, and walk around. Probably like many before us, we tried the doors and boarded-up windows, yearning for a peek inside. Surely these ghosts have seen whaling ships, frigates, and rumrunners crossing Long Island Sound. There must have been terrible storms and dreadful wrecks. Did they marvel over the canvasback ducks, sea turtles, and dolphins we never see anymore? A herring gull snuck out of a cracked vent, but we could only touch the rough stone and imagine.

When we got back in the boat, I noticed the gas hose had come off the fuel tank. I pushed it back in, but after an hour of trolling I could see we were sucking way too much fuel. We turned back toward Port Jefferson and made it halfway. "Shit. We're out of gas," I told them in the sudden silence of our starved engine. We were without a radio and adrift in water deeper than our anchor line. "Might as well keep drinking," Eugene said. And we did. Beer after beer, moving slowly east with the outgoing tide.

It was getting on four o'clock, and I started wondering what would happen if we didn't get picked up before dark. Huge ships crossed the sound. We had no running lights, no horn, no charts.

How would anyone know where we were? Then Eugene, head wrapped in a red bandana and cracked sunglasses, pointed and rasped, "Arg, mateys. Sail on the horizon."

We waved over a yacht named *Euphoria,* and they agreed to call the Coast Guard. We expected orange helicopters and an official boarding, so we flattened all our empty beer cans and hid them under the life jackets. An hour later, a sluggish cabin cruiser showed up, Coast Guard Auxiliary, skippered by our neighbor, ill-tempered Mr. O'Malley, whose house we egged every Halloween. He bull horned, "Put on your life jackets." It may have been the first time we ever wore them, and they smelled of mold and beer. Our rescuers approached, threw us a towline, and kindly dragged us back to the ramp in Port Jeff, where my father and Eugene's father were waiting. "What the hell happened?" they asked. We were late, tired, sun-dried, and beer fuzzled, but we explained, and Mr. Jones went over to make a donation while my father assisted getting the boat on the trailer.

"How many beers have you had?" my father asked.

"Just a couple. I'm fine."

Feeling too wasted to pilot, I once again gave the wheel of the family station wagon to Eugene—always a better driver—and we headed home. A few blocks from the water, we heard a terrible grinding noise and looked back to see a shower of sparks. Eugene did what any driver might do when something is wrong—he hit the brakes. But the trailer had come unhitched, and when our car stopped, the wheeling boat rolled on, crashing through the wagon's back door and widow, showering us in blue glass. "What the fuck!" Eugene screamed.

"I don't know," Birch calmly replied, "but I'd say we just got rear-ended by your boat," the fish chasing, seaweed festooned prow of the *China Cat* having joined him in the backseat.

My father must have felt some relief in my return to college. But when I called him to say that a student had been killed drinking and driving on a country road outside Mitchell, he got serious and said, "You better think about that."

I survived my senior year, and my father, Aunt Lil, twelve-year-old brother, David, and my friend, Tim, drove together to South Dakota for my graduation. The occasion raised much revelry, and Professor Ditta and his wife threw a party at their house. My father, who had never graduated high school, talked and laughed all night with professors, parents, and my friends. Woody, Xanti, Birch, and Ben Whitehorse were there. There was a keg of beer, a few bottles of booze, and discreet smokes available in the bushes.

Janet planned to bake a six-pound brown trout I caught a month before from the Missouri River, but while thawing on the counter, the fish was seized and eaten by her two golden retrievers. She instead brought out two pans of baked walleye she had caught with her dad.

"This is the best fish I ever tasted," Tim said.

"Fantastic," I quickly added.

Tim and Janet hit it off, and by the time the party was winding down and my family had returned to their motel, I thought something might happen between the three of us. We walked back to my room in Graham Hall, mostly packed up in boxes and suitcases. The little fridge was still plugged in, and there were a few remaining wine coolers, refreshing after the long night of talking. I sat on the couch with Janet while Tim stood above us admiring Janet's legs.

"Would you like to see some more of them?" she asked.

"Sure," Tim said. Janet smiled and pulled up her skirt.

Tim kneeled before her and began caressing her thighs, and Janet pulled him forward for a long kiss. I joined in.

At seven in the morning, the phone rang. It was my father. "Hey, where are you? Your brother is waiting. You taking him fishing or what?"

"Shit. Okay, right. I'm on my way." Janet was asleep on the bed, Tim snored on the couch, and I was a sticky, smelly, hungover mess. I shook Tim awake, and we both took hot showers in the communal dorm bathroom, looking a little awkwardly at each other.

Speed dressed and gear gathered, we raced Janet's pickup to the motel. We were an hour late, everyone was watching television, and my brother was upset. But Tim and I were in high spirits, despite the hangovers, and we promised donuts and plenty of good fishing. I made a big deal over my brother's new spinning outfit with a red Cardinal reel that Aunt Lil bought him the day before. "Be careful with him around the water," Lil said. My father gave me twenty dollars. "Hey," he looked right into my bloodshot eyes, "Watch your brother."

We stopped for donuts and coffee. My brother, chubby like me at twelve, gobbled down two Bismarcks, drained a strawberry milk, and said he felt sick. Tim and I savored the coffee but couldn't eat. We drove down a washboard gravel road—"I'm gonna puke," my brother threatened, but he didn't—to the grassy banks of the Jim River, where I told him we could catch some catfish. David could cast pretty well, but there were countless snags, and it was frustrating for him and us. I had to help him break off and retie a few times, and he said, "I hate this place."

I had not fished with my brother for many months, and now he was straining my patience. In this same way I surely must have exhausted my father, a man who doesn't even like fishing. But maybe that made it easier. I had expectations and got annoyed when my brother didn't follow instructions or when he complained. David made another swift cast, and the top half of his rod shot into the water. "My pole's gone! My new pole," he screamed. "I hate this."

"It's okay," I calmed him. "Just reel slowly." Somewhere out in the river the retrieved sinker stopped at the top guide and brought the launched section back to us. "Man, Dave. Are you trying to spear the fish or what?" He laughed, and I told him I had shot top sections off my rod many times, explaining how some ferrules are prone to it and that he needed to check that the two pieces were snug. He looked at me and laughed. "That was cool. Can I do it again?"

It had been a couple hours without a bite, so I rigged up a night crawler under a bobber and told David to cast upstream and let it drift with the current. I just wanted him to catch something.

The sun came out and I joined Tim under a railroad trestle and watched my brother cast his baited rig. My little brother had come all this way, and all I did was get drunk and stoned, debauch myself, show up late and hungover, poison him with donuts and abandon him on the bank to fish and fumble alone. He reeled in, lifted the rod straight up and the line wrapped around the tip. I watched him struggle with the tangle but felt too tired to get up and help. He finally unwrapped the line and made a good cast. "That's it," I yelled. "Just leave it there a while."

"That was pretty wild last night," Tim leaned back on his rolled sweatshirt.

"It sure was," I said.

"You're okay with it?" he asked.

"Yeah," I said.

"You think Janet's okay with it?" he asked.

"She seemed okay last night," I said. "We'll talk about it later."

Tim and I fell asleep, waking to my brother's cries. I looked over and saw him at the water's edge, rod bent deeply, and something splashing ten yards in front of him. We ran over and saw him battling a large bronze fish. "Take it easy, Dave," I coached him. "Don't horse it," Tim said. The fish fought well. I could see the bold scales and golden, barbeled face of a carp. Most Americans deem carp a trash fish, but this tenacious ten-pounder saved our day. "Good job, bro. He's huge." It was no mean achievement for a young angler to keep casting even after his brother passed out. And it takes skill to land a big fish on six-pound test. When the carp came up in the net, we high fived and hugged David. He looked like the happiest kid in the world.

We carried the fish back to town and showed it around. People took photos and congratulated my brother, asking if he planned on going to college in Mitchell. Ben Whitehorse hailed us, explaining that carp "was damn bony," but he also told us how to prepare it, cutting off the head, gutting, scaling, and then knifing deep slashes in the sides down to the bone. "Deep fry the whole thing," he made a gesture like a bounce pass. He said the little bones would dissolve and that the flesh was fine. We cleaned the carp and packed it in a squeaky Styrofoam cooler with ice from the motel. But there was so much going on with the move that I called up Ben and asked if he wanted the fish. "No Indian's gonna eat a damn carp," he said. "But I know a white lady who might."

"Norwegian?" I asked with a smile when he came by.

"I think maybe she is. Yeah, something like that," Ben smiled. "Real nice."

And that's the last time I saw Ben Whitehorse, driving off with another big fish in the backseat of his old car.

Schooling

Gazing down into the orange-brown Wabash River from the old State Street Bridge linking Lafayette and West Lafayette, Indiana, I could see large carp picking at what looked to be a fuzzy love seat jammed under the pilings. "Water's polluted," a man walking his dog told me when I asked him about fishing. "Eli Lilly upriver. PCBs, mercury. You don't want to eat those fish," he made a sour face, and his dog barked. But I wouldn't mind catching them, I thought.

It was August 1987, and I was starting the master's program in writing at Purdue University, an institution of nearly thirty thousand students. Driving the family's aging Buick station wagon with the boat-smashed back door past West Lafayette's blaring fraternity parties with bikinied girls water-sliding down palatial lawns, past Boilermaker fanfare, students queued to buy books, and grand brick buildings dedicated entirely to subjects like entomology, I found Burnham's hunting and fishing store in a red tin barn above the river. I got a fishing license, bought what little gear I could afford, and spent many hours talking with the proprietors, Luke and Edith Short. Luke also did boat motor repair, and the big building featured his outboard collection, including a skinny 1925

Johnson, famous for its reliable flywheel magneto made in South
Bend, Indiana. There were 1940s and '50s deco-finned Johnsons
and Evinrudes, dorky Sears Elgins, and slick Mercurys from the
'60s and '70s that reminded me of old Ralph's Fishing Station.
Luke always had time for my questions, and in the days before the
Internet, he'd pull atlases and old books off the shelf, pointing out
a spot or reading up on a fish. "I think you caught a mooneye,"
he said after looking at my photograph. "Always wondered what
the hell they were. Kinda like a shad, wouldn't ya say?" He would
thumb through thick catalogs and take my special orders—floating
jigs, a cross bar ceramic knife sharpener, a ten-gauge shotgun—
promising it would be there next Friday.

From Burnham's parking lot the Wabash looked like a wide,
muddy, slow-going southern river. Although teeming with life,
people often disparaged the river as "polluted, ugly, scary, and dis-
gusting." "Do you actually touch that thing?" other students asked
with horrified expressions as we drove over a bridge. I've fished
many troubled rivers—the Wabash, Hudson, Shinano, Nanchang,
Chao Phraya, Mississippi, Willamette—but would never write off
living water, no more than I would disown a sick friend. "It's a
lovely river," I'd say. Of course, I wanted healthier water, and I
attended meetings of the local Izaak Walton League, signed peti-
tions, voted on new legislation, and went door-to-door asking people not to throw oil down their storm drains. It's hard to know what
to do in the face of such a complex problem. "Start by getting to
know it," Luke at Burnham's told me when I expressed my worries
about the Wabash.

So I walked the banks and cast soft plastic lures and plugs
around brushy snags, bedsprings, woody sloughs, and tire-banked
flood ponds, hooking crappie, largemouth bass, sunfish, and sauger
with camouflaged bodies that reminded me of old fighter planes.

"It's great, but I can't seem to catch a walleye," I reported back to Luke.

"Maybe you're fishing the wrong school," he said, pulling straight his University of Minnesota sweatshirt and turning to his wife with a smile.

"He's been saying that silly thing for twenty years," Edith patted him on the back. "Tell him your secrets, honey."

Luke explained that in the murky Wabash I needed a lure that made noise. Following his advice and casting what he called the Minnesota maraca, a three-inch football-shaped Rattlin' Rapala, behind a downed sycamore, I caught my first decent walleye, maybe three pounds. I studied the large teeth, the golden, cross-hatched complexion, and namesake eyes that glowed like a lion's in safari lights.

At first there was something distant and inaccessible about the walleye's metallic stare. We emotionally connect with animals by looking into their eyes. I loved the warm eyes of my dogs and cats. The blinking eyes of a shot duck pulled flapping from the icy water made me uneasy. The stilling eyes of dying rabbits and the fox I killed haunt me still. "The soft eyes open," James Dickey writes in "The Heaven of Animals," illuminating the presence of an eternal animal spirit that challenges traditional Christian theology denying that animals have souls. The cold, shallow eyes of fish—bright and colorful as they are—may not move us as easily. That makes it easier for some of us to kill and eat them. Elizabeth Bishop says the large yellow eyes of the fish she caught "shifted a little, but not / to return my stare."

Fish can appear unfeeling until we get to know them, watch and feed them underwater or in an aquarium, exchanging bits of squid for liquid glints of appreciation. My brother's pet bergall seemed to express with his eyes the curiosity and hunger of a puppy as he poked out of his cave for a bit of turkey.

So what about the eyes of a fish that we're going to eat? Very few people look into the living eyes of their food. Walt Whitman looked into the eyes of an ox. "What is that you express in your eyes?" he asked. "It seems to me more than all the print I have read in my life." I held the walleye a few inches under the water and then tilted up the head and looked again into his eyes: *river, hunger, other walleye,* and terrible predators like *me.* Although I read hundreds of books in graduate school—many of those pages now forgotten—I shall never forget the telling gaze of that walleye I returned to the dark, swirling river.

The Wabash swirled with a multitude of fish eating and being eaten, among them vast schools of gizzard shad. I caught walleye, bass, and catfish bulging with shad and watched gulls dipping over the silver schools. In winter, flocks of the more delicate ring-billed gulls appeared on the river just as the shad were recruiting into

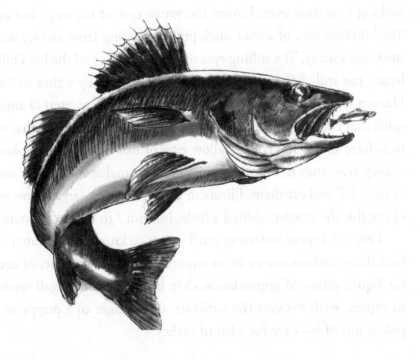

great shoals that sometimes choked the ponds linked to the river. On the Williamsburg Ponds connected to the Wabash River in West Lafayette, I watched in horror as a massive school of corralled and panicked shad began gasping and dying. The gulls fed on the silver fish while they were alive. When the fish died and floated, the birds rejected them, and thousands of pale shad, along with collaterally suffocated catfish and bass, lined the banks.

Staring at a raft of dead fish, I opened a letter from Janet telling me that she was doing great in school, had been elected student government president, and was dating another man. We had talked about staying together over the miles, but our letters and phone calls thinned out. When I didn't answer her last letter, she said she knew it was over. I felt guilty and tried to call her but chickened out. Instead I dashed off an apology letter. I had handled the breakup badly—I admitted that—but I didn't ask her to reconsider. I called a new friend.

Erin and I met at Harry's Chocolate Shop, an old tin-ceilinged, wide-windowed college bar that poured stiff drinks and tall beers and packed in crowds that usually became unbearably dense and loud. One got the sense that they never scrubbed Harry's, just swept and re-varnished the sticky palimpsest of conversation, flirtation, discovery, and delight—and plenty of wasted time—into another amber veneer of collegiate civilization.

We were sitting at a back table when we overheard the woman behind us talking about the fish kill. "Excuse me," I said, and we met Pamela, a doctoral student in biology. She explained that fish kills happen naturally but can be augmented by environmental degradation. Pamela was surprised that a couple of "literature types" were so aware of life and death on the river. "Of course," I said. "We're poets. Always attuned to nature." Pamela just looked at us and smiled, and I wasn't sure if she heard me.

Harry's was getting crowded and noisy. Erin asked if we should all get some dinner, and when we stepped out on the cold, quieter sidewalk, Pamela offered her place. We picked up some groceries, two bottles of wine, and walked up to Pamela's apartment, a neat one-bedroom with framed paintings of dark landscapes and a silver bass encircled in watercress. "This is pretty fine art for a biology type," I teased, and she told us that her mother painted and her father liked to fish. I asked about the image of the silver bass, conveying my nostalgia for the Long Island striped bass. "Yes," she said. "They're closely related." She talked about a hybrid of white and striped bass that were introduced into Indiana's rivers. "The hybrids are fertile," she said. "There's evidence of reproduction." I loved her knowledge. She put on some Tracy Chapman, made a salad, and heated bread. I opened and poured wine, and we drank, ate, and talked away the evening. Although Pamela and I had a fish connection, her eyes were on Erin, and she kept asking about her writing and what books she loved. When Pamela got up, she touched Erin's shoulder, and Erin stared at her. Around one, I said goodnight. "Can you get home all right?" I asked Erin, and Pamela reminded her of all the wine she'd had and said she could stay. I smiled, thanked Pamela, and walked home, feeling a little lonely.

By April the Wabash heated up, and the waxy strands of dead shad were decomposing along the shore, shoveler ducks and teal appeared, and at dusk beavers crossed the Williamsburg Ponds dragging freshly cut willow branches. I fish-walked the wooded peninsula to the inlet of the North Pond and zipped out a bucktail spinner. On the third cast I had a hit, always encouraging; on the fourth retrieve there was the solid, living thrill of a fish. A steely, black-striped silver bass came through the brown water. The silver or white bass, as they are called in different regions, is a handsome fish, compressed and deep with a spiny dorsal and a tail forked perfectly for speed and stability. Three silver bass and one larger fish that had the broken striped pattern of the hybrid came in and out of my hands. I thought of Erin and Pamela, who became lovers. I thought of poetry and biology, flowers and fish, and the watercress and white bass I'd like to taste.

"They are great eating," claimed the guy at the bar.

"From the Wabash?"

"From the Tippecanoe," he smiled and introduced himself as Sean McNerney. Sean was studying classics, didn't much like going to class or finishing papers, but could read Latin and some Greek and speak intelligently on many subjects, including history, literature, cooking, and *halieutics*—fishing—he repeated the Latin and wrote the original Greek letters on a bar napkin.

"Tippecanoe and Tyler, too," I repeated as we drove my old station wagon along the gray Wabash up North River Road, past the Prophetstown State Park and along the Tippecanoe River, listening to Bon Jovi's "Blaze of Glory" and discussing William Henry Harrison and the famous battle of 1811. Indiana has a lot of Native American history but, from what I could tell, few Native Americans. The new fields of corn and beans were coming up, flocks of waterfowl filled the sky, and the Tippecanoe River held a greenish clarity along its pebbly bank. Coming into the town of Monticello, one sensed the humble fruition of a working class dream. From small plots along and near the river sprang little bungalows, ticky-tack trailers, and prefabs in bright colors. There were trailered aluminum boats in driveways and canoes and dinghies tipped against fences.

People worked their whole lives in noisy, windowless Indiana factories, dreaming of such riverside retreats.

Sean directed us to Smitty's Bait Shop. The place felt like a pet store, warm and humid with bubbling tanks of minnows and walls of tackle. Smitty, an inveterate angler, card player, and bourbon drinker, looked a little rough around the edges this morning in May. We smiled, put a couple lures on the counter to stimulate conversation, and he coughed out a report and pointed to recent photos of walleye and the hybrid striped bass he called wipers. Flash-lit photos of fat red-faced men holding huge ten-pound wipers—their eyes shining—urged me on. "All right, Sean. Let's go." But Smitty said we should have some bait. His dusty gray cat jumped up on the mesh screen covering one of the tanks. Smitty netted out a two-inch minnow the cat pawed, bit, and ate before us. "They certainly work on cats," Sean said. We bought spinners, hooks, two Cokes, a minnow bucket, and two dozen fathead minnows, paid Smitty an extra dollar for parking, and drove down to the gravelly shore below the dam.

The water looked good, but the banks were garbage-strewn, and a number of people sat in folding chairs casting weighted bait into the current. "Beautiful water all to ourselves," Janet used to sing in South Dakota, but I had done a lot of urban fishing and the scene didn't bother me much. The catching, however, was slow. We touched and released two tiny silvers in two hours, and a guy in a monster truck pulled onto the gravel, rolled down his windows, and cranked Metallica. "And it's like their worst song," Sean groaned. I could see people fishing from the dam rail a few hundred feet upriver. "If we're gonna do this, we might as well go all the way," I told Sean.

We drove to where the road ends at The Oakdale Inn, boasting "The Best Dam Food Around" from its twenty-foot vertical marquis of a giant catfish holding a pitcher of beer. The earthen dam was walled in concrete and pouring water from the Tippecanoe River and Lake Freeman above. Worm containers, tackle packages, old line, cans, and bottles littered the packed dirt along spillway. "You really want to fish here?" Sean asked.

We tied on number four hooks and bit lead split shot onto the line. I reached my hand into the bait bucket and cupped a fluttering minnow, grasping it and gently piercing the hook through its lips. In the seventeenth century, Izaak Walton advised that one hooks a frog for bait "as though you loved him." And there are numerous accounts of anglers lovingly hooking live worms, insects, salamanders, mice, even cute little ducklings to lure a ferocious pike. I remembered flounder fishing as a boy and crucifying sandworms shortly before Good Friday. I had also just read David James Duncan's essay, "First Native," recalling a childhood trauma of using a live stonefly for trout bait and feeling "like this nine-year-old Roman asshole who'd just crucified a little winged Christian." Duncan meditates on the suffering bait, but his pierced offering is resurrected in a brilliant wild trout that saves the day and his spirits. This is a cycle I willingly accept, even celebrate.

Every fisherman should, at some time, contemplate the bait. Lures and artificial flies might be cleaner, more artistic, and even more sporting, but there's nothing like live bait to put one in touch with the savage world of a fish. I gently cast the hooked prey into the white churning water and imagined its horrible plunge, unable to swim for cover, the surprised and delighted bass unfolding its mouth. The words are human, but the action was real as I immediately had a bite and lost my minnow.

Most fish eat other fish, even their own young. And if we're to look only to nature for moral guidance, it could get ugly. Fish can, however, help us accept a predator-prey world of delicious

delights. Becalmed off Block Island, Benjamin Franklin, a practicing vegetarian, craved some of the fresh-caught codfish coming
out of the frying pan in the ship's galley. "I balanced some time
between principle and inclination, till I recollected that, when the
fish were opened, I saw smaller fish taken out of their stomachs.
Then thought I, 'If you eat one another, I don't see why we mayn't
eat you.' So I dined upon cod very heartily . . ." I've always admired
Franklin's Enlightenment thinking, though he admits the dangers
of rationalizing, "So convenient a thing it is be a *reasonable Creature*,
since it enables one to find or make a Reason for everything one has
a mind to do."

Sean had a strike, set the hook, and reeled up a ten-inch silver.
"That'll fry up nicely," I saluted him. He smiled, waving his fish
toward the foam, "I bet there's a whole school down there." Fish
school for safety, feeding, and breeding. Some species swim close
and tight in schools of thousands, their eyes and lateral lines func-
tioning better than Volvo cross-traffic monitors, their nerves and
fins wired for high performance synchronous maneuvers. I thought
of my own place in the big university, the support and safety of
its name and numbers, my direction coursed by the motions of
the class, program, and department. But there were risks, too. The
odd fish out is the first to be eaten. The writing workshops tended
to reward a well-behaved poem that everybody liked rather than
something wild, edgy, or bizarre. But these workshops also taught
me how to understand and get along with other writers and readers
and how to consider, and even support, styles and philosophies
unlike my own. We might be different people, but we shared many
of the same passions, the same essential goals, and the same school.
And so it is with anglers.

We heard the Metallica-blaring monster truck pull into the
Oakdale Inn parking lot. "Shit," Sean said. A few minutes later the

driver came down the trail with his fishing gear, said "Howdy," and found a place at the rail. He was in his thirties, a big guy in work boots, worn jeans, and a flannel shirt. Under a black Ford cap his stubbly face looked like it had seen some trouble. In ten minutes he hooked a big fish.

The fish flashed silver in the foamy water and the man's drag sang. Sean and I reeled in and let him pass over us. He took the cigarette out of his mouth and threw it into the rocks. There was no way he could bring this fish straight up. Just as one would do on a party boat with a big salmon or bluefish, he worked his way down the rail and over people who were generally accommodating, following his fish downriver. When he scrambled over the boulders into the tail out, I grabbed our net and followed him. "I'll give you a hand, if you want."

"Yeah, thanks."

This was a fine fish, more than two feet long and fighting fiercely. It swam through the rocks and into the flatter water, bolting for the opposite shore. It did not leap, but its broad flanks caught current and strained the line. We walked down river and the man looked at me, "I don't know, guy. This might take a while."

"No problem," I said.

After fifteen minutes we had walked past a Latino family using hand lines, a white fly fisherman in L.L. Bean regalia, two black guys drinking Colt 45 who said, "That's what we're after," a fat couple who told us they had one like that yesterday and it broke the line, and a jerk who kept casting right in front of us. We ended up almost to the spot where Sean and I started, disturbing the reclined and arousing tremendous interest from children. Smitty had come down to nab a guy for evading the one-dollar parking fee. The great silver fish slowly came into view and then tore out a couple more times. "He's scared," a boy said, staring at the action. The fish was fighting for its life, but we all wanted him. I walked into the water to the top of my boots, and the trembling man steered the bass headfirst into the long-handled net. A gorgeous thirty-inch wiper.

"Great fish. Nicely done," I said.

"Thanks, man. I owe you," he shook my hand, still dizzy with disbelief that he actually caught such a fish. "That's the best thing to happen to me in while," he looked at the fish and smiled. A few kids gathered around, and the same sensitive boy pointed to a rusted hook and broken leader trailing from the fish's jaw. "He got away from somebody," the boy said. I felt sympathy for the great, gasping fish but was also pleased to see it caught. Santiago's words echoed once more: "Fish, I love you and respect you very much. But I will kill you . . ." Something twisted inside me, and the man cracked the fish's head with a stone and it lay quiet. Smitty asked the happy angler to come up for a picture.

I walked back to the dam and found Sean coming down the rocks, fighting another nice fish, and I netted it, too. A fifteen-inch wiper. "Damn," I said. "This is all right." Sean and I put a dozen good silvers and his wiper in our bucket and called it a day. At the Oakdale Inn we had two beers with two sidecars of celebratory bourbon, taking in the shiny mounted fish, vintage tackle, boat parts, and park signs screwed to the wood paneling. The bartender smiled and blinked her big lashes at us, her shirt printed with that beer swilling catfish snug between her round breasts.

Back at Sean's apartment in an old wooden house in West Lafayette, I filleted the bass, and Sean prepared them for dinner. "With fish, be gentle," he spoke in scholarly tones. "They live without gravity. That's why their muscle is flaky and breaks apart so easily." His method of steaming the fillets with lemongrass for ten minutes seemed both sophisticated and profoundly simple, differing so much from the egg and breadcrumbs, milk and mayonnaise, the butter fried, and over-broiled fish that I grew up on. He pulled out a bottle of sake and filled a couple small ceramic cups. We toasted to the fishing and the food.

Schooling was good for me. I took classes in literature and writing, composed poems and essays, and helped start Purdue's first literary magazine, *Sycamore Review*. As the magazine's editor, I enjoyed a lively correspondence with dozens of writers, some of them yet unknown, such as Ron Rash, who sent us a gripping poem about an Arkansas bass fisherman who, in trying to free a snagged lure, puts a hook through his eye. There were letters and submissions from John Updike, Diane Wakoski, Marge Piercy, Mary Oliver, James Dickey—who said he wished he fished more—and the beloved Charles Bukowski. Bukowski sent us several poems with a mustard-stained cover letter warning that any magazine called *Sycamore* was in danger of getting too many "Good doggie poems." He drew a picture of a dog and a man drinking in bed. We exchanged several letters, and when I asked Mr. Bukowski about fishing, he said he used to go down to the pier in San Pedro, where people caught sharks, mackerel, and croakers. His poem "The Fisherman" tells of an old man who walks every day to the pier and fishes, only to return to a small apartment and an indifferent wife who throws his catch in the trash. Sadness, waste, but also a sense of endurance in the act of fishing. "Yup," Bukowski said.

Drinking a couple beers up in the *Sycamore* office, as we often did in the late 1980s, I fell into more and more conversations with Caitlin, our best intern and a star among the undergraduate English majors. One dark night with no one around, we just started kissing.

The currents rose—her tongue in my mouth, my hand moving down her soft neck and over her sweet chest. I pulled back and just looked at her—Dutch blue eyes, fair eyebrows, and straight blonde hair that fell to her shoulders. Her muscular body tuned easily to running, hiking, swimming, and lovemaking. Notwithstanding her parents' concerns, we moved in together in a little house on Dodge Street. Caitlin was affectionate yet demanding, insisting we eat more fresh vegetables, boycott certain products and stores, clean the apartment every Saturday, and meditate.

In the spring of 1990, Caitlin and I attended a reading by the famous Caribbean poet Derek Walcott. At the tweedy evening reception, we nervously approached the poet to thank him and present a copy of *Sycamore Review*. Walcott gave Caitlin a long up and down look, rubbed a finger over his thick, graying mustache, and smiled. Then he looked at me and asked, "Do you have a car?" I nodded. "Let's get out of here," he said. We rumbled across town in my old station wagon, picked up beer and cigarettes, and headed toward his hotel. Walcott noticed the fishing rods in the back of the wagon.

"You like fishing?" he asked.

"Yes. I love it."

"That's good," he said.

In the dimly lit hotel room, the three of us talked for hours. Walcott did not drink but smoked cigarette after cigarette. He told us about the islands and the local fishermen. He was interested that I grew up in a fishing town on Long Island. I praised his poem "Tarpon," and he described the fish in detail, regretting that they were often just killed for sport. He talked about living in the States, relationships, and sex. He loved talking about women, and I watched his eyes move over Caitlin's body. I steered him toward the topic of publishing and asked if he might give us something for

Sycamore Review. He pointed through the smoky haze to a spiraled manuscript on the night table. "Take something from that—okay?" It was entitled *Omeros,* and at the time I didn't know what the hell that meant. "Go make copies," Caitlin urged. "I'll be okay." I gave her a questioning look, hesitated, and then ran to the all-night copy shop. When I got back, Caitlin and Mr. Walcott were sitting in the same places talking about ceviche. She smiled, and I knew everything was okay.

Reading the manuscript for *Omeros* (the Greek pronunciation for Homer) in the days that followed, Caitlin and I found a vivid, musical, oceanic epic about the people of St. Lucia—many fishermen among them—and we published a section in our magazine. In 1992, Derek Walcott received the Nobel Prize for literature, and *Omeros* was deemed his masterpiece.

Caitlin grew more and more curious about my love of fishing. Once or twice a week, Sean and I brought back bodies, photos, or stories of catfish, carp, sturgeon, gar, bowfin, paddlefish, and the usual assortment of bass and panfish. Two French women, graduate students in linguistics, rented the downstairs, and they talked with us as we cleaned fish in the backyard. "In France, seafood is considered very sexy," one of the women said to Sean as he rinsed a bass with the garden hose. He blushed and gave them fillets, which they later told him were *délicieux.* Sitting with Caitlin on the backsteps one evening, the French women came home and asked when I was going to take them fishing. "Hold on," Caitlin said. "I'm first."

I had been exploring Wildcat Creek, a beautiful stream with abundant smallmouth bass, accessible 15 miles east of Lafayette near the town of Monitor. The clear run of the south fork had nice gravelly stretches, and on a warm afternoon, Caitlin and I waded in shorts and old sneakers, casting little jigs into brushy pockets and deep holes for willing bronze-backed bass. We saw heron, whitetail deer, and a black mink that slinked down the buttery bank. Caitlin enjoyed the river so much I thought a more expeditionary adventure would befit us.

A couple weeks later when we showed up at Wildcat Canoe Rentals, the unshaven, sticky-haired owner greeted us glumly, explaining that we were the only ones paddling that day. "Perfect," I whispered to Caitlin, imagining secluded stops for fishing and picnicking. I had two rods and a bag of gear; Caitlin packed a small lunch cooler; we had towels and a jug of Gallo red for the ten-mile paddle. While filling out the rental and release forms, the man told us the creek was running a little high, but he'd been down with a chainsaw the other day, and it was okay.

"You done a lot of canoeing?" he asked.

"A little," I said.

"Just around a lake," Caitlin flashed a smile.

"Well, you'll wanna sit in the back," he looked at me. "Try to steer clear of shit."

He shuttled us upstream in his pickup truck with a canoe in the back to a spot under a graffiti-covered bridge. Standing creekside and describing the landmarks for the takeout, he seemed to remember something in the truck and scuttled up the bank, stopping halfway and doubling over in a coughing fit. Caitlin and I looked at each other. The man's face was red and confused. "I'll see you around three." He waved, walked to his truck, and drove away.

We packed the canoe, and I tied the wine to the seat frame. Caitlin got in while I steadied and then eased us off the gravelly bank, taking the back seat and pushing with my paddle. From Ralph's rental skiff off Long Island to this gliding arrow in Indiana, I have always loved the sensation of being suspended and moving over water. Gravity can be a real drag on our terrestrial lives, but water offers buoyant possibilities. Caitlin smiled brightly, getting a feel for the paddle and stroke. A pair of mallards swam up to us, and she said they were "ducky little lovers."

The water was moving swiftly, and as it narrowed, its speed and power rose more like a river, the red canoe glancing off rocks and bumping logs. I was looking for a good place to stop and do some fishing, but the water was higher than anticipated, and it seemed best to keep moving. Shooting through a timbered flume, an overhanging branch caught one of the fishing rods. Reaching to grab it, I felt how tippy we were, and Caitlin was having trouble bringing the bow around. I tried to rudder with my paddle, but we swung diagonally across the river, hitting a large rock.

"That was scary," Caitlin turned back to me once we settled into calmer water.

"We're fine," I said. "Just relax."

We turned another corner and the river funneled into a rapid passage dammed by a huge fallen tree. "Get to the side," I yelled. "Paddle left, hard." There was a moment of confusion about whether I meant left direction or left paddle, and then we dug hard, powering the canoe across and down the river. But the current was overwhelming and we slammed into the tree. There was that moment of *what do I do?* The roar of water, the canoe smashed lengthwise against the trunk, river pouring in my lower end. As I plunged, I saw Caitlin above me, her body falling in a scream. There was a cold blast, dark noise, my head rubbing against the rough bark of the tree and popping up on the other side. I looked for Caitlin. In a moment she was there, frightened but swimming, and we touched ground together, hugging and shaking. I helped her to a rock and waded out to retrieve our swamped canoe. There was only one rod, no cooler, no floating cushions, one paddle, and the tethered jug of wine. I took a long drink and handed the bottle to Caitlin.

Caitlin and I drank some wine and shivered on the shadowed rocks. Her wet shirt stuck to her chest, her nipples sharp and dark.

"We weren't even wearing life jackets," she said.

"I know. I think he forgot them."

"What about you? Jesus, Henry. You're supposed to know about this shit. That was so fucking stupid."

"I'm sorry."

I got up and looked for my other rod, the cooler, and the second paddle but found only a straw hat snagged in the bushes, perhaps the bobbing farewell of another hapless paddler on the spring river.

"You okay, Cait?" I asked again, helping her back into the canoe. She nodded, but I knew she was cold and shaken. A few hundred feet down river we found our other paddle and one cushion. The movement was good for Caitlin, and as we got into a wide, calm stretch of river, the sun came out like a golden blessing, and she smiled. After a half hour of sun, Caitlin stripped off her wet clothes down to her swimsuit, the blonde light returning to her hair, the muscles in her back and shoulders flexing to the rhythm of each stroke. I took off everything but my underpants and the straw hat, and we dried and warmed and paddled. Passing the wine, the fear washed away, and we talked about the accident and how it felt to go under the tree. We might have gotten snagged and drowned, but we didn't. We rose shining and alive. For those of us with safe, calm, and steady lives, perhaps dozing on the warm ferry ride of middle-class America, a survived shipwreck brings quite a high. Worth the risk, I thought. Definitely worth the risk.

I drank more wine and, without any lunch, felt quite buzzed. "You wanna stop here for a bit?" I asked, and we glided into a sandy pocket, scattering a school of minnows. Caitlin stepped out and stretched. She looked beautiful. We held each other and kissed, pulling off our remaining clothes and lying back on the river-softened trunk of a downed elm. Our lovemaking was a little wilder that day on Wildcat Creek.

The Big Hard

For spring break 1990, Caitlin and I drove down to New Orleans to visit Woody, my old friend from college who was studying chemistry at Tulane. We savored the increasingly warmer winds of Kentucky, Tennessee, and Alabama, playing and replaying Paul Simon's *Graceland* album, loving the voices and rhythms of Ladysmith Black Mambazo. Just a month before, South Africa's President De Klerk announced that he would repeal apartheid and free Nelson Mandela after more than twenty-seven years in prison. We drove past Civil War monuments and, somewhere in Alabama, pulled into a park and slept in our car. I got up early, pissed, and walked down a trail, staring into the deep woods and out past a fresh green field. I imagined a line of slaves working the rows while a white overseer rode on a horse above them. The fields were hemmed by a pretty creek. There was no one fishing.

We drove into New Orleans, following Woody's handwritten directions down Carrolton Avenue toward the river, parking on Short Street, and knocking on his chipped door. He had a small dark apartment. There was no bed, just a sleeping bag and some blankets folded on the floor. The place had been picked up a bit, but the kitchen counter and sink were piled with pots and pans and crimson crab shells. "I'm gonna make you a nice Cajun dinner," he said. It was great to see Woody, and he and Caitlin got talking about New Orleans and poverty segregation and liberal reform. The city had shined up during the 1980s oil boom, but there were still poor parishes, political corruption, and countless social problems. Woody was informed and fairly open-minded but more cynical than usual. "It's all bullshit," he would say over and over as we talked politics. "This ain't no Big Easy," he said. "It's a Big Hard." When I asked about graduate school, he said it was bringing him down.

"You're a TA now, right?" I asked. "How's the teaching?"

"Shit, Hughes, you know it's work. And my supervisor's a prick."

We drank some cheap wine and ate Woody's fine supper of wild rice covered in a zesty crab sauce with a side of smothered okra. Woody led us down St. Charles, and Caitlin admired the mansions draped with sleeping cats. "It would be great to live here," she said. "Expensive as shit," Woody scowled. Back on Carrolton at a lowbrow blues bar, we had a round of bourbon and just listened. I felt relaxed walking back to Woody's. He wanted to do a bit more drinking, but we said we were tired. We stopped by his car, the side window taped up in plastic.

"Last month they fucking broke in and stole my fishing poles," Woody said.

"No."

"Fuck, yeah. This ain't a great neighborhood."

"I'll bring my rods inside."

"What about my car?" Caitlin asked.

"Maybe we better park it up by Cheryl's." Woody's girlfriend lived a few blocks away in a safer neighborhood. Woody and Caitlin drove off to park, and I sat on some steps and looked over the railroad tracks and levee to a flickering stretch of the Mississippi. Two teenaged black guys walked by.

"Hey, you need a little weed, man?"

"No, thanks," I said.

"A'right. We's right up the street. You ask for Whisker."

"Okay, thanks," I answered and smiled but didn't want to get too friendly.

The next morning Woody had to set up a lab at school. I drank a cup of instant coffee, ate a couple stale beignets from on top of the fridge, kissed Caitlin, donned my new fishing vest, grabbed my medium spinning rod, and stepped onto the cool and quiet streets, past a couple homeless guys sleeping under a tree, over the tracks, and up and down the levee. At the base of the levee were long pools of trapped floodwater, and I walked around them and found a trail down through the brush to the river. *This river is huge*, I thought, looking out over the Mississippi's oily gray complexion shifting with the cloudy sky. Heavy tugboats pushed barges. There were smaller boats and some kind of dredge chewing away upstream. I wasn't sure what to do with all this water, so I just started casting a chubby auger-tailed white worm on a quarter-ounce jig head.

Without any bites, I kept moving upriver, where I met an older black man with a meaty catfish on a stringer. "Nice fish," I said.

"Once in a while the good Lord gives me one," he said. We had a long talk about fishing and the river. He looked at my lures and said I might catch a green trout, a largemouth bass, but if I wanted catfish I better use some bait. "You wanna lit'l bit of dis here?" he asked. "I make it." He showed me marble-size balls of dark clayish bait. I found an old bleached chicken liver container in the bushes, and he dropped in a few pieces. "Good things come to those who bait," he chuckled. "Now if you got time an' a car, you ought to go over da river to da West Bank towards Belle Chasse or Lafitte and try for some redfish an speckled trout. They bitin' right now I heard. An artificial wid a piece of shrimp on it no problem." I thanked him and told him my name. "I'm Delmar, nice to meet ya," he said and made another cast.

Upriver beside a bight where the water swirled and stalled, I rigged for catfish, stuck on Delmar's special bait, cast, and sat down. I fished for three hours without a bite, listening to the sounds of industry and commerce along the river. Two men in their thirties set up chairs nearby and fished lazily into the weekday morning. I thought of Bing Crosby and Louis Armstrong singing about skipping work and hanging a sign, "Gone Fishin'," though I preferred a more discreet approach, calling in sick and angling far from campus where my students wouldn't see me. In any case, a fishing escape from the workday seemed in keeping with what I still wanted to believe was the Big Easy, a city reputed for its laid-back, love-to-play attitude. Things were different back in the busy Big Apple, but there was the New York legend of Rip Van Winkle, who avoided profitable labor to "fish all day without a murmur, even though he should not be encouraged by a single nibble." Then again, old Rip caught hell from his wife. I looked at my watch and reluctantly started back over the levee.

Down in the long flood pool, I saw a fish. Getting closer, the lines and scales of a huge carp, three feet long, became clear. I approached gently and presented the bait near his head, but it only spooked him and he yawed off a few feet. I made my next cast way ahead of him, and gently dragged the bait along the bottom toward his barbels. "Come on," I whispered. For a moment he seemed interested, and then he moved away. I took off the catfish bait, lightened my lead, and looked in the grass for a worm or grub, finding only a torn pretzel. It was rock hard, but I managed to drill the hook into a shard. The bait floated nicely above the split shot, and I gently presented it to the carp. I could see everything. The carp slowly approached the pretzel, touched it—its thick lips round in low note embouchure—then turned away. "Come on!" I couldn't believe it. I tried for another half hour, but this fish wouldn't bite. The carp was in shallow water, clooping at the end of a tapering pool. Maybe I could drive him up the shore and grab him. It would be great to show up at the apartment with this Mississippi monster.

I took off my vest, set down my rod, and, with jeans and sneakers on, I waded into the pool up to my knees and then turned and walked toward the carp. He faced away from me, hovering in a foot of water. This looked promising. I came up slowly, watching the feathery undulations of his fins and fanning gills, got right over him, and sent my hands down into the water—ready, so ready. The moment I touched him he bolted, plowing a wake through the shallows and into the deep end of the pool. When I stepped out of the water to higher ground I could see him. He composed himself and swam back into the shallows. I composed myself and made one more ursine effort but failed.

Walking across the grass toward River Road I saw that weed-selling kid, Whisker, talking to Delmar. Delmar walked on, carrying his gear and two fine catfish. I waved, he stopped, and I told him about the carp. "You try doughballs?" he asked.

"Pretzel," I said.

"It's been a day of blessings," he smiled. "Maybe I'll give it a try."

"Good luck, Delmar."

When I got in, Caitlin was a little annoyed. I was over an hour late and soaked below the waist. "Did you fall in?" she asked.

"No, I tried to grab a carp."

Woody came in, set down his bag, and listened to my account of the huge fish trapped in the levee.

"Let's shoot 'im," Woody said, grabbing his duck poaching .22 from the corner of the room. "Let me get some more rounds."

"Great!" I said.

"Are you two crazy?" Caitlin boiled. "You're just gonna walk through the streets with a gun?"

"Dis here is N'awlins, dahling," Woody exaggerated an accent and grin. "Just a little redneck recreation."

"Shooting a fish? No, I'm not sticking around for this. I've been waiting here to do something in this city. This is ridiculous."

I knew what I had to do. "All right, Woody. We'll let this one go."

Sensible, mature women have on several occasions saved me from reckless folly. I changed into some dry clothes, and we picked up Woody's girlfriend, Cheryl, and drove south to Magazine Street, where we spent a lovely, languorous, drink-and-food filled afternoon at Miss May's and The Club. Cheryl was a bright, attractive woman with full strawberry hair and green eyes, and Caitlin and I enjoyed her company very much. She did have more conservative viewpoints and made some comments about affirmative action and the failure of African Americans to educate themselves that angered Woody and led to a low-level fight that clouded the afternoon.

I told Woody about Delmar and asked about catching some redfish. The next day, Caitlin, Woody, and I got an early start and drove Caitlin's car south over the bridge and down the expressway across Harvey Canal, where Woody said he caught some big catfish, one with a bird in its stomach and another stuffed with cigarette butts. Fish, like people, put the craziest things in their mouths. We stopped at a tackle and charter shop in Lafitte. The air was muggy and fishy. Gulls and pelicans billed around the canal. A chartered boat trip was out of our price range, but Woody pressed a blubbery, bald man behind the counter with questions, and I listened. "You know where dat strip club used to be?—try behind there," the man drawled, rubbing his belly. There were other conversations about "ditch crawfish, if you know where they's at" and some kind of fish gravy "made wit carrots, onyun, and celry."

Past the long town of Lafitte and down a gloomy gravel road, we found a bayou that looked promising. Caitlin was worried about leaving her car parked in a "creepy swamp," and I was dying to explore the place and start fishing. "Come on, Cait," I said. "We're here," as if that settled it. We walked a spongy trail to its swampy margin. There were tall trees draped in Spanish moss and the eyes and snout of a small alligator ventured into the sticky air. We caught nothing, and Caitlin insisted we check on the car. "Another half hour," I begged. Something swirled in the tea-colored water. There were turtles, mud hens, and the distinct crack of a gunshot a few hundred yards away. I thought of the pirate Jean Lafitte slipping through the mist with his rum and gold. "That's it," Caitlin said when we heard another gunshot. We found the car unmolested and drove to a lunch dive where the waiter's tie was so stained and flecked with food it would have boiled down into a nice fish gravy. The special was redfish and rice. "I hope I don't get sick," Caitlin held her spotted water glass up to the light. You could buy alcohol almost anywhere in Louisiana, and I ordered a round of straight vodkas as a preventive measure against microbes. After lunch we stopped at a bulkhead along a brackish canal and tried plunking some shrimp for redfish. Two rough-looking white guys whistled at Caitlin and asked if they could buy beer from us. We gave them a couple cans from our cooler and were glad to see them move along. Again, no fish.

Woody popped in a Stevie Ray Vaughn cassette tape, and we picked up some catfish fillets from the market and drove back to Cheryl's for dinner. She and Woody seemed okay. Cheryl made her mother's recipe of blackened cat, dipping the fillets in melted butter and rolling them in a bowl of paprika, cayenne pepper, black pepper, white pepper, salt, garlic powder, onion powder, dried basil, thyme, and God knows what else. She dribbled a little more butter on the crusty fillets and set them in a red-hot cast iron skillet and covered it. We drank wine, heard crackling sounds, and after three minutes she lifted the lid to a cloud of delicious smoke. Cheryl turned the fillets and dampened the chimney once more. The very air had become a tantalizing appetizer. After a few more minutes, the catfish came smoking out of the pan, the spices roasted dark to the flesh. I had no trouble telling Cheryl, "This is some of the best fish I've ever eaten."

Caitlin and I took long walks downtown and through the French Quarter. We talked, listened to music, admired the filigreed ironwork, ate oysters, shopped, drank different things, toured graveyards and little museums, and lingered around buskers and bookstores. Sometimes tensions rose between us about what we might eat or buy, what we might do in the next hour or in the next year, and I felt this must be the continuous challenge of a relationship. One time New Orleans author Kate Chopin wrote about marriage and that "blind persistence with which men and women believe they have a right to impose a private will upon a fellow-creature." Caitlin stroked a black cat stretched out on a shop counter.

"I wish we could get a cat," she said.

"Won't that be a hassle with school and everything?" I frowned.

"You love cats," she said. "You don't even know what you want."

But when things were right with us, they were very right. Out in the sun we sat on a bench and kissed long and deep. "The Big Easy," I whispered, swimming a hand up her skirt. Caitlin smelled of lavender and clean sweat. "Not here," she smiled and pushed my hand down. I felt close to her body, and at night, with Woody snoring, we made love.

Still, I would sneak out for a couple hours each morning and explore the Mississippi. At the end of the week, I saw Delmar talking to Whisker again. When Whisker walked off, I went down to Delmar. "You know that guy?" I couldn't resist asking.

"Yeah, he's my son."

"Really? Whisker?"

"Sounds like you know him, too. That name's from fishing, cause he's good at it. Or was, when he did it. The Lord ain't done with that boy, that's for sure."

I considered Delmar a man with far fewer opportunities than someone like Woody, yet he seemed much happier and hopeful—a man who knew how to keep himself afloat in the big waters of life. Delmar went on to tell me about the stranded carp. It just wouldn't bite, but now it was gone and maybe somebody got it with a pitchfork. "I'm heading home tomorrow," I said, and he looked right at me. "May God bless you, son, and grant you a safe trip."

On the last morning, Woody and I walked up to the north end of Audubon Park. Delmar was there. "You get around," I said and introduced him to Woody. Woody nodded, "I've seen you around. At least someone's catching fish." Delmar had another catfish on his stringer.

I was glad to be in Audubon Park. I had recently read a biography of John James Audubon and knew that he spent time in New Orleans when he was still an emerging artist. I told Woody that here in 1821 Audubon met a beautiful young woman who commissioned him to draw her in the nude. He was nervous, but he did a good job, and she paid him with a fine new gun, asking only that he keep her name a secret. "New Orleans got all kinds of secrets," Woody said and smiled over the story. Audubon loved hunting, but he found fishing a bit boring. He may have appreciated wading a stream and casting flies to trout, but there wasn't enough action in plunking bait. I felt the same way today and tied on that oily white auger-tail, worming it around the pilings. After twenty minutes, a fish hit like thunder and made erratic runs back and forth between the poles. "Hallelujah," I cried. Woody came over, and Delmar watched. It looked like a big pewter porgy but longer, swirling up to the bank, where I reached down and pinched its gills. Whatever it was, somebody in this town will eat it. Deep bodied with a divided dorsal of sharp spines and soft rays, it felt to be a solid three pounds. When I set it down it creaked and groaned like a tight lid on wooden box. This creaking-groaning-croaking voice reminded me of the Long Island weakfish, a member of the drum family that includes redfish. Males of these species vibrate muscles against their swim bladders to create what some call a drumming sound. I told Woody it must be a drum.

"Dat d're is a gaspergoo," Delmar declared.

"Gasper-goo?" I repeated, relishing the word.

"It's good eating. With fish gravy."

We wouldn't have time to prepare the fish, and we offered it with respect to Delmar. "Sure," he said. I was curious what the drum was eating and asked if we could gut it right there. "Don't see why not," Delmar said. The stomach was heavy and crunchy with small snail and mussel shells. I later learned that the gaspergoo, a freshwater drum, could live more than seventy years and that the older males make the most noise. "You keep that fiber in your diet, and you'll be grunting into old age, too," Woody told me on the phone months later when we reminisced. School hadn't worked out too well for Woody.

"What about New Orleans?" I asked him.

"There's a lot of good and a lot of bad. It's tempting to stay in a place like this, but it could do you in. I'm telling you, man. It's the Big Hard."

Maybe drink and cynicism got the best of Woody, but he kept on fishing. "Sure, I'm still fishing," he'd say in a late night drunken phone call. "What else is there?"

Caitlin and I had a good relationship, but our prospects waned. I finished my degree in 1990, hung around West Lafayette, and taught part time, while Caitlin applied and got into graduate school. We celebrated, but everyday life felt increasingly low and muddy. I had little money, my car was breaking down, and Aunt Lil had just been diagnosed with cancer. Should I go back to Long Island? Maybe follow Caitlin to grad school in Pennsylvania? "You should go to Japan," my fishing friend Sean advised. "They love drinking and fishing. And there are jobs for English teachers." When I told Caitlin that I had applied to teach in Japan, she was upset.

"Don't you think that's something we need to talk about?"

"You're off to grad school. What am I gonna do?"

"Come with me?"

"And do what?"

"Maybe I'd like to go to Japan."

"Would you?"

"We should at least talk about it."

We talked, meditated, jogged together, talked some more, but it was clear that we were going to be apart. "How long?" Caitlin asked, and I said I didn't know.

Men are afraid of commitment, it is often said. Is it because they fear it will limit their pleasure or power? Everything from evolutionary biology to pop psychology has been used to explain or excuse male behavior that favors multiple partners and social roving. True or not, it's a shame that these fears and forces prevent some men from ever enjoying the kind of deep and lasting union that rewards so much better than a dozen flings. I would eventually come to understand that commitment is not restriction but rather *form*—like the meter and lines of a sonnet or the angle and rhythm of a fly cast—that shapes a crucial part of our relationships. There are conventions that dictate these arts—including the art of being together—but every couple must also find its own way of getting along. So much is possible if one is sensitive, creative, and flexible within certain boundaries.

I appreciate that form now in my late forties, but I didn't much at twenty-five. My reluctance to renew living together with Caitlin was a rejection of form. I wanted the freedom to come and go as I pleased. I wanted to fish like crazy. At least I was honest with Caitlin about my ambivalent feelings and my increasing desire to be on my own. It was the Big Hard of loving and enjoying someone very much but still feeling incomplete and unsatisfied in the wider world of wonder.

The summer after her graduation, Caitlin came out to Long Island. The traffic was heavier. More forest, field, and farmland had been turned over to housing and shopping centers. We drank tea and talked in the backyard with Aunt Lil. Lil put seed out every day for the birds. Caitlin smiled and asked, "What's that one?" pointing to what I thought was some kind of warbler. My brother, David, came quietly through the gate and called the delicate flit of green and brown a vireo. David was almost six foot, broad shouldered and barrel-chested, his straight sandy hair cut short like a guy going into the Army. He was going to be a junior in high school, and he reported on his summer job down on the docks. Caitlin told Lil she had "done a good job raising her boys." Lil smiled and said she thanked God every day for his help. We could see that Lil was sick, but her spirits were steady, and she was glad to be retired. "Would you like a little pickled herring?" she asked. It was one of her favorite snacks, served with sour cream on little squares of rye bread.

Lil had taken part of her pension purse and bought my brother a new boat, a seventeen-foot center console Mako with an eighty-horsepower Evinrude outboard motor. Lil spoiled David, telling me quite explicitly that she was trying to make up for the loss of his mother. "Well, that's one mother of a boat," I said to Lil, suddenly realizing how stupid and insensitive that sounded. I was jealous. "You are one lucky kid," I told David. "I never had a boat like that." My father gave the old *China Cat* to a carpenter friend who wanted to restore it, but the boat rotted away in his yard.

Material jealousies wear off fast if we really like someone, and Caitlin and I happily crewed on David's craft, which he let me christen *Queequeg*, after our beloved pagan hero from *Moby-Dick*. Trolling around Buoy 11, not only did we hook the familiar schooling blues but ten- and fifteen-pound striped bass, one after another. "Where did all these stripers come from?" I asked my brother, and we would both learn that commercial restrictions, habitat restoration, pollution controls, and sport management had brought them back. These were large fish but under the thirty-six inch limit, and we carefully released them back into their schools. After comparable environmental and catch management efforts, fluke were also on the rise. Fluke, sometimes called summer flounder, are predatory, toothy flatfish that hunt the shoals for sand eels and other small fish and squid. We rigged for fluke with a two-ounce sinker, three-foot leader, and a feather-dressed wide-gapped hook baited with shiners. A fluke grabs its prey and swims off before swallowing, so we drifted along the shoal with the sinker just tapping the gravelly bottom, feeling for the tug and letting out another few feet of line before setting the hook.

"Now," I shouted, and Caitlin set the hook on a bolting fish.

"That's no fluke," my brother punned when the net slipped under its creamy belly. We caught several, their topside colors varying from speckled tan to dark gray, according to the bottom. Caitlin landed the only keeper—a chocolate brown, lightly spotted, twenty-seven-inch doormat of a fish. That night I steamed the thick fillets the way Sean showed me, and Aunt Lil said it was so good and healthy. "Who needs all that grease?"

The fish news wasn't all rosy, however. The winter flounder of my childhood were all but gone. Sea bass and weakfish numbers were way down, and for some reason the mackerel no longer recruited to the north shore in great numbers. A variety of depleted stocks meant that far fewer draggers, lobstermen, and clammers were able to make a living off Long Island. For many, the old ways of life on the water were disappearing.

"Plenty of eels still around," Herbie said, trying to cheer us up despite reports that American eels were also diminishing. Having just retired as a union laborer, Herbie devoted himself to eeling and fishing. Life hadn't been easy for Herb, but as Washington Irving once said of a venerable old angler and seaman, "His face bore the marks of former storms, but present fair weather." Herbie hired a friend to build him a wooden skiff, and he paid cash for a new outboard, mooring his simple craft in Setauket Harbor. Looking out over the green haven made me think of William Sidney Mount's painting, *Eel Spearing in Setauket Harbor*, 1845. It was on the cover of our college American literature anthology, and when I was in South Dakota and Indiana I would stare at the image of the black woman, spear poised, as the young white boy paddled in the stern, thinking about my home waters.

Herbie took Caitlin and me trolling for blues, and I admired his new outfits, graphite rods with carbolite guides and deep, narrow Daiwa reels loaded with bright wire. "It's all Japanese now," Herbie said. "Good stuff." We trolled the old spots but couldn't find the schools and didn't get a single hit. We talked and drank a little beer. When Caitlin had to pee, he pulled out a low cut bucket and told me to lift the bench cushion as a privacy screen. "He's more of a gentleman than you let on," Caitlin told me as we crossed the inlet. When we docked and Caitlin walked up to the car, Herb squinted and said, "Nice ass. I bet she's fun in the sack." Herbie was born poor on rural Long Island, had little schooling, served in a tank crew during the allied invasion of France, and then shoveled dirt and hauled bricks for forty years. He made a few extra dollars selling furs and eels, and he ate what he caught. "Stay in school," he used to say. "You don't wanna do the shit I did." At sixty-two, he was retired and smiling from his boat, telling me a story about some old lady trying to pick him up at the hardware store. "I'll show her some hardware," he laughed, rod between his legs. But just as suddenly as he earned his time, his time was gone. At the end of that summer he complained of abdominal pain, thought he pulled a muscle, and asked his doctor, an old fishing buddy, to give him some Vicodin. People helped Herbie when they could. He finally drove himself to the hospital, but his appendix had burst and he died. His car was packed with rods and tackle for the next morning.

There are some days I need to fish alone. In the dark of early morning, I parked by the Port Jefferson docks where my mother and I released the shark. I slipped on my fishing vest, picked up my spinning rod and fish-walked East Beach, past where Theresa and I had our goodbye swim, rounding Seaboard Hole as the sun came up. There were the black wooden ribs of the Priscilla Alden, the old ferry that carried my father's family from New England in the 1920s, and fox tracks under the wild plum bushes that made me smile. Tucked in the strand line I found a little dried seahorse, maybe two inches long, that somehow crystallized my sweet sadness. There was the dawn-burnished Long Island Sound of so many fish and people come and gone. "The water's the last good thing about this place," Herbie would say as they bulldozed the topsoil off another field for a car dealership. But he was dead. Caitlin was inland at school; my brother was still in bed. I had no idea what Tim, Theresa, Birch, Janet, Woody, or Sean were doing. I stepped to the water and made a cast.

"Some things will be hard," Eugene said, driving me to the airport later in the week.

I nodded.

"You'll miss people," he went on. "You'll have to learn Japanese and sit on the floor. But some things will come easy. You'll see."

"Like what?" I asked.

"Like fishing," he said.

Sashimi

I had been in Japan just one week, and I was thinking about Eugene and my brother on Long Island, how we could fish together for hours, speaking few words over the water in early light but feeling close. Then I thought of silent days fishing alone—sometimes sad, troubled, or unsure—when angling became the language of asking, the fish a hoped-for answer, as easy, elusive, or complicated as any deep truth. Some days there were no fish, some days there were many.

Here, at dusk, the fishing party of fifteen men shouted back and forth above the roar of the engine, rigging outrageously long poles with *sabiki* rigs, consisting of five small hooks dressed in capes of pearlescent plastic and tinsel that twinkled like holiday lights. "Like Christmas," I said, singing a bit of Jingle Bells. The men laughed. I was aboard the fifty-five foot *Yutaka Maru*. "It means boat of plenty," explained Usami Manabu, one of the English teachers I would be working with that year. The school was in Niigata Prefecture on a river-crossed rice plain twenty minutes from the Sea of Japan and fishing ports such as Teradomari, where we sailed from that evening. Usami and a few other teachers from the junior high had offered to take me *sakana tsuri*, fishing, when they heard it was my *shumi*, my hobby, said to be an important part of everyone's identity in Japan. Unlike the duties of family and job, which are often foisted upon us, a hobby was something one pursued for pure pleasure, which may have been particularly important in a culture where social forms and responsibilities seemed greater and stricter. Wherever and however we live, it's good to have a *shumi*.

The steel boat plowed north beyond the jetty, the mountainous mainland creased in cedar ravine shadows behind us. Japan was greener than I imagined, but this was the first foreign port from which I ever sailed. I had never been abroad, hadn't yet learned a sentence of Japanese, but I understood the familiar pitch of the boat, the smell of salt air, the rods and reels ready in their holders.

We cruised a couple miles offshore, the engine idled down, and the whole deck lit up like a baseball stadium under large clear bulbs swinging from a wire running the length of the boat. The captain set the anchor and then lowered four submersible lamps into the sea, igniting a glowing emerald ring around us. Within ten minutes I started seeing small fish drawn to the chum of our light.

I was told to fish the bottom, but I stopped on the way down and jigged a little—I knew it as a way of locating fish. The man next to me said "*dame,*" no good, "*tana o awasete,*" on the bottom. He gestured with his fist pressed hard against the gunnel and reached over to flip the clutch on my reel. I pulled away, a little annoyed. *I know how to fish,* I thought. A few minutes later, the first fish were caught, and true enough, it wasn't until I bounced the bottom that I hooked one myself, an eight-inch silver *aji* that I swung over the railing.

I studied the *aji* that were now being caught in great numbers. Usami pulled a paperback dictionary from his bag and said, "Horse mackerel." I knew it wasn't a mackerel, but it certainly shared its schooling and feeding behavior and was caught in a similar fashion.

One of the science teachers approached holding another book. "Jackusu famuly," he said.

"Jacuzzi family?" I cocked my head.

"This fish is jacku's family," Usami peered at the book and tried to help.

"Who's Jack?" I asked.

But when I looked at the page it became clear. There was the Japanese word, *aji*; the Latin, *Trachurus japonicus*; and the English with a study sentence, "Jack mackerel (Japanese horse mackerel), belonging to the family of jacks, among them the amberjack and trevally." "Okay," I smiled. "It's a jack." The relieved and joyous faculty repeated, "Jacku, jacku, okay."

As the evening progressed, a wild arena unfolded in the green glow below us. Schools of small mackerel and yellowtail (another species of jack) skittered across the surface, squid and swimming crabs hunted the shadows, and a pair of gulls sat at the light's soft edge. It was a magical world surrounding our boat, and we started catching fish at various depths, sometimes a bonus squid groping an imperiled *aji*.

The captain, a short sinewy man who wore a cap eerily similar to Japanese naval officers in World War II, came down to chat with me through Usami. The captain told of a huge sea turtle that once swam into the light of the *Yutaka Maru*, its swollen flippers entangled in fishing line. He tried to net the turtle so it could be brought on board and the lines cut away, but the alarmed creature dove, and he never saw it again. "That's sad," I said, telling him about a dead swan I once found, its beautiful long neck choked in fishing line. "*Hakucho*," swan, the captain raised his hands into the sky, telling us that they came every fall from Siberia to winter in Niigata. "*Taihen, ně*," that's terrible, he acknowledged the fate of our turtle and swan. Although such casualties may seem insignificant in the face of vast human interferences on the planet, we nodded solemnly, knowing that every angler has lost harmful line, hooks, and lead, every angler has released fish that would not survive, everyone has injured and killed creatures unintentionally.

With the captain watching, I reeled in two *aji* and suddenly felt a fierce strike. Something like a dragon broke into the glowing arena. "*Tachiuo, tachiuo,*" the men called from the deck. The long bright fish had swallowed one of my hooked *aji* and hooked itself. The captain swept down a landing net and scooped up the yard-long beast. *Tachi* means long sword, a much better name than ribbonfish, as the species is commonly called in English. Stretched over a bladelike body the fish's skin was preternaturally silver, brilliantly reflecting the lights on deck, and its dragon head narrowed into a mouth of long needle teeth. It twisted powerfully out of the net, the live *aji* still fluttering in its jaws.

As the fishing slowed, a few of the men sat around the stern drinking Asahi beer and cutting squid and *aji* into *sashimi*, thin strips of raw fish dipped in soy sauce. I had never eaten raw fish before. Watanabe Jun, a broad-shouldered, handsome teacher with a crew cut, pulled a knife from his bag. He held up my stiffening *tachiuo* and gestured, bringing the two beams of silver together, creating a triangle between us. "Okay?" he asked. "Okay, okay," I affirmed. He slit the fish lengthwise and skinned it. Then he sliced the pale flesh into thin ribbons, handed me a pair of chopsticks and asked, "*Sashimi oishī desu ka?*" Is sashimi delicious? I sampled the flesh of the dragon. It was tender and delicate. "*Oishī desu,*" It's delicious, I said, learning my first bit of Japanese.

One of the men aboard the *Yutaka Maru* that night was the tall, thin, and very fishy Kanamaru Mitsuru, who asked me to call him Ken. Ken often took me fishing along the Niigata coast, where we cast from rocks and tetrapod jetties for *tai*, a bottom dwelling sea bream that reminded me of its cousin in the *Sparidae* family, the Long Island porgy. For twelve hours we would stand, slip, sit, talk, or stare silently into the waves, angling long rods and strange baits, Ken chirping "*kita-kita-kita*" when he felt a bite, which wasn't often. The first time out we each caught one *kurodai*, the black sea bream, about the size and shape of an average freshwater sunfish, and Ken said it was wonderful. "One fish is worth twenty dollars."

"No way," I said.

"Way," he countered with a smile, having watched and loved the new movie, *Wayne's World*.

Ken insisted we eat the fish the next day, explaining that it takes hours for the flavor of some fish to develop. I was incredulous, thinking the fresher the better, but with dictionaries and patience, he explained that the proteins had to break down into mouthwatering amino acids. I told him about aging beef, and he said, "Fish, too. But not too long." The following afternoon at his house, Ken filleted the *kurodai* with surgical precision. He then set out small dipping dishes with his preferred mixture of soy sauce, a sweet cooking sake called *mirin*, and a broth called *dashi* made with the flakes of a cured bonito. His wife, young son, and I all had a slice of *kurodai* that we dipped gently in the sauce. Firm, almost crunchy, imparting the subtle flavors of the ocean, it seemed the epitome of seafood sophistication yet required no cooking. "*Oishī* amino acids," I said. Ken didn't catch my joke and asked, "Okay?" with brow-lined concern. "*Oishī desu*," I smiled. Never had I eaten a fish with such a heightened awareness of its delicacy and value. Around the Kanamaru house were *gyotaku* ink prints of trophy fish Ken had landed over the years, and in the family room alcove hung a scroll featuring an ink painting of a carp rising in a lotus pond. The tapestries of the Sistine Chapel and Coventry Cathedral could not have felt more holy.

Ken may have exaggerated the value of the little black bream, but its red-skinned relative, the famous *tai*, often called red snapper in America, was a truly precious fish; I saw four-pounders on ice at the market for six thousand yen, about sixty dollars. When I attended the elaborate wedding of a friend, each guest was served a whole cooked *tai* in a lacquered box, the very name of the fish the tail end of *omedetai*, meaning congratulations. Honored at shrines, pursued by emperors, revered by the people, the *tai* seemed almost sacred. But it was also being fished to death. The difficulty of catching a single *tai* indicates not only the rocky elusiveness of these creatures but also their relative scarcity in many areas. Even on a bad day off Long Island, we could catch a few porgies. Japan's seas have been supporting human predators for thousands of years, but the population density and industrialization of the twentieth century had taken a serious toll. The thought of a hundred well-armed Japanese men and women dropping lines down on a few lonely *tai* hiding in their mossy grottoes was discomfiting. I angled Ken toward the more abundant *aji* and yellowtail, feeling better, but perhaps just hiding my own head from the truth of man's deep-reaching predations.

"Don't get too deep," the dive master warned before we rolled off the side of the fiberglass skiff. Scuba diving around Niigata's Sado Island, a couple friends and I chased a football-sized octopus that changed color and shape as it squeezed into a new cave. I followed another octopus into seventy feet of water before the cold and darkness turned me around. We swam with the honored bream and the famous *fugu*, a blowfish with delicious or, if improperly prepared, deadly flesh. And a huge, bulb-headed *kobudai*, an Asian sheeps-head, dogged us around the rocks, eating squid from our hands.

On the boat ride back to the island we also saw the Japanese fishing fleet chasing bluefin tuna, *kuro maguro*. As Japan and the West craved fattier melting bites of sushi, the bluefin's value exceeded the snapper, sole, swordfish, and every other fish in the sea. In the 1990s, bluefin prices were already on the rise at hundreds of dollars per pound; in January 2013, a 489-pound bluefin tuna sold for $1.8 million, more than $3,600 a pound. At these rates, very few Japanese or American sport anglers will ever catch a bluefin tuna on rod and reel like Hemingway and Zane Gray.

"Imagine hooking one those giants?" I prompted Ken.

"They're too expensive to play with," he said.

"That's a crazy way of looking at it," I argued. "If we stop fishing commercially for bluefin tuna, or any rare fish, they're likely to recover." I'd happily give up eating any fish for a few years or forever if it meant the species' survival. And if the big fleets would lay off the bluefin maybe the average sport angler could, one day, catch one. "The schools would return," I said, dreamy-eyed. "Like the great herds of buffalo."

"Japanese don't like buffalo," Ken snorted, fluffing up his tight curly hair with a pick. "They like Kobe beef."

Under the cover of a language misunderstanding or by poetic tangent, Ken would often evade my questions and contrary opinions.

One afternoon, under a beautiful October sky, I saw salmon leaping and rolling up the Shinano River not far from where I lived. A fisherman casting for mullet told me only commercial netters could pursue them. *Fuck that*, I thought to myself, making plans to cast some big spinners. When I told Ken, he snapped, "You must never!" His face was red, his tight hair vibrating.

"Just catch-and-release," I shrugged. "I'll say I'm mullet fishing. What's the problem?"

"It's against the law, and Japanese people obey the law. You have no right."

It was the first time Ken got upset with me, and I backed down. But I thought it wrong to deny a few anglers the experience of pursuing, hooking, and battling a salmon while gill nets hung across the river. Why should commercial operations have exclusive rights to the tuna and salmon, especially when these rights were abused? Ken was a passionate angler but sheepishly obedient to customs, systems, and laws that favored government-supported industrial fishing over sport angling. And he almost blew a gasket when I told him I was going to fake a few sick days and fish in the mountains.

"Are you sick?"

"No," I laughed.

"Then you shouldn't do that."

"I haven't used any of my sick days, and they're in my contract. Just a couple days."

"You're a teacher. That's not right."

Despite some cultural differences, Ken and I got along. A hair stylist who had studied in England, Ken ran a salon that became an after-hours fishing social club. Ken's English was excellent, but two languages as different as Japanese and English are prone to pratfalls, and I smiled at his expensive sign, Hair Craps, depicting two friendly looking crabs with scissoring claws. Even if spelled correctly, Hair Crabs is not a great English name for any sort of salon. Sitting in state-of-the-art styling chairs, drinking beer and sake, and eating dried squid and miso mackerel, we would discuss hair, women, pornography, food, fishing, travel—everything under the rising sun.

Through Ken and the salon, I made more friends, including Teiko, a beautiful woman in her early thirties who seemed, nonetheless, to carry sadness in her dark eyes. I sat in her pottery studio one afternoon, watching her hands press and pull a dull mound of spinning clay into the cylindrical form of a sake flask. "You love to drink," she said. "So I make you a *chōsi*. But this one will have fish." Teiko called herself a modern Japanese woman. An artist who graduated from the Women's Art College in Tokyo, she attended English conversation clubs, watched new movies, listened to cool music, and dated me, a twenty-six-year-old American. But she confided her increasing problems at home. "Now I embarrass my parents. They want me to marry. Then I will have no time for this," she said, shaving the inside of the *chōsi* with a long wooden tool. "My father gets very mad. He say I'm wasting my time with art and you." She picked up a wide wet paintbrush and groomed the outer walls, leaving them smooth and unreflective, then took another wooden stylus and, with a few lines, engraved a lovely fish. "I'm sorry," I said. She suddenly smiled, flaring the *chōsi's* mouth and pinching a pouring spout where the fish rose.

Teiko liked the water. We took trips to the sea and walked along the beach. Beaches in Japan are full of delights: people swimming, flying kites, surfing, and racing motorcycles. There were interesting dead creatures and debris printed in bright characters. But I was always surprised by the tide of garbage—bottles, cans, tires, plastic wrappers, even a washed-up female manikin, entirely nude but for a piece of kelp across her eyes as if she were a sea bandit turned to plastic by the dragon, Ryūjin, for trying to steal his jewels. Every culture has its paradoxes, and the law abiding Japanese, with all their civic mindfulness, order, cleanliness, efficiency, cultivated arts, and an obvious love of natural beauty, were still capable of trashing the sea. "Maybe it comes from Korea," Teiko said. And though oceanic garbage can travel thousands of miles, this empty can of Asahi beer had the stamp of a local distributor.

Teiko would often stay the night at my apartment. We'd wake on the futon, I'd make tea and slide open the *shōgi* screens to a field and marsh waving gently with new rushes. Spared by the plow and bulldozer, the wedge of land behind my apartment provided a small sanctuary for egrets, warblers, and shrikes. The waters teemed with frogs, crayfish, dragonfly larvae, and small fish. Stepping onto the gravel along the train tracks directly behind my building, a cock pheasant warily pecked. We noted the iridescent blue-green neck without a white ring and the long gray tail striped in black. I told Teiko about the ring-necked pheasants of South Dakota and Indiana, how they'd been introduced to America from the far fields of China and Japan. She put her hands around my neck and said, "You go the other way, *nē*?"

Some mornings I would get up early and fish the town's river and canals. One drizzly dawn I saw a man riding his bicycle down the cinder path under a line of ash trees, once grown to support bamboo poles for drying rice. Very old, wearing a shoulder cape and a round hat of woven rushes, he may indeed have dried rice stalks on these very trees before the war. Dismounting from his rusted one-speed, I noticed his mitten style rubber boots, which separated the big toe from the other digits. From the rear basket he pulled out a bag and a plastic bucket and then assembled a long two-piece bamboo handle and attached a semicircular net. He began dipping for *funa*, small crucian carp abundant in the warm rivers, muddy irrigation ditches, and polluted canals of East Asia. *Funa*, like all carp, seem to flourish almost anywhere, swimming through murky debris, feeding on vegetation, plankton, and small insects. Carp are tough, enduring fish, perhaps that is why they named Hiroshima's major league baseball team the Hiroshima Carp just four years after the devastation of the atomic bomb dropped on that city in August 1945.

Following the example of the young boys in town, I was also *funa* fishing but with a light wand, hair-thin line, and tiny hooks baited with maggots plucked from a dead cat. Catching finger-size fish from an irrigation ditch may not sound like great angling, but it brought me out into the fields where I could watch birds and insects, follow water, and bring home enough tiddlers for Teiko to make *kanroi*. Back in my apartment, I scaled and gutted the little fish, and then Teiko grilled them lightly over the gas burner and placed them in a pot with soy sauce, sugar, and *mirin*. The fish simmered all day while we played around, drank sake, and watched a movie until late afternoon when the *funa* became soft and dark. Served in Teiko's elegant little bowls with sides of white rice and pickled eggplant, we picked up our chopsticks and ate the sweet stewed fish of the fields.

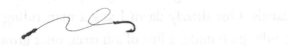

Up at school during the week, I was frequently visited by one of our textbook salesmen, Mr. Masugata, the characters in his name meaning "trout inlet." "I must take you *ayu* fishing," he said over and over. "*Tomo zuri, né?*" Friend fishing, okay? I had no idea what he was talking about, but his snapshots of the beautiful trout-like fish and the sparkling rocky rivers were enticing.

It was late July, and Masugata picked me up early in the morning. He knew little English, and my Japanese was basic, but we had a fishing language between us until he popped in a cassette tape of Kabuki, his other hobby, and tried to explain what was going on. We stopped at a 7-Eleven, the popular mini-mart of Japan, and bought some canned coffee and *onigiri*, hand-size triangles of rice stuffed with salmon or pickled plum and wrapped with crispy seaweed. I loved *onigiri*. We ate and drove to the river, stopping on a bridge so he could eye the water level and strategize our approach. At a nearby bait shop, Masugata parked the car and said, "Now buy *ayu*."

"Aren't we fishing for *ayu*?" I asked.

Masugata laughed. "I'll show you friend catch friend fishing. Okay?"

"Okay," I said.

I had gotten used to entering into events or taking trips where I really wasn't sure what was going on. One of the young teachers once brought me to a Beach Love Party that I thought would be a blast only to discover I was captive among a dozen missionaries from Kansas, sipping Coke and eating *yaki soba* while they discussed the Lord's work in Japan. I saw sharks in the waves and feigned stomach upset, getting home and calling Teiko for some sake and a long surf on the blue futon.

The tackle shop was busy, but the proprietor greeted us with a smile and netted ten live *ayu*, about nine inches in length, from a bubbling cement tank, securing them in Masugata's hi-tech aerated cooler. We drove down to a river looking very much like a North American trout stream, clear water braiding over rocks with riffles and blue-green pockets. The banks and islands bloomed in violet wildflowers and small bright bushes. There was little garbage, and birds flitted through the willows.

At streamside, we assembled the rods, incredible lances some thirty feet long. "Samurai fished *ayu*," Masugata spoke in deep charcoal tones. "Instead of sword when no more war." I watched an angler downriver. There was, indeed, something of the *nodachi*, the long sword, in the grace and power of his motions, and I could imagine a scarred warrior finding solace in a summer day wielding a bamboo rod below the cascades. Like Hemingway's Nick Adams trying to heal after the horrors of World War I, mindfully preparing his gear and casting for trout on Michigan's Big Two-Hearted River, sometimes one had to practice deliberately at peace in order to find and keep it.

"No reel but many lines," Masugata instructed, handing me about a foot of top line that I tied directly to the rod tip and then to about fifteen feet of aerial line running to a marker and a new ten-foot length of underwater line made of fine monofilament to minimize the strain on the bait. The bait, decoy, or friend, was a live *ayu*, detained by a braided line leading to a nose ring snapped through the fish's nostrils. From the nose ring, another span of braid runs along the body of the unfortunate hostage, ending in a monofilament leader and a single hook pierced through its anus, another treble hook trailing an inch behind.

Would you do this to a trout? Live minnows for trout, maybe, but never a live trout to catch a trout, though artificial lures are manufactured to mimic small trout, and I've had a large brown trout attack a little rainbow I was reeling in. Trout are cannibals, but we still grant them respect. When it comes to speciesism, we differ, sometimes arbitrarily, in the way we treat animals. We love and pamper our dogs and cats yet slaughter and eat cows and pigs. As an angler, I have happily snagged bunker and shad, jerking weighted treble hooks through their bright schools, yet I'd never dream of doing that to trout. Why not? Sportsmen extol the ethics of fair chase, thus we ban snagging and restrict the baits and lures that may be deployed on those game fish we privilege. In some cases, these laws make catching more challenging and less injurious to wild species whose numbers are threatened. That's good conservation. But even in a pond stocked with hatchery-raised trout, it would be considered unsporting and downright savage to snag fish or use baby trout for bait. Fishing laws and attitudes often reflect the way we *feel* about certain fish. So how should we feel about *ayu*?

Ayu are cousins to the smelt, I reasoned, associated in America with creel limits by the ton, fund-raising fish fries, cheap beer, bowling alleys, and Michigan all-nighters. So in the end, however spurious my logic, I felt okay lowering this store-bought smelt into the river for his friends to attack.

The territorial, wild *ayu* becomes "angry," Masugata said. The fish rams the intruder's flanks and belly, possibly hooking himself. "So they are not friends?" I retorted. Earlier, Masugata had acted out this drama with finny gestures and butts of the head, and now it was making sense. We both smiled, walked out into the river, and dropped our fake friends into likely living rooms. Masugata was a master angler, and with his conical straw paddy hat, red neckerchief, techy vest, and the graceful motions of his lance, he conjured the time-traveling samurai cowboy or perhaps the mysterious conductions of the ribbon-wanded Kabuki actor. Emitting deep humming sounds and holding firm, he swam the leashed *ayu* upriver a few feet. His rod tip pulsed with the living decoy, and then suddenly he felt the pull of another fish and swung back, launching two gold rockets through the air and into his fine-meshed net.

The name *ayu* nicely translates as sweet fish, and it has the lovely golden colors and grace of a trout. In winter, *ayu* hatch upriver and head out to sea, returning in spring and early summer and continuing to feed on vegetation and small insects, growing up to thirteen inches.

Masugata took the tired decoy off the hooks and creeled it in a little floating bow-nosed holder he towed like a toy boat behind him. The freshly caught wild *ayu* was hooked as the new bait and the show went on. The water was deep and swift, and I knifed my hips into the current, found some sure footing, and swung my flipping friend into a likely lie. But I had trouble knowing if the wiggling action was my bait, the rushing flow, or an ensnared quarry, and I pulled up too often to check, wrecking my set and, in a couple cases, knocking off a nearly hooked wild fish. Masugata coached the best he could, but I exhausted a couple baits and had to start fresh. This time when I felt something like an attack, I yanked fiercely and shot two fish way over my head onto the gravel.

We waded and fished until early afternoon. Small sculpins fled from our steps, and sulfur butterflies fanned the mud. Masugata landed *ayu* like a lacrosse goalie stopping double shots with ease, while I caught only one more, admiring the sunburst on its side and the orange trimmed adipose fin. "Smell it," Masugata urged. "Maybe melon, *ne*?" There was something fruity to the ayu's skin. The subtle and various smells of fresh fish were always pleasing to me. Fresh bluefish smelled of garden cucumbers, and grayling earned their Latin name, *Thymallus*, from their air of thyme. Oregon writer Ben Hur Lampman found smallmouth bass "as fragrant as flowers," and old Izaak Walton wrote that English smelt "smell like violets." *The Oxford English Dictionary* notes the peculiar odor of smelt but does not suggest a connection to the word "smell." With words, I say, it's not so much where you begin but where you end up, and this sweet smelt smelled swell.

We built a small fire on the bank, and as the wood burned down, we drank sake from pull-cap glass cups. Masugata drank little, observing the enforced zero-tolerance for alcohol and driving in Japan. The Japanese were really good about this—they loved to drink and party but knew enough to arrange a ride or call a cab. Today I could drain a few cups of sake, eat strawberries his wife packed, sit back, and watch the river and the other anglers.

Down at the water's edge, Masugata splashed some river on himself and me and said "River spirit." I asked if it was a Shinto rite, and he laughed and said, "Cheap shower." The Japanese seemed to be the most and least religious people in the world, but either way, they worshipped the spirit of all things fishy.

I helped Masugata clean the fish, friends and all, and he reminded me to carefully scrape the bloodline, the dark purple artery and kidney in the body cavity along the spine. I then followed as he raked his knife back against the tiny scales, patting the fish dry with a clean rag. He pushed a long metal skewer longways through each one, salted them, and, like an installation artist, positioned the fish over the fire in a way that suggested a swimming school. The perfectly fatted fish sizzled and twisted, turning golden brown. With a pair of gloves, Masugata pulled out a couple stakes and pushed off the cooked fish on black plastic plates. *Ah, sweetfish*, I thought, chewing slowly. The skin was salty and crisp, the flesh extraordinarily moist and, yes, slightly melony—indeed, some wild fruit, some sweet sacrament of the river.

In November of 1992, my old friend Eugene Jones came to visit me in Japan. I picked him up at Narita airport, and we rode the Shinkansen, the bullet train, back to Niigata, sipping fugu sake from cans that activated a heater upon opening, gently warming the fish-infused brew. "Not bad," Eugene said. Many of my *gaijin* friends reviled treats like fugu sake, sea urchin sushi, jellyfish salad, roasted squid on a stick, or savory bar snacks of nuts and minnows called *iriko*. "Bait" was the common joke. Japan was, indeed, a fishy place, but Eugene was a fishy guy, and I figured he'd like fugu sake.

Opening up the English edition of *The Daily Yomiuri*, he started asking questions about Japan and then said, "Holy shit," pointing to a small headline, "Man Dies of Fugu Poisoning." But this fugu sake had only positive effects that we chased with a couple beers, arriving in the Tsubame-Sanjo station where Teiko and her friend, Yuko, met us with a car.

Teiko hugged me, put on her hip blue-framed glasses, and drove us to a local *izakaya* for more drinks and food. Cushioned on tatami, Eugene and I were getting pretty loaded, eating *gyōza, yakitori,* and fried crickets, croaking karaoke, pawing our dates, and at one point reaching into a large aquarium to grab a dinner-fatted carp. We paid our bill, and Teiko was herding us toward the door when Eugene stumbled. I tried to steady him and also lost balance, both of us crashing through a shōgi screen and into a room of celebrating businessmen who found the intrusion hilarious, unlike sober Teiko and the tavern keeper.

The next day demanded recovery. "Did we really eat crickets?" Eugene rasped as I poured cups of green tea. In the morning mail I received a long letter from Caitlin that reminded me of her beauty and brilliance. She was flourishing in graduate school, excited about new books and her own writing. I read parts of the letter to Eugene, and he said, "She's pretty amazing. But so is Teiko."

Hungover but dutiful, we made it up to the junior high, where Eugene was a big hit with the kids, talking, asking simple questions, and handing out half dollars, *I Love New York* stickers, and little tin models of the Statue of Liberty. This went a long way, especially since my principal received a phone call from the *izakaya* owner reporting that *Hendy sensei* and his big *gaijin tomodachi* had trashed his tavern last night. My supervisor, Sagi, was not happy, but he deftly repaired the situation. "You pay nothing this time," he told me. "Bring present and say, 'Sorry.' Next big teachers party, we have there." I brought the tavern keeper a good bottle of sake and bowed in apology. He smiled and said, "Okay."

Sagi was a wise and warm friend, and he and his wife hosted Eugene and me at his home with a feast, including superbly grilled wedges of salmon and a seemingly endless sampling of fine Niigata sakes. A year later, Sagi and his wife visited New York, and Eugene and I took them out dining, drinking, and porgy fishing.

During Eugene's stay in Japan, Sagi arranged for the two of us to go cod fishing with his old friend who ran a boat out of Teradomari. I never got the man's name, but everyone called him *Senchō san*, Mr. Captain, and we stepped aboard his creaky boat on a cold, drizzly November morning. The seas were rough, the tops of big swells blowing off like snow in a stormy Hokusai print. Eugene and I sat in the cabin with two silent fishermen, rolling and tossing, unable to do or say much of anything. *Senchō san* was probably in his early sixties, but he jumped around the deck like a teenager. We stopped, anchored, picked up the heavy rods and reels, pierced bits of squid on a set of three hooks, and sent them down into the dark. I could feel the lead hit bottom, but it was hard to keep it there with the high pitch and fall of the boat. *Senchō san* smiled and showed us how to click the rod butts into the holders. "Sit down and watch the poles," he said in Japanese. Eugene and I were both feeling cold and queasy, and it was one of those rare moments when I wasn't entirely happy to be fishing. At *Senchō san*'s command, we reeled in and tried another spot, catching a couple tiny fish, including a small fugu, its pectoral fins buzzing away like a hummingbird. The little spotted puffer inflated in my hand as I unhooked and tossed it back, floating for a moment until the waves washed it away. Finally Eugene's rod showed some life, and he reeled up from a hundred feet, with hardly a fight, an eighteen-inch *tara*, codfish, that I netted. It didn't look like much, but the captain was delighted. Within the next four hours, the other three fishermen and I caught one cod each of identical size. I had to wonder if, like the Atlantic stocks off North America and Europe, these cod were pursued beyond the brink of survival? Should the Japanese, like the Canadians, put a moratorium on catching cod before it was too late? Should we even be out here?

When the boat turned back toward land, Eugene and I felt relief. And when we got into the calm harbor, we felt damn good, cracking a couple beers and eyeing the sights. *Senchō san* tied up and invited us into his dockside house. Past the runkled tin exterior, the wooden two-story displayed an impressive timbering of cedar and smelled strongly of fish, the bottom floor a kind of shop with nets, rods, tools, and large boiling cauldrons. We climbed wooden steps to a loft that served as a casual parlor where we sat on cushions beside a kerosene heater. The captain's wife appeared. A short, thick woman, gold-toothed and friendly, she poured us sake and set down a dish of shredded dried fish. Eugene and I looked around. There were old family portraits in tortoise shell frames tilting down from the wall: a young man in a Japanese naval uniform, a handsome couple in formal *yukata* and *kimono*, perhaps a wedding photo. When *Senchō san* returned we asked him about the photos, and he said, "Father and mother," and nothing more. I was fascinated by Japan's World War II history, but most Japanese were reluctant to discuss those dark times. After a couple more sakes, I asked *Senchō san* about his father. Was he in the war? "Yes. His ship went down at Leyte. I was just a boy." Eugene and I both said we were sorry. Eugene spoke briefly of his father, a surviving veteran of D-Day wounded at Battle of the Bulge. I mentioned my father's service in Korea. "To our fathers," Eugene raised his glass. I translated, and we drank.

The captain's wife brought three steaming bowls of soup on a lacquered tray. "*Tara jiru*," cod soup, she said over the yellowish broth amalgamated with leeks, white radishes, and big hunks of cod. Mine contained a head. We lifted the bowls to slurp the misoed broth, then chivied out bits with our chopsticks. Working on the head, I pulled lovely white meat from behind the cheeks then plucked out one of the eyeballs. "*Oishī*," delicious, pointed *Senchō san*, his face reddened by the sake. So I put it in my mouth, the lens was a bit chewy, the ball bursting briny between my teeth. The captain clapped his hands and laughed in approval. Eugene downed his sake and said, "Okay, bring me a head."

Cool Hot Chance

Eugene kept his head during the software boom and bust and moved up as a systems designer for a pharmaceutical company. "But the best drug is fishing," he'd always say, and in 1993, while I was still in Japan and riding a strong yen, we arranged a late summer rendezvous in Alaska. My father's older sister, Aunt Shirley, lived in Anchorage, and she met us at the airport. I didn't know Shirley well. She was sixty-nine with the tan, creased skin and lean figure of a lifelong skier and hiker, her wind-whipped hair suggesting a recent flight from a grizzly bear or ex-boyfriend. On the drive back to her house, Shirley said, "My son, Doug—your cousin who you met when you were just a little boy—wants to take you to church tonight." Eugene shot me a severe look. I hesitated, then spoke.

"We've had a long trip, Aunt Shirley."

"Well, we'll go over to my place and have a drink first."

I'd heard that Aunt Shirley liked gin and tonics, so my panic turned to confusion. When we got to her house the Tanqueray and Schweppes were on the counter. "I've got ice and limes. You boys make yourself at home," Shirley said, smiled, and crossed the room decorated with watercolor paintings she'd done of her favorite ski runs. Eugene and I knocked back a couple drinks, and when my cousin Doug and his wife arrived, he asked about Japan and our fishing plans. "Well," he finally said. "I hear you're up for a little church tonight." His wife laughed and walked into the kitchen. My gin-tuned receptors sensed a code cracking moment, and after a fine supper of moose stew and local squash, Doug drove us to his favorite strip joint for a few hours of worship and hymns like Def Leppard's "Pour Some Sugar on Me" and Warrant's "Cherry Pie," the elastic offering plate frequently filled. The drink-serving altar girls wore T-shirts depicting lady anglers above the testimony, "I Love a Good Pole Dance."

The next morning, after pleasant reflections on the evening service, Eugene and I gave thanks and took to the skies in a small plane for Fish Lake, seventy miles northwest of Anchorage.

"There must be a thousand Fish Lakes in Alaska," Eugene spoke to the pilot through the headset mic as we leveled off below the clouds. "How will I know where I am?"

"Because in a couple days I'll be back to get you on this one," the pilot answered and laughed.

Looking past the wing strut over the woods, rivers, and vast wetlands of Alaska, spotting moose and caribou, it's easy to believe that the planet is still a wild and beautiful place.

"It's all ours," Eugene cried as we landed. The outfitters provided an A-frame cabin and a small aluminum boat tied to a wooden dock. Unpacking our simple gear, we launched within minutes, casting floating Rapalas, twitching, and retrieving until a pike attacked. The northern pike is a magnificent predator with sight grooves down its snout to target prey and a vast mouth of needle-sharp teeth to seize and swallow anything that moves. I had caught pike in South Dakota and Indiana but never of this size and number. We landed several long fish up to eight pounds and kept one, from which I cut translucent white slices of sashimi that we dipped in soy sauce and wasabi brought from Japan.

On the second day of fishing, Eugene hooked and fought a tremendous pike. It ran and jumped and rolled like an alligator, and I swear it was more than four feet long. "Of submarine delicacy and horror / A hundred feet long in their world," the poet Ted Hughes imagined the pike's powerful place in the little lake community. This fish thrashed and circled the boat, but those brilliant teeth sawed away the twelve-pound-test leader, and it was gone. "I can't believe I lost it," Eugene groaned, and I reminded him of that time he was so cool after hooking and losing a five-pound bass on Lake Ronkonkoma. He groaned on. Then I offered Izaak Walton's adage that, "No man can lose what he never had." He groaned some more. Big fish lost haunt us more than big fish caught, but they deepen the angler's soul, reminding us that it's not "all ours," that there are still great, ungraspable forces alive and free in the universe.

Big fish lost can also deepen our worries and guilt. I fretted over the pike swimming around with a Rapala stitched to its mouth. Hooks rust quickly in water, I told myself, and this beast was a survivor. But we can't deny that anglers injure some of those fish we lose or let go. I love fishing, but I know it does harm. It's a dilemma I've never resolved.

Fly fishing is gentler. I brought along my fly rod, which I owned for years but used only occasionally to whip poppers over sunfish and bass, not thinking much of the style or efficiency. The beautiful film *A River Runs Through It* had just played in Japan, and I went on to read the novella by Norman Maclean. It was a deeply moving, lyric story about an early twentieth-century family and fly fishing in Montana. The angling metaphors spoke clearly to me, and I was ready to seek grace through the metronomic rhythm of the fly cast. "Come on, Yooze. Will you get that serve—that cast—down," Eugene ducked from my wild delivery. At first the fly cast felt all whippy, my tippet hopelessly tangling, and the back cast requiring much more rear tolerance than I was used to. Perhaps I wasn't ready for grace. But I slapped out enough line to put my streamer near a log, stripped back a few inches and there was the fantastic strike of an over-willing pike. All aspiring fly anglers should be brought to an Alaskan pike for confidence counseling, which sometimes doubles as the illusion, perhaps the sensation, of art and grace.

Flown back to Anchorage, we rented a camper and drove up the Alaska Highway—for many miles a gravel, washboard, two-lane road—toward Denali and got stuck behind a slow moving Army convoy. When the sign for Willow Creek appeared, we pulled off and parked. The air was heavy with spruce, fish, and the cries of gulls. Walking past a stand of birch to the river, where a few people were casting, I could see a silver-gray parade moving upstream. I had never seen salmon so close and dense in a river, and my hands trembled as I snapped on a bright spoon and cast into the school, immediately snagging a twenty-inch fish and putting it on our chain. A boy with a crew cut and bright red jacket walked up to me and said, "You're not suppose to snag them. You can't keep them when you snag them." His father nodded approvingly from a distance. "I had no idea," I said, thanking the boy, bowing humbly to the father, and adjusting my practice. We caught several three- and four-pound pink salmon, still quite bright and full of fight. Gulls and eagles crossed the sky, and boot and bear tracks dented the sand.

Back at the camper, Eugene sliced up raw salmon for a nice plate of sashimi, while I marinated the jewel-like eggs from one fat hen in a little soy sauce. Eugene vinegared and sweetened some leftover white rice, and I reconstituted miso soup from shiny packets. We sat down for lunch with the pink salmon. This pretty fish spent two years at sea dining on herring and anchovies and then journeyed up Cook Inlet into the Susitna River and Willow Creek, where she met two humans who were born on Long Island but traveled thousands of miles to catch and kill her. A crazy lunch date, I thought, spooning her eggs into my mouth, divining over the briny, creamy crunch. "The essence of fish," I pronounced. "Now the essence of us."

"Okay, Mr. Poet," Eugene took it down a notch. "To us and the fish," he raised his beer.

We felt good in Alaska, napping and driving on, encountering more caribou, a drunk woman who wanted a ride but smelled horrible and dangerous, and an abandoned Chevron station overrun with rabbits. In Denali, we followed the lumbering rumps of grizzly bears, watched them stop and rake berries, their dark faces and blonde backs inspiring our own wildness. So we drove on, sipped whiskey, popped a couple beers, and parked along the Jack River looking for more fish.

In was August on the Taiga, and where the wide gray sky met the icy Jack, arctic grayling ran. Eugene threw spinners, and I walked upstream and cast a Royal Coachman—for no other reason than it was the prettiest fly in my box. I started feeling the rhythm, setting those white wings long across the river and sharply following the fly's drift and bob downstream. Such pleasure, even without a strike. Then a grayling grabbed the coachman, ran, somersaulted out of the river, fighting hard and veering twice from my net before I lifted it—its sail-like dorsal fringed in red and dotted iridescent. As the fish died it grew as gray as the sky. After a couple hours of casting, catching, and releasing, I walked to the riverbank and set the one dead grayling on piece of driftwood. Knife-scoring one side, I pulled off some skin and then lifted the fish to my mouth and took a bite.

In the eighteenth century, Jean de Crèvecoeur, living in the American wilds, posited that eating wild meat could make a man wild. "I'm worried about you," Eugene said, counseling toward a hamburger and some noontime human exposure at the Cantwell Lodge. The bartender, Ron, a big bearded man around thirty, set us up with draft Molsons and bourbons on the side. There was a quiet, friendly mood to the place, and we started talking with Ron and a bony, smudged, retired old railroad man who said he was cutting wood all week and needed to get home and cut some more. Ron seemed delighted to have the extra company, and we threw dice to see who would coin up the jukebox. Larry, a middle-aged man who once tended the Cantwell bar, regaled us with local history—gold mining, snowmobiling, fishing, trucking, women, and drinking. A dark varnished clock on the wall was said to hold actual gold nuggets. The clock maker left the bar drunk and angry one night and drove his snowmobile right into the spinning prop of plane. His clock keeps the time he lost.

"Any shootings around here?" we asked.

"Oh, yeah," Larry said. "I was behind the bar, and this woman came in and she was mad at me cause I wouldn't go out with her."

We laughed and whooed. "Larry, you lady killer."

"Other way around. She comes in and pulls out this pistol and starts shooting. There's the hole." He pointed to a bullet hole under the bar labeled in pencil *.44 Mag.*

"She was shooting right for your family jewels," Eugene speculated.

"Well, I was already way down the bar and took my jewels with me. But she hit a jar of mustard that went all over the place."

"Like mustard gas in the Great War," the old railroad man mused.

We drank, talked, and laughed. More people gathered around. Tom Petty's "Free Falling" played, and we sang over with, "Free, free pouring." And that's how it began to feel. The currents of the universal being flowing through us as we relived fish caught and lost, bought a couple rounds for the bar, tipped Ron, absorbed and told more stories. I bought a silver ring from a mustachioed woman and promised to give it first "to my girlfriend, Teiko," then "to my girlfriend, Caitlin."

"You got some things to figure out," Larry said and tipped his beer at me. "Be careful."

Down at the end of the bar was a man they called Second Chief, an Athabascan Indian neatly coiffed and dressed in a collared shirt and sweater. His discerning eyes behind square-rimmed glasses reminded me of the Japanese teachers with whom I worked. We asked Second Chief about the fishing. His soft voice was hard to hear over the jukebox, so we leaned in close, and he told us about the mountain lakes to the south, "Good fishing. Nobody 'round. But you'll need horses. Take a few days."

"Better try a plane," Larry interrupted. "Go see the bush pilot, Ray Atkins. He'll fly you in."

At 5:30 in the afternoon we were drunk but full of energy. We brushed our teeth in the camper and followed Larry's directions to Ray Atkins' house. His pleasant wife answered the door and showed us into the living room dominated by a television set and a massive moose head, the animal's taxidermied face glued to endless reruns of *Cheers* and *Frasier*. Ray and his wife must have known we'd had a few, but we held it together, asked his advice, and hired him to fly us to Caribou Lake for lake trout. "Pack light," he said.

We drove our camper down the rough road to a long pond where Ray docked his plane. In those days we drove drunk too often, regretting it the next day and swearing never to do it again. But when you're drunk, it seems fine, even necessary.

Ray's plane filled quickly with a cooler, shotgun, ammo, fishing gear, and our heavy selves and seemed to barely lift off the water before the ground smeared below. Eugene and I looked anxiously at each other. "She was a little dead under that left wing," Ray spoke calmly into his headset.

Ray flew us south through deep, craggy canyons and pointed out mountain goats and bighorn sheep. It was grand, but the long day of fishing and drinking had stirred my pool. Hunched in the back seat, shifting to the banking turns and turbulence, I felt increasingly sick and uneasy. The plane suddenly dropped, and I clawed Eugene's shoulders, saw the approaching ridge, heard the engine accelerate, turned away, and nearly vomited as we cleared the rock. We flew another ten minutes, and Ray put us down smoothly on the lake. "Thanks, Ray," I said. "That was a lot of fun." A few years later Ray and a client crashed in those mountains but survived.

Above four thousand feet under a leaden sky, Caribou Lake winked against a bare shore of lichen and moss-printed rocks. Amid the low brush and a colony of curious ground squirrels, our cabin was a simple wood frame covered in tent plastic with a stove and cots. With plenty of light and our heads clearing, we stepped down to the water, threw small green spoons, and caught a brace of lake trout for dinner. Grizzly bear tracks followed the shore, and I glanced back at our shotgun leaning against the cabin.

The little lakers turned out bright orange fillets that I fried in some bacon grease glommed from a jar above the stove. We ate, poured light vodkas, and talked. "God's country, all to ourselves," Eugene said, chewing a piece of lake trout.

I nodded, knowing what he meant, but skeptical about there being any God, any sort of mystical realm beyond the human imagination that could conceive of a metaphor like "God's coun-try" and our rights to it.

"So, trips like this bring us closer to God?" I asked.

"Absolutely," he said.

"What about people around the world who can't fly to Alaska or some pristine wilderness for a little spiritually uplifting fishing? How are they gonna see God?"

"A park, television, shrooms? I don't know. Church?"

"Seriously, man. Not many people could afford to take a trip like this. Do we really deserve it?"

"Hell, yeah," he said. "There's no shame in spending money on a fishing trip."

"So it's like money well spent on your spiritual enrichment?"

"Sure."

"Don't get me wrong, I'm having the time of my life. But just think of the fuel alone it took to get us here. For what? A little recreation?"

"No, to get us closer to God. Aren't you paying attention?"

I lay down confused, thinking maybe we should have ridden up here on horses like Second Chief counseled. This country and its fish needed to be earned more physically, more intimately. But we were modern, first-world pilgrims who had to get back to our jobs and credit card statements. I slept fitfully and rose hungover, stepping out of the cabin to the mad chirping of ground squirrels. Then, on the ridge behind our cabin, a wolf—its unmistakable sil-houette a sharp symbol of—what? Wildness? Maybe. And perhaps even the rightness of my being here to see and feel it. "We need the tonic of wildness," an educated but financially strapped Henry Thoreau declared. I watched the wolf until it disappeared and then put away my guilt about being a privileged American and grabbed my fishing rod.

Eugene said he needed some exercise, and he headed off on a long fish-walk to the west. I worked the lake before me, fly casting a high floating White Wulff and raising fish after fish. They were heavy-headed, lanky lakers—each one fourteen inches long—from a long lean lake. Although Alaska has a reputation for big game, high altitude waters surrounded by so little flora and with a long winter freeze just manage to sustain their fish. Conversely, shaggy shallow ponds in the South get too hot—the oxygen drops, and the fish gulp at the surface, dodging herons and good ole boys with bows and arrows. It's a tough world at all latitudes, I thought. Gray clouds massed and shifted behind dark ridges, a peregrine falcon glided high and away, and I felt far from the peopled world, drinking in the "tonic of wildness," both humbled and exalted by its sublimity. A good feeling, a spiritual feeling, at least while it lasted. After a few hours of casting, I walked back to the cabin and mixed myself a Bloody Mary. One good tonic deserves another. Our light packing did not exclude olives and celery. Eugene walked up with a stringer of fish and a huge caribou rack over his shoulder. "Yea, I wrestled it right off the beast," he said and smiled.

"Well done, man. Have a drink." He had gone several miles to the next lake over, glimpsed the wolf, caught fish, napped in the sun, and found some fresh antlers. Ray Atkins picked us up in a couple days. We handed him a bag of fillets, lashed our antlers to the wing strut, enjoyed the return flight to Cantwell, and rested on the warm rocks beside the Jack River, watching grayling rise.

Back in Japan in the autumn of 1993, I brought Teiko persimmons and a bottle of sake. She smiled and thanked me, but I knew she wasn't happy.

"I don't want to be your girlfriend anymore," Teiko said.

"Your father is still angry?"

"No, me. You just want to play. It's hard for me."

I had been with other women during the time that Teiko and I were together, but there were no stated expectations or exclusivities in our relationship. On one extended weekend in Tokyo, I met a younger woman who asked if I had any marijuana—extremely illegal in Japan. I did, and we got high in her little apartment. She had magazines depicting women with elaborate tattoos, and she said she wanted a phoenix or a koi on her back. "They'll think you're a gangster," I said, and she ran her fingers over my mouth to close it. We underdressed, and I traced a koi across her lower back, its wide tail caressing the rise of her ass, my hand a pale fin over smooth stones at the base of a waterfall. We spent a few wild hours together. When I tried calling her the next day there was no answer. I called again and discovered it was the wrong number.

I had been reading the thirteenth-century Zen master Dogen, who described emancipation using the term *todatsu*, a fish slipping from the net. Dogen referred to the Buddhist-inspired freedoms from desire, materialism, and selfishness, and I twisted the application to sexual freedom from social conventions. When I tried to explain some of this to Teiko, she laughed at me—"You are too selfish." She was right. The desire for independence is a selfish desire. Then later she told me, "You hurt my heart."

I did not want to hurt Teiko's heart, but I could not marry her. Through many talks and my apologies we remained friends, but it was never the same. There were other women, Japanese and *gaijin*, delights, disappointments, and some downright regrets.

Under the pretext of English lessons, a Niigata housewife invited me over while her husband was away on business. Like King Leontes in *The Winter's Tale*, I knew that many a man has "his pond fish'd by his next neighbor," but when this woman served me glass after glass of whiskey and a bowl of whale stew—the dark meat tasting like soapy corned beef grazed on seaweed—I felt like the prey. Like one of those sharks Frank Mundus of Long Island chummed in with ground grampus. I vaguely remember rolling around on the futon, and I'll never forget waking up in the middle of the night on the salty sheets with an earthquaking hangover, the agonizing, seismic cries of a dying whale sounding through my brain.

There were love notes from Caitlin, and we talked about getting back together. Would I meet her in New York for Christmas? She even sent me a photo of herself in a tight top, licking her lips, the inscription, "You'll never catch another like me," drawn out in luring, looping pink ink. I wanted to send her the ring I bought in Alaska, but I couldn't find it. She was always beautiful in my mind, and I thought long and hard about Caitlin, but I didn't want to settle down.

I got handwritten letters from Aunt Lil. She was receiving radiation treatment for cancer, but her words were full of life from home: the mums were in bloom, my brother caught two big blackfish, she liked the scarf and silk slippers I sent, the cat ate some old bait in the garage and threw up, a dusting of snow made the oaks in the backyard glow. Lil's letters pulled on me. Friends and family from New York urged me to come home, even my colleagues in Japan suggested I be with my family at a time like this. My supervisor, Sagi, said he'd understand. The Japanese honored family responsibilities. But when I spoke to my father on the phone he said I should stay in Asia, travel around, "See how Korea is doing."

"It's your life," my father said. "You gotta do what you really want to do. Don't live your life for other people—not now, not at your age."

"What about Lil?" I asked.

"She's sleeping," he said and fell silent. "Go on. Go."

My father knew what I wouldn't admit—that I wanted to see and fish more of the world. His words, "It's your life . . . do what you want," stayed with me. I know some of my Japanese friends saw my actions as selfish, even reckless, but I packed my bags and tackle and headed to South Korea, where a friend, Jon, and I hiked through Seoraksan National park and down into the fishing town of Sokcho, where I caught herring off the dock, tossing a few to a pride of cats that had gathered around me. They clawed the flipping fish, biting off pieces, chewing and purring loudly.

Jon and I found a seafood restaurant in Sokcho, knocked back a few glasses of the local firewater, *soju,* devoured a seaweed salad, and then stared at a flatfish pulled directly from a glass tank and sashimied, still breathing, before our eyes. I'm not sure how we ordered it, but the neatly sliced flesh was replaced on the fish's horizontal bones so the living creature became its own platter. I had eaten living sashimi in Japan but without Jon's imagination comparing it to an Aztec priest cutting the beating heart out of a sacrificed slave and showing it to him in the last moments of his life.

"Fish and people are very different," I said.

"Yeah, still," Jon said, nodding. "Can't they just put the thing out of its misery?"

I had read several studies arguing that the simple nervous system of a fish did not allow it to register "pain" the way it is experienced by mammals. Perhaps that's true, but fish express an obvious physical reaction to being bitten or hooked. They don't like it. Maybe the human words "pain" and "like" are impossibly distant from what this flatfish was feeling. "Who knows what birds and fish feel?" Basho wrote in a seventeenth century haiku, "Or how the year's end party will feel to us," suggesting that the inner workings of nature are as unknowable as our own means of handling sorrow, aging, and death. I suddenly thought of Aunt Lil lying in her sick bed and my father encouraging me to make this trip instead of returning home. I looked at the pulsing flatfish and recalled my father's conflicted feelings on killing foxes and eating veal, his only advice, "If you can live with it, go ahead." Living flesh between my chopsticks, I chewed and swallowed an allowance that I'd never fully digest.

In December, I traveled alone to Malaysia, walking the colorful streets of Kuala Lumpur, past throngs of people, mosques, and Chinese altars, stopping at Yong Soo Pets Shop, hung with Moorish wooden cages, fluttering chocolate brown finches, tear-eyed thrushes, and brilliant blue and green leafbirds plucked from the trees of Southeast Asia. Deeper into the dark store, I studied fish glowing in glass aquariums. There were tanks of tarantulas, and turtles in tile tubs. Near the back door, guarded by a goose on a foot leash, gasping eels thrust their heads out of a dirty aquarium while a flat black catfish glummed below the tangle. I wanted to let them go. You might ask how the same person who eats a still quivering flounder could worry about a bunch of choking eels? I don't know, but this felt like neglect. The animals' suffering was completely unnecessary. From a barred window I could see a canal running down the alley behind the store. I might be able to tip the whole tank into the canal, at least giving the eels and catfish a chance. When I reached to test the back door, the goose honked.

Down the road from Yong Soo's, I stopped at a restaurant that rivaled the pet shop with its wide glass tanks of live *arowana* and catfish. I sat down, flipped through my phrase book, and ordered what sounded like "bee chew," (I would later learn it was the Chinese word *baijiu*) the popular spirit among ethnically Chinese Malays and a good buy at fifty cents a glass. Antique refrigerators hummed away with shelves of Coke, Sprite, and Carlsberg Beer. One of the men spoke some English and noticing I liked to drink, pointed to museum-like jars of *baijiu* infused with hairy ginseng roots and whole snakes. "Good for man," he said, gesturing a fist in front of his groin. "Okay," I said, waving in a glass. The sapor of musty root was fine, but I felt no special effects from the reptilian promise except a growing sympathy for creatures crowded in glass. I ordered stingray, flapping my arms for clarity, and it arrived grilled and very dead, wrapped in banana leaves and topped with a sweet and sour sauce. I ate, paid, bowed to the staff, and sailed into the cooling night alone with my freedom.

On Christmas day 1993, during an hour flight to Malaysia's Langkawi Island, a stewardess in a blue hijab delivered a "Meddy Christmas Mister Hug-gess" over the intercom. I smiled and picked up a magazine advertising "Tundra to Tropics—Make You A Cool Hot Chance," and thought of the wild Alaskan tundra and the broiled confines of the Kuala Lumpur pet shop. How does one ever make sense of the wide world, compressing space and time inside a jet, the place we stand, or right inside our own head? I once dated a brilliant and overweight nutritional psychologist. We were talking about conflict and contradiction, and I quoted F. Scott Fitzgerald from the "The Crack Up"—"The test of a first rate intelligence is the ability to hold two opposed ideas in the mind at the same time, and still retain the ability to function." She smiled, chewed a buttery hunk of lobster, swallowed, wiped her mouth, and said that a mental breakdown is more likely to occur in a first-rate intelligence because the person is aware that so many ideas are opposed and still true. Unable to reconcile the constant barrage of contradictions in the human condition, I simply dismiss them with a cocktail and a nap, saving myself from the dangers of a first-rate intelligence or insanity.

Langkawi's December jungles were insanely hot and wet. A civet cat sprang behind a bamboo fence, and I watched leggy, eye-ringed myna birds, so like our common starlings, pick crumbs from the yard where I sat sweating, eating *nasi goring*—fried rice and veggies that tasted like something Caitlin once made from a recipe snipped out of her mother's *Good Housekeeping*. Everything felt both exotic and familiar, and I wasn't cracking up.

The next morning I took a long fish-walk to a swampy village and arranged for a boat trip through the root-tangled mangrove swamps. I had walked several miles and was glad to be sitting in the wooden pirogue watching rusty red sea eagles, iguanas, turtles, and mudskippers—small fish that walk on shore and breathe air—while my guide rambled on about a snake in his wife's bed. The blue-spotted, bubble-eyed mudskippers flashed their high dorsals and pulled themselves in and out of holes, sometimes jumping for joy or something that seemed like joy in this wild world of possibilities.

The Malay guide spoke a few languages, and after he calmed down about the snake we started talking about fish and fishing, using some French and Japanese words to fill in the gaps. Knowing this was a wildlife preserve, I asked him about some men pulling nets starred with crabs and small fish. My guide was easy. "*Chari makan*," he said. "Everybody has a right to get their food." I told him I was also looking for some fish to catch and eat. "Go to the restaurant," he laughed, gesturing cash fanned from a fat wallet. I felt a little embarrassed and quickly mimed the actions of a man casting and reeling. "Oh, okay," he said, wriggling his ropey arm. I thought he was back on the snake, but he described an aggressive fish called *murrel* swimming through the rice fields and marshes.

After we docked, my mangrove guide set me up with a handsome young man in a splashy green sarong and Hard Rock Café T-shirt who drove me to a village where two older men agreed to walk me to the reedy edge of a murky, steamy pond fed by a slow river. They had bamboo poles, and I extended the telescopic spinning rod I brought from Japan. Using minnows on rusted hooks, within a few minutes one man pulled in a foot-long fish that I recognized by reputation—snakehead, a dreaded invasive species in the United States but rightfully at home here in Southeast Asia. I tossed and retrieved a blueish plug, raising something on the third try and hooking one on the next cast. Dark and long, like a meaty eel, this seventeen-inch snakehead fought well and made the men smile. "*Ikan hantu*," they said, "fish for dinner." A number of children had gathered around, and they asked me questions in Malay and English: "What is your hometown? Do you like soccer?" They giggled when I turned to answer. The snakehead was well-toothed and slick, but I wrangled it into the plastic laundry basket with the other fish and carried them up to an open pavilion-style eatery where a woman scrubbed off the slime and large scales. She asked me questions I could only answer with a smile. She smiled back, sliced fillets, and dropped them into a wok crackling with oil and red pepper. Despite its muddy home, the fried, pink flesh was firm, fine grained, and mild. I thanked the woman and ate heartily.

A growing taste for Southeast Asia also drew me to Jakarta, Indonesia, and on to Bali Island the following spring. The beautiful, saronged Balinese woman at the *losman* where I lodged kept an almost equally beautiful blue betta fish in a pickle jar on the shelf. The villages and temples were green and calming, but I couldn't resist spending a couple days in the touristy southern city of Kuta, checking out the clubs and bars full of young men and women from Australia and Germany. After a night of too much drinking and some reckless sex, I took a long shower and visited a Hindu temple to light incense and reflect. A young man outside the temple said he was a driver and could show me the island.

Andres was bright and friendly, chatting away as we crossed terraced rice fields and cascading jungles. Stopping at another Hindu temple with luxuriant lotus ponds, I reflected further on my promiscuous lifestyle, watching a swirling school of pretty striped cichlids. Was I as simple and milt driven as these cavorting fish? I certainly admired their beauty and freedom, cherishing their fishy place in the world. I loved to catch fish, feel, see, and hold them for a moment. Sometimes I killed and ate them. I admired and sought women for their intelligence, beauty, and difference, and I loved having sex with them, but I would never coerce or force a woman into my bed. I admit to using some deception, to playing down one relationship in hopes of securing a new one, to making claims about myself that weren't entirely true. I am not proud of these lures, these deceptions. Although comparable desires at some playful metaphoric level—*There are a lot of fish in the sea*—fish and people are very different.

Andres' English was excellent, and when I told him that I loved fish and women in different ways—in ways I couldn't yet fully understand—he squinted in confusion, paused, and then explained that Vishnu once appeared as a great fish and warned of a world-cleansing deluge, instructing the good king, who was tender to Vishnu-the-fish when he was just a minnow, to build an ark and spare the useful creatures of the land and few decent people. The story rang some Christian bell buoys, to be sure, but I wondered how a fish eating, philandering fisherman from afar would fair under an admonishing Hindu fish god. Vegetarianism and sexual abstinence honors the gods and brings us closer to Nirvana. When I explained my quandary to Andres, he laughed. "You're not Hindu, so don't worry."

Andres dropped me off near Tulaben, where I planned to scuba dive on the wreck of the *Liberty*, a US Army transport ship that was torpedoed by a Japanese submarine in 1942. The remains of the ship lay just off the northwest shore of Bali in thirty to a hundred feet of water. Getting my gear ready on the beach, I saw and heard several Japanese travelers, including a couple from Niigata, and we chatted a bit. The Indonesian dive master came over, buddied me with a German named Herman, and we dove the wreck, following each other under rusted archways that scraped my tank. Although the wreck was heavily encrusted in coral, we could still see portals, chains, ladders, and the guns of the old ship. The profusion of fish life was remarkable—striped angels, parrotfish, snappers, sweetlips, grouper, anemonefish, and a beautiful, poisonous lionfish hovering in an orange cave. Gazing up with our bubbles into the silvery-blue light, we watched a circling school of bigeye jacks and, above them, a small boat. It was a fish's view of the world, and I saw myself in the boat, dropping a line and hoping again and again for something I believed in but often couldn't see.

Herman and I had a beer together on the beach, talked diving, and joked about the Japanese and Germans returning to Bali with a better attitude. The Germans I knew were always more willing than the Japanese to talk about history's darker chapters. Herman and I hiked up to a village of bamboo houses and rickety little shops with signs for San Miguel Beer and Salem Cigarettes. Small black pigs and brown chickens scavenged, and people came down from the coffee plantations and napped in elevated pavilions. We walked out on a promontory and looked down on the Bali Sea. Herman said his friend went on a fishing charter and caught giant trevally and red snapper. But right before us we could see locals using Bali *jukungs*, outrigger canoes with crab claw sails, plying their nets and hand lines. "You should join them," Herman pointed to the beach. "That's real fishing."

I spoke to a young man who said his father would take me out fishing with hand lines. I left my fishing rod in my hut and at mid-morning met the father, who I called *Nelayan*, Fisherman, which made him laugh. He was in his forties, dark skinned, and sinewy with great veins running down his biceps. He wore light cotton shorts, a worn T-shirt, and a Japanese-style jungle hat with a neck flap that read "Bali Fun." Freshly painted in red, white, and green, his wooden *jukung* stretched a narrow fifteen feet crossed by two timbered outriggers pontooned port and starboard with bamboo. Nelayan, his son, and I, with the help of another man, picked up the boat and carried it the forty feet down to the water. I hopped in, and Nelayan followed, grabbing his double-ended paddle and moving us out. A couple hundred feet from the shore, something dark breached, and I shuddered—sharks?—but it was a pair of spinner dolphins gracefully coasting the island. When we got to a spot he liked, Nelayan handed me a bamboo spool wrapped with monofilament that ended in a well-used hook weighted with a spark plug. We pulled salted sardine-like baits from a round cookie tin.

Nelayan spoke no English except "Okay" and "No," and I knew only a couple polite expressions in Bahasa Indonesian, but we got on fine. Fishing often found the shared language that sustained my travels. I dropped the baited hook down, letting the line roll off the spool and holding it out with my right hand, feeling for the bite.

We caught a couple small snappers and tossed them into a reed basket. Most Balinese ate fish.

But it was a slow morning. The sun got high, and flies buzzed around our bait as we drifted closer to shore. We paddled in and were greeted by Nelayan's son. I told him that I enjoyed myself, but I wanted to try it again, "Tomorrow morning before daybreak, 5:30 am, okay?" The son translated, and Nelayan smiled and nodded. I would pay him twenty dollars.

That evening I skipped drinking, wrote in my journal, set my travel clock, and woke to the sound of roosters in the cool ocean air of Bali. A couple geckos scurried up the bamboo walls of my rented hut, and I dressed and brushed my teeth. Out on the dark beach, men were preparing boats and equipment. Nelayan and his son helped me put my camera in a plastic bag and tuck it under the bench. There was a little bit of surf that morning, and we had to make a piercing launch into the waves. I was given a paddle this time, digging hard as we arrowed through the breakers and into the moon-frosted roll of open water. Nelayan directed us to a different spot, a better spot, I reasoned, now that he knew I was serious, and by sunrise we were catching some hearty reef fish and filling our basket.

I liked the physical intimacy of the hand line but can't deny that I missed the fishing rod, a wonderful instrument that seems to amplify and heighten life at the other end while also absorbing its shock and power. With the hand line, I could hook fish easily with a firm jerk of my wrist, but fighting the fish had less of a sensory thrill. And with a large grouper, it was harder to absorb the fish's power and administer drag.

Sitting comfortably, spool in my left hand, line played out in my extended right hand, my mind was musing on the virtues of fine graphite drawn to a smooth, progressive taper, and I was yanked off balance and nearly pulled overboard. Something huge had my bait.

Line blistered out, burning my fingers and sending the bamboo bobbin bouncing across the belly of the canoe. I grabbed the spool with both hands and tried to pay out line, but there were stops and runs and our canoe was jerked sideways and then towed backward. Nelayan yelled something and gestured, but I had no idea what to do other than give some line and hold on. The monofilament was pretty heavy, maybe forty-pound test, and with our canoe underway I felt like Santiago in *The Old Man and the Sea* or Ishmael in the whale boat. The Bali sleigh ride lasted a hundred feet and then everything went slack. "Oh God," I moaned, my legs shaking from the adrenaline. I pulled in the line and saw that it was bitten through. Nelayan made more painful sounds and then put his flat hands together and pointed over his head, like a tall prayer. I recognized the diver's sign for shark. We must have hooked a big shark or ray. "What else could it have been?" I asked his son when we pushed up on the beach. "Nobody know," he said. I sucked my scored fingers and picked up our basket of fish. "Good it got away, maybe," the young man said. "My father try to catch everything. He crazy."

My father seemed quite the opposite of Nelayan. Stories tell of a wild teenager, dropping out of high school to play ball, work, drink, and tear around Port Jefferson on his Harley. But the man I knew was careful and measured. He was faithful to his wife and job. He never remarried after my mother's death, telling us, "One good marriage is enough for me." And he declined offers for more challenging work or promotions with heavier responsibilities. When his aging boss offered him the small crane business, he said "No thanks," accepting easier work on oiler's wages with other outfits. "I want nothing to do with running a business," he told me. My father was steady and hardworking but not emotionally or professionally adventuresome or ambitious. Maybe there was something dangerous about trying to catch everything, but I was willing to try.

Younger than Santiago and older than Ishmael, I wanted to be close to something wilder and bigger than myself.

It must be this hubris in some men that leads them to greatness or dramatic failure—or worse, shame.

Other fishermen came ashore and held up some small tuna and shouted to us. Nelayan, his son, and I walked over. One of the men filleted the tuna and set it out on an old board and then someone else doused the red flesh in lime juice. We all picked up hunks and started eating. It was good. One of the men carried a few pieces up the beach to a thatched hut where an old woman was pulling fishing nets off the potted plants outside her door. When the man walked up, the woman threw down the nets in anger. It looked like the man was trying to apologize as he offered the fish. Island to island, I thought, things are different and the same. Back on Long Island I remembered Aunt Lil getting frustrated with me as she pulled yards of monofilament from the vacuum's roller brush. "Damn this fishing line," she cursed. "It's all over the place." But I had just gotten a hot tip on weakfish close to shore, and I dashed out of the house to grab my surf gear, pick up a friend, and head to the beach. Now I wanted to go back to that moment as a different kind of man. I wanted another chance. "Sorry Lil," I'd say. "I'll take care of it. You relax." Maybe bring her some pickled herring on a cracker.

Kings and Emperors

I sat at the edge of Aunt Lil's bed. She was dying of cancer. "Read something to me," she asked and squeezed my hand. "Read me one of those stories you like so much." I pulled a collection off the shelf. So many stories were draped in death, so I started Updike's "A&P," suddenly thinking it too adolescent. Lil liked it. "I spent a lotta time in supermarkets," she said, her cracked lips turned up in a smile. And she found it funny that the bikinied girls went to so much trouble to buy a jar of pickled herring. When Sammy in the story quits his job, angry and embarrassed over the way his manager scolds the scantily clad girls, Lil said, "I'd bet you'd do that."

"I don't know, Lil. I need a job."

I did need work, and a letter from China offered a university teaching position in Beijing if I wanted it. It was the summer of 1994, and I had been home for a month. "You should go," my father said, lifting the lid on the Crock-Pot to check his beef stew. He had just retired and was doing a little cooking. My brother was starting his first year of college in Massachusetts.

"But what about Lil?" I asked.

"What can you do?" he said. "I'll take care of her."

I accepted the teaching job in Beijing, hoping I could get home at Christmas. Eugene came by to visit. He and Aunt Lil were good friends, and the three of us sat around the kitchen table, sipping tea and talking. Our marmalade cat, Twain, jumped on the table, and I reached over to grab him. "Let 'im stay," Lil said, stroking the cat as he dropped and rolled over some newspapers, purring. After an hour, I walked Lil back to bed, then lifted Twain and set him down beside her. Eugene and I stepped out on the back steps to talk and watch the birds. He and his brother were going fishing in Thailand and wanted me to come along. "It's on the way to China," he said. "We'll pay for the boat. Come on. I won't see you for a while. Let's fish together."

On an August morning I said goodbye to Aunt Lil. She wanted to come out into the driveway and see me off the way she always did, but she couldn't make it. We sat on the breezeway couch and held hands until my father warned I'd miss my plane.

"I'll see you at Christmas," I promised.

"You be careful, now." She hugged and kissed me, smiling over her tears. "Don't fall in that Yellow River."

Bangkok's pungent humidity smelled familiar. I had been here before, checked into ten dollar a night guest houses with paint-chipped rooms, wobbly ceiling fans, and leaky toilets that sashayed water across the floor. There were crazy, careening tuk-tuk taxi rides across the city, always to a cousin's jewelry store or a friend's travel agency. Over the course of three visits from Japan, I befriended a Thai driver named Sang, who took me to meet his family outside the city, where his father raised and fought bettas, Siamese fighting fish. Dropped in a tank together, the cocky males fin-flashed and then charged and nipped each other while men shouted bets with fistfuls of red *baht*. Back in Bangkok, Sang drove us to restaurants overlooking the Chao Phraya River, the River of Kings, where we slurped the gingery heat of turtle soup and feasted on *tom yam goong*, steamed stingray, spicy prawns, fried swim bladders, braised grouper, and endless varieties of pad thai. Sauces and soups brought the fire of chilies to the mellow milk of coconuts and coriander.

There was plenty of Singha beer, Mekong whisky, and good smoke that opened the gate to other sensations: bizarre sex shows and the lurid nightlife around Patpong, where numbered women danced or slumped like used cars on a sales lot. I took some pleasure at Patpong—and it might've been okay, had I not broken a condom and woke the next morning in the horrible shadow of AIDS and the impassive face of the purchased woman. Confused and disgusted with myself, I wandered alone through smoky neighborhoods and a Buddhist temple veined by a canal that came alive at dusk with fish rising in endless swirls and splashes. The next evening I returned to the temple with my telescopic spinning rod. The rubber worm plopped into the dark canal, and I instantly hooked a large, eel-like monster—God knows what it was—that overpowered me and broke off. A young monk in saffron robes ran up. "No, no," he said, fanning his hands. Another monk joined him and said, "We not fishing here." I opened my wallet, repeating, "I'm very sorry, very sorry," and gave them five dollars each. Although an obvious purchase of religious indulgence, they smiled and bowed. I bowed and hurried out of the grounds with my rod and spirits unstrung.

There was the Grand Palace with its fantastic murals depicting a bow-drawn King Rama lured from home and wife by an enemy disguised as a trophy stag. The story came from ancient India and seemed relevant to the modern world. Resting on a bench, I heard an older American man talking with his family about the Vietnam War, when he was on "R & R in '67." His wife stepped closer to study the mural. "Never thought of coming here," the man confided softly to his grown son. "We just wanted a good time." It was swelteringly hot and humid. His wife undid a couple buttons and sat at the other end of the bench. The stag's twisted antlers raked an orange sky, and the crazed hunter pursued blindly while ogres surrounded his wife.

One December, my friend Dan and I took a rumbling night bus up to the mountain jungles of Chiang Mai, trekking with a group of Swiss travelers through the foggy mountains, staying overnight at a Karen village where we smoked a little opium and Dan played guitar for a smiling family. In the morning we mounted elephants for a lumbering ride down to a brown river. The elephants seemed happy with the water, taking long drinks and wading out into the flow. Our guides used old bicycle tire tubes to lash bamboo into rafts while Dan and I walked along the grassy bank. People hawked small pipes, bracelets, and spangled bags, and one man came up with a homemade rifle. "You try?" He muzzle loaded powder, wadding, and a lead ball, handing me the gun and pointing to some plastic jugs floating by. I pulled the hammer back, aimed, and fired, miraculously blasting a jug. A small cheer went up in the crowd. I paid the man a few *baht,* and we moved on. We had asked the Thai guide about getting a little smoke, and he came up with a joint that Dan and I burned on the sunny bank, watching the elephants blast water over their dusty backs. It was powerful herb, and we felt very high. The guides called us back to the group and explained that the last leg of our journey would be a four-mile raft ride. Dan and I stepped onto our wobbly raft, little more than a four by fifteen foot bath mat, and picked up our long bamboo push poles. The two Swiss couples each had their own raft, and the guides shared a larger raft with our bags. My elevated state played nicely to the easy float downriver from the thatch-roofed village under huge trees and some boys checking their fishing nets, but the river narrowed and picked up speed, cascading over rocks and the rusted wreck of a bus. As we bounced over more rocks, the lashings loosened and my feet started slipping between the bamboo. I grew anxious and scared, imagining my ankle snapping off, and I just tried to focus on keeping my feet and watching the river. We pushed off boulders and snags, but the bamboo took some terrifying hits, and I fell to my knees just to stay aboard. Up ahead, the first Swiss couple bashed a boulder and spun out of control. We poled up to them and saw that the bamboo had split and cut the woman's leg. It looked deep and serious—blood ran down her calf, and her boyfriend was trying to bind the wound with his shirt. I called for the guides who waved us forward. There was nothing to do but raft on. When we reached the next village, our guide ran up to call a doctor. But the doctor was upriver for another emergency, a man had been blinded and badly injured when the breech of a homemade gun exploded in his face.

Thailand was beautiful, freeing, and full of dangers. Arriving that August in 1994 with Eugene and his brother Ken, I was troubled about leaving Aunt Lil and unsure about my work in China. "Let's get you a drink," Eugene said and put his arm on my shoulder. We checked into the Phuket Fishing Lodge on Chalong Bay. At $12.50 a night, the clean, balconied waterfront rooms were idyllic. We walked under coconut trees into the adjacent yacht club pavilion—a laid-back Key West sort of scene—and were greeted by the lodge owner, Siri, a neatly dressed Thai man in a crisp Panama hat, and Crazy Bill, a wild-haired American wrapped in sunglasses and a flowery bandanna. Bill, a local charter-boat captain, regaled us with legends of the seventeenth-century Englishman Samuel White, who abused the King of Siam's favor and became the pirate of Phuket, ravishing women and plundering the island's riches. When we told him about our booking with English captain John Pearce, he went silent. "Pearce, hah?" he said after a moment.

"Is he a pirate?" Ken asked.

"No." Bill adjusted his sunglasses. "He's a serious fucking guy. But you'll catch fish."

That evening, Ken, Eugene, and I rented scooters and rode into Patong, one of the stinkiest, craziest, wildest party towns I've ever roamed. Bob Marley played over crackly speakers, and we waded through a steamy carnival market of clothing, jewelry, fruit, birds, monkeys, and sex. A transgender woman wrapped in a python invited us to inspect her shapely chest while young women in miniskirts and tiny tops sidled up with, "Come on. Have some fun." Increasingly thirsty, we broke through to an open arcade with canopied bars and people in various states of intoxication, including a large Buddha-like man, passed-out and completely naked, lying flat on his back on a table while his friends tried to rouse him by pitching peanuts and fried shrimp at his balls.

Nearby, a young Thai boy quietly hand-fed a small monkey, and two German-speaking men felt up a creamy blonde leaning against the bar. We had a couple drinks and just watched. "Well, we gotta big day of fishing tomorrow," Ken, the older brother, reminded us. Early morning fishing commitments—often waking up at 3:30 or 4 a.m.—have saved me from many nights of overindulgence. There were times, however, when we drank all night and, hearing the first robins of dawn, decided to go fishing. Spirits high on the first cast, the flesh rarely held up for much longer, and we never experienced our best mornings in such a state. *Don't tie one on if you really want to tie one on* is my wellness slogan.

That bright morning in Thailand, my head was clear. Brown puddles stretched across the streets from the night's rain, palms glistened, and we sat on plastic stools at a card table near the beach and met John Pearce at 7 am. Pearce, in his late twenties, was a tall, lean, handsomely clean-cut Englishman with beautiful teeth. Friendly, professional, but not overly warm, he talked briefly about the planned three days of fishing, collected some money, and said sailfish over and over again. I asked about tuna and wahoo. "Sailfish is king around here. You want a sailfish," he insisted.

We stepped aboard the *Andaman Hooker*, a trig forty-foot game-fishing vessel, and met his Thai crew: Saron, the pilot, and Don, the tackle mate. In need of live bait, Saron motored us out to Monk Island, and Don and Pearce began jigging sabiki rigs like those used for *aji* and herring. "We can do that," Eugene said.

"Yeah, I'd like to fish," I rubbed my hands together and stepped to the stern.

"I'd rather if you didn't. We know how to do it," Pearce frowned.

"We know how to jig," I persisted. "We grew up jigging for mackerel in New York."

"These guys are fishermen," Ken added, happy to lean back in the warming sun.

Pearce reluctantly handed us the rods, grumbling, "You got about twenty feet of water." We clutched, thumbed, dropped, engaged, jigged, retrieved, and dropped again without a whisker of backlash, bringing in slim pairs of slivery queenfish. Eugene reeled in a seven-inch yellowtail. "That's what we want," Pearce rejoiced, carefully placing the yellowtail in a live well. He half apologized. "I get a lot of people who never fish. They screw things up." When I reeled in another line of dancing queenfish, Pearce cursed, "Damn those things." Apparently only the crew found queenfish desirable. "Good to eat," Don smiled at me, slipping them into a plastic bag. We caught six yellowtail for bait, rigged for sailfish, and began trolling off Koh Racha Yai, a lush, steeply cliffed island at the southern tip of Phuket. Only one other boat was in view. While we trolled, Pearce inquired about our evening. "So how many birds did you bag?"

"How many birds?" Ken asked.

"Sea eagles?" I queried, remembering the raptors for sale at the bazaar. Pearce laughed, "Come on, don't play innocent with me. I recommend two each. In case one's a dud." Pearce ordered Saron to steer off from the other boat and then went on talking about Thai prostitutes in the most crude and mercantile manner. "Cheap birds, right?" he nudged the Thai mate, Don. I felt embarrassed. Pearce then moved on to the "German and Australian bimbos who come down thinking they're gonna liven up their sex lives and end up getting a sunburn and pussy rot from their blokes." It was hard talk. A movement over our lines refocused him in silence, and then he cried, "Fish!"

A sailfish bill-thrashed around the inside bait and then bit and bolted across our wake. It was an unlucky moment for a strike with the other boat close behind us, and Pearce yelled for Ken to set the hook. "Now!" he screamed. Ken fumbled a bit with the rod and then pulled up hard. The fish made a magnificent leap, shining through a purple pirouette and crashing back into the water, throwing the hook.

"Bloody hell!" Pearce shouted. He waved a fist at the other boat, "Bugger off," and glared at Ken. "When I say 'Now,' I mean *Now!*"

We rebaited, and Ken caught what locals call a *longtom*, a garlike needlefish with a beaked mouth full of teeth. "Good to eat," Don said, slipping it into the plastic bag. Pearce grew even madder.

"There goes another good bait." We were savaged further by barracuda and a mystery fish. An hour later, I picked up a jumping rod and zinging reel and felt the amazing speed and power of a wahoo, the Maserati of mackerel, that thrilled me with its racing runs and black tiger stripes, coming up finally on the point of Don's gaff. "Good to eat," Don said.

At 5:30 we pulled in the sailfish baits and turned home, cruising at fifteen knots and trolling pink and blue tuna skirts. "We're always fishing," Pearce repeated. "Always fishing," I nodded in approval.

When we pulled into the dock, a beautiful Thai woman in a flowered dress with two young children smiled and waved. Pearce hugged the woman, kissed her, and reached over to take the little child from her arms. It was his family. "Let's make it eight tomorrow morning," Pearce said. "I've got to help my wife with the kids." I was amazed. Was this the same chauvinist who called women "cheap birds?"

Siri came by and arranged for our wahoo to be cooked and served at the corner restaurant. Wahoo, or *ono* in Hawaiian, is one of the least expensive fish at world markets, so I'm reluctant to boast of its flavor. Fillets from our fish were soaked for a half hour in olive oil, lime, paprika, and red pepper and then grilled for fifteen minutes over hot coals. It was rich and delicious. While we were eating, Crazy Bill stopped by. "No sailfish, hah?" We told him how close we'd come. "Pearce didn't torpedo the other boat? He's gettin' soft. Oh well, plenty of wahoo around."

That night Ken went to bed early while Eugene and I returned to Patong, petting a baby elephant and chatting up two Australian women, Monica and Alexa, who told us they were graduate students in chemistry. They had a lot to say about Thailand and the ocean. Alexa grew up in Perth and liked to fish. "Among the aboriginals, it's the women who do the fishing," she said.

"Are you an Aboriginal?" Eugene asked.

"She's an O-riginal," Monica quipped, and we laughed.

"Why don't you two join us tomorrow?" I said. "There's plenty of room." Monica bowed out, but she encouraged Alexa to go. "All right," Alexa lifted her hands from the table. "What time do we sail?"

"Pearce is gonna flip," Eugene grumbled, looking up at the stars on the way back to the lodge. Two cats wandered onto the road, and I reached down to pet one.

"It's about time he met a bimbo who was smarter than him," I said, stroking the cat.

"That thing's probably got fleas," Eugene walked on.

"Come on, it will be fun with Alexa."

"It's fine with me, but I don't wanna piss off Pearce."

"I'll talk to him in the morning."

"And Kenny," Eugene said.

Lying in bed, I had misgivings about my offer. I should've asked Ken first. He and Eugene were paying for the boat. And maybe it would upset Pearce and the fishing. What was I looking for? Was I that lonely? I thought of Aunt Lil cuddling her cat, slowly slipping away on the other side of the world. What would my family think of me wandering the streets of Patong? What was I doing here?

In the morning over fruit and coffee, Ken liked the idea of having an Australian woman aboard. Eugene said, "Whatever." Alexa arrived at 7:50 looking beautiful and prepared. When Pearce drove up, I walked over to him.

"Good morning, captain."

"Hello," he said without looking at me.

"If it's okay with you, we'll have another guest with us."

"No hookers on the *Hooker*."

"It's my Australian friend, Alexa. She's a chemist."

"I bet. Hey, that wasn't the arrangement. If you guys wanna fuck around, fine. But if you want to catch a sailfish, you need to concentrate on fishing."

Eugene was correct, Pearce was not happy about our guest. We fast-trolled grass-skirted pink and green tuna lures out to Monk Island. "Always fishing," I said to Pearce, but he hardly smiled when we picked up two skipjack tuna in the five-pound range. Alexa handled the rod nicely, bringing a black-striped silver bullet of a fish to the transom, where Don swung it into the cockpit. She turned a wonderful smile, and I took her photo. We stopped to jig for baitfish, refreshed Alexa on how to clutch and thumb a conventional reel, and she caught a couple queenfish, a lizard fish, a small snapper, and a trumpet fish. Eugene and Kenny hooked three yellowtail, but that's the only live bait we had. "Bad luck," Pearce growled.

Trolling for sailfish in thirty feet of water off the northern end of Koh Racha Yai, we went three hours without a strike. Terns dipped in our wake, and Pearce pointed to some dolphins playing a hundred feet off our bow. Pearce was an excellent captain, in command of his vessel and a great body of knowledge concerning southern Thailand's waters and marine life. We listened to him talk about his beloved sailfish, how they migrate, change colors, and use their sails to herd squid. "Must be great to work out here," Ken said. Ken was an insurance agent. He made excellent money, but there were long, sometimes stressful hours in the office. Eugene was a computer systems manager for a large pharmaceutical company. He made great money, but there were long, sometimes stressful hours. I was off to China to teach English for three hundred dollars a month. "A month?" Ken exclaimed. "Hey," Alexa touched my shoulder, "What an adventure for you." She was wearing denim shorts, and she pulled off her T-shirt to a blue bikini top. Pearce held the rail at the cabin entrance and watched the lines, finally addressing Alexa: "So you're a chemist? Like home economics?"

"Sure," she said. "You want me to bake brownies for everybody?" We laughed. "I'm a biochemist," she answered again. "Been doing work on lipid metabolism. Maybe save you guys from having heart attacks when you're sixty." Pearce, stripped down to his swim trunks and a tennis visor, had a lean runner's build. "I'll keep you in mind," he chuckled.

About one o'clock a squall blew heavy rain and wind across our decks. We retreated to the cabin, and the water turned choppy. In ten minutes, the rain passed, but with the tide ripping out and the wind blowing in, the seas grew rougher. A reel clicked off and Alexa jumped to the far rod. "Fish on," I yelled to Saron at the wheel. Pearce stepped behind Alexa, coaching. "Let it take line. There's nothing you can do now." But the fish got off. "Bloody bad luck," Pearce shook his head. Ken and Eugene played a game of cards in the cabin, and Alexa and I went up on the flybridge. Now rolling in seven-foot waves, the bridge of the *Andaman Hooker* felt like a wild amusement ride. We held tight to the rails, laughed, talked, and rejoiced over another pair of glistening dolphins.

At 4:30 a sailfish startled us. Making a play for the live bait, the black bill sliced the waves and turned away. Then the fish struck back, grabbing the yellowtail and running. After many quiet hours of concentration, lapse, distraction, reconcentration, hope, wonder, even despair, a large striking fish feels like a miracle. They do exist, they are here—by God, there's one on the line!

Line peeled off the reel, the rod bent, and the disciples stared, wave-lulled and awed, except Pearce, who snatched the rod from the holder, waited, and then arced back on a hook set. The sailfish made an incredible leap, its brilliant blue-bronzed flanks and namesake dorsal glistening cobalt against the gray horizon. And that was all. The hook pulled free, and the fish disappeared. "Goddamn it!" Pearce shouted, looking up at the sky and closing his eyes. "Bugger all. What a fucked up day."

With the late afternoon seas still beating on us, we turned for home. "What a great day," Alexa smiled. "Thanks so much."

"Will you join us for dinner?" I asked. Ken groaned on the edge of seasickness. Eugene leaned back against the padded bench and closed his eyes. "We'll have some sashimi," I forecasted, holding a tuna by the tail.

A long day on rough seas can wear out a person. We all felt tired and achy, and dinner was shorter and quieter than I had hoped. I spoke to the chef about tuna sashimi, and with lots of Japanese tourists, he knew exactly what to do. "This is wonderful," Alexa said, dipping the bright red flesh in soy sauce and bringing it to her lovely mouth. Siri came by to report that a virago monsoon was swirling over India and we would feel her skirts. "No fishing tomorrow," he said. Eugene and Ken bade goodnight, and I sat with Alexa and ordered a Mekong Mountain, Mekong whisky and Mountain Dew, hoping it would perk me up. A couple German men walked in with their skin and bling Thai dates.

"So, do you sample the local ladies here?" Alexa asked with a raised eyebrow.

"No," I said resolutely. "Well, I did on my first time to Bangkok a few years ago. It was disappointing. I'm no longer inclined."

"What, to screw twelve year olds?"

"I would never do that," I squinted in disgust.

"Have you been tested?"

"For AIDS? Yes," I said, sipping my drink. "Had to, for the China job."

Alexa was attractive and interesting, and I thought we might come together that night, but perhaps my admissions, her attitude toward Western men in Thailand, or our bruised weariness ruined that opportunity. Still, I thought it worth asking. "Would you like to hang out in my room? There's a nice view of the bay."

"Sure," she said, and I felt my dull heart leap.

We were up half the night, and by morning it was good that a storm swept Phuket, as I was in no shape to fish. I went out and found instant coffee and sweet cookies, and Alexa and I watched the bay and talked easily. Siri's boat wallowed in the chop, a string of Christmas lights and its bright red cabin ports made it look heavy and clownish compared to the lean athleticism and naval grace of the *Andaman Hooker.*

Alexa told me that she was once engaged, but she discovered that the man was obsessed with his own success. "He worked all the time, and I was okay with that for a while. But when we were together, he couldn't talk about anything else. I stopped asking him questions and stopped listening."

So I asked Alexa more questions and listened.

"'A woman needs a man like a fish needs a bicycle.' Have you heard that?" Alexa put a finger on my chest. "Irina Dunn, an Australian activist, said that."

"I thought it was U2. So you don't need a man?"

"Not sure about 'need.' I like men," she said and smiled.

"I've seen a lot of bicycles in rivers," I said. "The fish seem okay with them."

I told her about Aunt Lil, who never dated or married but seemed happy with her life. Alexa listened and said she was sorry about Lil's illness but that our family was lucky to have had Lil all those years after my mother died.

Alexa had to go. She and Monica were heading back to Bangkok later that day. "Time to get back to work," she said, slipping on her shoes.

"I guess you work pretty hard yourself," I said, not wanting her leave.

"You must've guessed I also like to play."

"Or at least fish."

"You should visit me in Perth. I'll be there next spring. There's lots of fishing."

Alexa and I walked out into the wind and rain. In the distance, waves crashed the coral shoal, and I hailed a covered tuk-tuk. Alexa kissed me. "Write me when you get to China. Good luck. Be safe, okay?"

"Thanks. You, too."

I would never see her again, but would never regret or lament the brevity of our relationship. Brief, intimate encounters with people can leave us with powerfully formative and remembered sensations, joys, and insights unsullied by the efforts of getting along for years or under the stresses of work and family. I wouldn't want an emotional life composed solely of short episodes, but I wouldn't want a life without them.

The weather can change so suddenly in Thailand. Clouds lifted, the sun shone, and you could hear the popping snarl of the local long boats as their pole shafted props churned Chalong Bay. "Always fishing," I thought. Eugene and Kenny waved to me from the restaurant. "So, if it isn't Captain Horny," Eugene smiled broadly. "Good night of fishing?"

"Looks like *he* was the fish," Ken smiled, folding his newspaper. "Alexa caught a *longtom* last night."

"And the price was right, hah," Eugene laughed.

"Okay, okay. We had a nice time. She's a cool woman."

"I'll miss her," Ken said, nosing back into his paper. I laughed and ordered coffee. In an hour the skies turned dark again, and wind and rain drove us inside.

After a day of rest we were eager to fish, but we wanted to forgo the sailfish and head to open water for more action and variety.

"Didn't you come here to catch a sailfish?" Pearce looked severe when we met him the next morning. "Sailfish is a prize worth working for."

"No need for prizes, John," I said.

"We're on vacation," Ken smiled.

"We'd like to get into some tuna, maybe some dolphin fish or more wahoo," Eugene added.

"Fine, it's your money."

When we started loading up, Pearce asked, "Where's your chemist friend?"

"She threw us back," Ken said. "You know, catch-and-release."

I shook my head. Pearce smiled and said, "She was all right. Probably high maintenance, but all right."

We steamed into the Andaman Sea for a bluewater drop 23 miles to the west. After a three hour ride—with flying fish bursting and gliding off the waves—a nasty squall blew in. "Normally I'd blame a woman," Pearce joked. It poured and poured, but the wind never mounted, and the seas softened in fifteen minutes. We trolled over long blue swells, and just after 11 a.m. the first rod went down. Ken battled a beautiful wahoo, shouting a deliberate, "Wahoo!" when it ran and took line. It was a big fish crowned in a long low dorsal sail; when it came up on the gaff, Pearce smiled. "Well, at least you caught the king of mackerel." There were more flying fish, and at 11:30 a school of dolphin fish—also called mahi-mahi or dorado—crashed our lures. With three rods alive, the fun ran wild, and I reeled in a mahi-mahi that fought like crazy, jumping all over the deck until Pearce trapped it in the hatch door. Eugene landed another one that slapped my leg, snapping its teeth and blushing radiant yellows and greens, while starry spots blinked on and off above its silver belly. Light and color refracting and pulsing through the wet scales of fish make them some of the most beautiful creatures on the planet. When Ken reeled in the third mahi-mahi, color rippling down its body, I just stared.

We cleared the cockpit, resumed trolling, caught several skipjack tuna, and then endured a fifteen-minute lull while Pearce tutored his mate, Don, on preparing a mullet bait. Don butchered a couple baits, and then filleted and hooked a split-tail mullet to the boss's satisfaction. Set out on one of the outriggers, it immediately got a take. "It must be one helluva fight for food down there if they'll eat this miserable mullet," Pearce speculated as Ken reeled in a large barracuda. Just then another rod went down, and Eugene worked on a tuna that suddenly felt like a submarine. "What the hell?" he looked down at a half-eaten fish surfacing in blood. "Shark," Don said. We all stared into the blue water, and I thought of Melville's "universal cannibalism of the sea." And if we turned the world upside down and considered our own sharkish business—from religious wars in the Middle East, tribal slashings in Africa, New York's predacious Wall Street, right down to the flesh markets of Thailand—things wouldn't look so different. Indeed, I shuddered over some of our captain's Ahabian traits, but measuring my topside friends I felt relief. It might be a sharkish world, but they were warm, trusted shipmates. And when Eugene and Ken dropped me off at the airport the next day, I didn't know how to say goodbye, so I just walked away, then turned and waved, articulate as a fish.

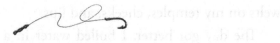

Unlike the lavish welcome I was shown in Japan, no one at Bei Wai, Beijing Foreign Studies University, seemed to know who I was or what I wanted. After a couple sweating hours of confusion and neglect, I just sat on the rim of a dry, cracked fountain in the tile lobby of the Foreign Experts Building and waited. A British professor, James, stopped by to ask if he could help. I explained what happened, and he assured me it was not unusual. "Welcome to China," he chortled. After another hour, a fit-looking, crew-cut, senior citizen rode up on his bicycle and introduced himself as Chen Lin, my supervisor. The attitude around me changed. Professor Chen had been the celebrated host of the first television program teaching English during the reform years under Deng Xiaoping. "Chen's friend?" the grim woman at the counter suddenly smiled.

Despite my connections, I was placed in a "temporary room" in Building 9. Chen and I climbed six flights of concrete steps, and he opened a sheet-metaled door to a filthy, stifling apartment. "Remember, only drink boiled water," he warned, setting down a complimentary Thermos. The sun was going down and Chen was eager to get home. "We will arrange everything in the morning. Thank you for coming."

I sat on the edge of a broken bed and looked at the pocked and peeling walls, exposed pipe, and sticky concrete floors. I was twenty-nine years old. Was this where I wanted to be? Tired and thirsty, I drank the few warm ounces left in the Thermos and brushed my teeth with tap water, trying not to swallow. There were no drapes or screens, so I turned off the lights, stripped naked, and lay on the tick mattress, sweating myself to sleep. I woke to sunlight and some amplified music. Touching my hot, itchy face, I found mosquito welts on my temples, cheeks, and lips.

The day got better. I boiled water in a tin pan, drank heartily, and brushed my teeth. Then I took a shower, rubbed cortisone cream on my bites, dressed, and ventured across campus. Even at a major university in the capital, you could see that life was closer to the bone in mainland China. An old woman wheeled a broom cart down the cracked sidewalk, pimpled students crowded and pushed into a bleak dining room where cooks in filthy aprons yelled back and forth. I drank tea and ate steamed bread that cost a few cents. The man next to me coughed up something thick and spat on the floor.

There were handsome buildings in gray brick crowned with wing-cornered Oriental roofs, but their cement interiors were hard and spare. I reported to Chen Lin's office. He wore a well-cut tan suit, greeted me warmly, offered concern over my mosquito bites, and insisted on a proper breakfast. We walked through the campus, past a mopped entranceway and a sign reading "Slip Carefully," and then stopped before a tailor's. "They can make your suits," Chen said, but I thought of custom fishing vests and shirts with big pockets. There were bike repair stations, book shops, and a market where a fishmonger set out his frozen fare on a makeshift wooden table. I stopped to examine the fish. "You like fish?" Chen looked surprised.

My classes didn't start until the following week, and I had some time to explore, get my bearings, make some friends, and learn a little Chinese. I stopped at a campus snack shop with a patio where a number of *laowai*, Westerners, and some Chinese were hanging out. I met a bald, elderly American professor named Art who had spent several years in China. He gave me sound advice on navigating the bureaucracy—"make friends, smile, and bring gifts"—and ordered us a couple Wuxing beers. As we were chatting, two young Chinese women approached our table. Art introduced me to Li, and Li introduced us to Jin Lei, a travel agent from Yunnan hoping to improve her English. They declined beer and sipped 7Ups, smiling and charming us with their limited but spirited English. Learning that I had just arrived in China, the women offered to help me shop and set up my room. I thanked them, and we made plans to meet the following morning. They sugared a "Goodnight," and walked away. Art raised a finger to me. "Be careful," he said. "The ladies like to cruise for free English lessons and free passports, if you know what I mean."

I quickly figured out that my temporary room would be my permanent room and that if I wanted to fix it up, I couldn't rely on the university. Art introduced me to his Chinese cleaning lady, whose husband's brother worked in the campus maintenance shop. For a carton of cigarettes I got new screens. Li and Jin Lei took me shopping, and I bought curtains, sheets, blankets, towels, and some lumber to fix the bed, bringing it all back in a *miandi*, a cheap yellow taxi built like a tinny VW bus. Through more smiles, gifts, friends, and favors—what the Chinese call *guanxi*, connections developed through friendship and reciprocity—we procured tools, university furniture, a working refrigerator, and got half of my apartment painted. "Now you need a bicycle," Jin Lei declared. We haggled for a used one-speed Flying Pigeon. "What other kind of pigeon is there?" I mocked the name. Jin Lei arched her black eyebrows. "Dead pigeon," she said—a Chinese philosopher dispatching the philistine.

The smoggy heat of Beijing still lingered through the first days of September, and Jin Lei suggested a bike ride to Yi He Yuan, the Summer Palace. We cycled north, finding safety in a long school of bicycles, finning in like a pair of mackerel fearful of the sharkish blue trucks and yellow taxis. Leaving the main thoroughfare, we pedaled down a quiet cottonwood-lined lane shared by donkey carts, as well as along canals, sorghum fields, and fish ponds. Jin Lei explained that they were raising carp. "Can I fish there?" I asked. She laughed, and then said, "Maybe," and I wasn't sure if she understood.

Passing through the red gates of the Summer Palace, we walked up to the Hall of Benevolence and Longevity, staring at the massive hardwood throne flanked by life-size bronze cranes holding thick fish-shaped candles in their long bills. We smelled a rose garden and gazed at more ornate pavilions, statues, and strange rocks, suddenly feeling the cool breeze of Kunming Lake. "Named after my hometown," Jin Lei said. "Kunming—in Yunnan. A very mountain and cool place."

To escape the heat of Beijing and the Forbidden City, the royal family retreated to this hilly, breezy, lake-cooled resort. In the eighteenth century, the successful emperor Qianlong expanded and deepened the lake, using it for naval drills and to angle for his beloved carp. The palace fell into disrepair but was restored a century later by the Empress Dowager Cixi. "Empress Sex-sy?" I read aloud the sign, remembering that crusty old hag from the film, *The Last Emperor*, until Jin Lei corrected my pronunciation to something like "Empress Sushi." In the late 1880s, the empress siphoned the military budget into the Summer Palace, and instead of buying a modern battleship she commissioned a crazy-looking marble boat hulked at the edge of the lake. Cixi might have been an ugly and terrible head of state, but she loved to fish, swinging a line from the marble boat or drifting happily in a Cleopatra-style barge while eunuchs baited her hook and removed the slippery catch. In one old photo, a eunuch holds a brown fish that might easily have been the size and shape of his missing member, and I wondered if a wave of regret passed over his loins as he tossed the hapless dart into a royal bucket.

For a couple of dollars, I rented a rowboat and two bamboo fishing poles, and we trolled Cixi's lake. "Oh, *fishing. Diaoyu*," Jin Lei exclaimed, understanding the word *fishing*, saying it again and teaching me the Chinese equivalent. Her long black hair shined, and her smile lit up the stern as I pulled on the oars. One pole twitched, and I swung in a seven-inch carp that, in fact, sized up pretty close to my own security. When I held the fish up and shared my reflections on sad and happy *memento penile*, Jin Lei blushed laughter and declared me a "so crazy *laowai*." I threw the fish back, hoping it would grow larger.

Teaching in China was fun. Unlike Japan, where I worked primarily with children in endlessly repeated dialogues of, "I like baseball. Do you like baseball?" Bei Wai assigned me adults, graduate students, and professionals—doctors, lawyers, and PLA (People's Liberation Army) officers—who would say things like, "Wine is good for your pancreas," or "America has many crime. Why?" or "We will buy America," and then laugh and offer me a mooncake. Five years before I arrived, China was rocked by the 1989 Tiananmen Square democracy protests and the brutal government crackdown. Sometimes people would discreetly tell me about the bloodshed they witnessed or friends and family gunned down or dragged away in the night. By 1994, political tensions had eased, and there was a general atmosphere of increasing openness in China, but some topics remained explosive, and one day my students and I fell into a tense discussion about the status of Taiwan, which I asserted was a sovereign nation separate from the People's Republic of China. "That's Western propaganda," one man shouted. And when another burly student with a crew cut tried to defend my view, a thin young lady wearing a kitten blouse yelled: "Traitor say that! We'll fight the US." After a couple days of cooling off, the students recognized the need for healing, so they gave me a carp.

"You're kidding me," I said when Captain Zhou, always neatly dressed in his dark green, red- and gold-trimmed PLA uniform, handed me a jumping plastic bag with a live grass carp.

"What's 'kidding?'" he tilted his head.

"No, I just mean that I'm surprised. Thank you." I tried to teach the class while eyeing the still-flipping fish hanging over a chair back.

"Today is Friday," the kitten lady said. "This is your Christian food."

Fish has always been a cherished food in China. An old Han proverb, "The fewer the feet, the better the meat," obviously ranks fish above two-legged chicken and four-legged pork. Thumbing through little red dictionaries, my students explained that the word fish, *yú*, is an up-tone homophone and symbol for "abundance," *yù*—and among fish, carp is emperor. Images of golden carp in baskets or in the arms of smiling children adorned red and gilt greeting cards and Spring Festival posters, signifying the blessings of fertility and plenty. Numerous myths and tales star a golden carp. In some stories, the resplendent carp is adored and cared for by a lonely student who is rewarded when the fish transforms into a gorgeous, enamored lover. Jin Lei retold a ninth-century Tang dynasty tale remarkably similar to the Western Cinderella story. A mistreated stepdaughter, Yexian, raises an affectionate golden carp in her family's pond, but her cruel stepmother resents the girl's loving attentions and kills and eats the fish. The heartbroken Yexian is told by a mysterious old man that any wishes she makes over the fish's bones will come true, and she provides herself with dresses, pearls, and shoes. Of course, Yexian secretly attends a ball, dazzles everyone, and loses a pretty little shoe that is picked up by a handsome prince.

Over the centuries, wild carp were cultivated into several colorful domestic varieties, including goldfish, which swam into fame on the scrolls and vases of the Song dynasty (960–1279). Although carp and goldfish are revered throughout East Asia—the Japanese certainly fancy their ornamental koi and sport a major league baseball team called the Hiroshima Carp—it seems China, with its vast, dusty interior and still-developing refrigerated infrastructure, has held on most tightly to the original durable fish. Carp can be raised in murky, warm water and eaten fresh when the sun is high and the sea is distant. I put the grass carp in the front basket of my bicycle and pedaled back to Building 9, where I met Jin Lei.

"*Hen hao*! That's great," she peeked into the bag. "We cook it." Jin Lei zipped off to get a few ingredients, returning to the apartment with a bag of vegetables and Miss Li. Then Art showed up, breathing heavily but safely escorting two German women who carried beer and shrimp chips. We had no phone, but people found us, and a Friday afternoon party was born.

It was a cool, sunny September day and we opened all the windows, popped big green bottles of Wuxing beer, crunched shrimp chips, and started cooking. Dime-size scales flew all over the kitchen, and then Jin Lei gutted, gilled, and rinsed the carp, patting it dry with my new bath towel. She asked for a sharp knife, and I honed and handed her my best Japanese steel. The head and tail remained, but she made several vertical cuts through the meaty flanks down to the spine. "Too bone," she said. We ignited a blue flame under a deep wok of oil, and I remembered Ben Whitehorse's advice on cooking carp, though I had never tried it. When the fish hit the hot oil, every head in the apartment turned, and I shielded us with a pot lid.

Simultaneously, Li prepared a sweet crimson sauce. The fish emerged crisp and curled, and we glazed it with Li's sauce. Beers lifted, I made a toast to Fish Fridays in Beijing.

The firm white chunks of carp were delicious and with a dab of the candied glaze, even better. Quickly following the fish, Jin Lei and Li brought out platters of vegetables—glistening eggplant and milky bok choy. The British gentleman I met on the first day, James, arrived with an older Chinese man who presented a bottle wrapped in red paper. "Have you tried the Chinese spirit, *baijiu*?" the man asked. I recalled the strong liquor of Malaysia but at this moment just said, "Not yet. Thank you. Let's have some."

"*Gan bei*," the cheers went up again. More people arrived. Neighbors banged on the wall. We hushed then rose again, riding beer and *baijiu* into the evening.

By eight o'clock people headed home. Jin Lei and I sat on the couch, dazed, exhausted, and happy. My newly painted kitchen was covered in fish scales and sticky grease, and a pile of dishes crowned by a carp skeleton towered like a pagoda over the sink. I started cleaning then gave up, dropping into bed. Jin Lei slept on the couch, but I heard her get up before dawn and sneak away, fearing the moral censure of my Chinese neighbors.

I was sound asleep when a firm knock shook the door. I jumped up and opened it to Chen Lin in a dark suit. He looked serious. "I'm very sorry. You must go home," he said.

"What?"

"Your Aunt Lillian passed out."

Auld Lang Syne

I called my father from Chen Lin's office. Aunt Lil died peacefully in a hospital bed with my father by her side—"Passed away," I explained to Chen Lin, who nodded sympathetically and made us tea. The trip back to New York was long and doleful. Eugene hugged me at the airport and drove us home to Port Jefferson. My father, brother, Eugene, and I sat around the kitchen table and talked about Lil. Our cat, Twain, jumped on my lap. "He keeps going in her room looking for her," my father said. My brother, David, had just started college, and I knew this would be hardest on him. David was two years old when our mother died. Lil was really the only mother he knew and loved. There was the wake and funeral. I looked into her casket; *Aunt Lil is not a fish*, I thought of Faulkner's bizarre story, Bud's giant catfish suddenly in my head. Flower fragrance soaked the room. *She's dead*, I said to myself. "She's in heaven," her friends consoled, and I smiled politely.

There were long dinners and long talks. Birch, Janet, and Caitlin called with kind words of condolence. After an exhausting week, my brother had to get back to school. I looked into his tired blue eyes and said, "Lil was so happy to see you start college."

"I don't know if I can do it," he coughed and looked down at the floor. He had gained some weight and seemed to shift uncomfortably in his clothes.

"What? School? It's okay. Do what you can. Next term you start fresh."

"Yeah, maybe," he said.

"What do you say we go fishing tomorrow?"

"I don't know. I gotta get back."

There was a long pause as he fiddled with his keys. "Fuck it. Yeah. Let's go," he brightened as he spoke. Dave drove us out early to Old Field Point and parked in the driveway of his friend. It wasn't a great tide and some wind came up, but we had the beach to ourselves and threw big plugs, hoping for striped bass or bluefish. Sea ducks skittered low across the sound; fiddler crabs and starfish brightened the pebbly shallows. We reminisced about the old saltwater aquarium, the clams, crabs, starfish, and pet bergal. Lil would come down into the basement, peer into the tank, and ask questions. Maybe drop in a little turkey for everybody.

"But the crabs creeped her out," David said.

"They creep out a lot of people," I said, whipping another plug into the gray water behind the surf.

"They're morbid, like worms."

"Yeah, but Lil had her heaven," I reminded him, honoring her belief in Jesus and everlasting life. After our mother's death, Lil testified to a visit from Jesus Christ in our basement while she was doing laundry. Christ appeared next to the dryer and told Lil that her duty was to take care of her sister's children, that she would be guided and kept strong. Lil was quite serious about this revelation. We teased her a bit and then left it alone, willing to accept that this divine charge may be keeping our family afloat.

"Still," David said, poking a small rock crab with his rod tip. "I mean…"

"Yeah, I know."

"Crabs, man. That's it. Crabs."

⁓

"Hey, you're back?" Art yelled to me as I crossed the Bei Wai campus with my bags. "They were gonna sell all your stuff."

"I said I'd be back."

"A lotta foreign teachers ditch this place. It's good to see you." Art shook my hand. "I'm sorry about your mother."

"My Aunt. Yeah, thanks," I said. "She was like a mother to me."

I walked into my apartment and found it clean, and there was a bright new spinning rod on the folded bedspread. Someone believed in my return. When I answered the door an hour later, it was Jin Lei. "So sorry about your *a yi*," she hugged me. "That's so sad. We missing you."

The fishing rod was from Jin Lei. She didn't have a lot of money. And after the emergency trip home, I was pretty broke, too. So I gave her one of the fishing rods I'd brought from home. "This is for you," I said.

She looked puzzled.

"We think alike," I said, pulling spools of line and a bag of fishing gear from my suitcase.

"Yes, I like you," Jin Lei smiled.

"I mean, we both like fishing. Now we'll both have fishing rods."

But I soon realized there were other likes developing. And there were better gifts for this woman. I pulled one of Aunt Lil's pocket books from my carry-on, reached into the dark folds, and lifted a gold necklace. "This was Aunt Lil's favorite," I said to Jin Lei. "I want you to have it."

It was a cold winter in Beijing. Chen Lin took me out for dinner, ordering three kinds of fish, counseling that "one should eat the foods they love to overcome grief."

Light snow accented the gray campus, and I woke with black coal dust lining my mouth and nose. On the way to class I bought delicious sweet potatoes pulled from sidewalk ovens made from old oil drums. The classrooms were cold, students bundled up and laced their fingers around jars of hot tea, but we worked together on English and broke for wonderful lunches of steamed dumplings dipped in a gingery sauce. Back at the apartment, I spread millet over my balcony. Jin Lei came over, and we spent afternoons reading, writing, and looking up to see the growing flocks of sparrows and pigeons—the only birds I ever saw on campus—until they scattered one day under a broad sweeping shadow. *Ying!* Jin Lei exclaimed. The pale wings of a great hawk flared inches from the window. There was still some wild nature in this hungry old capital.

For the end of December, Jin Lei and I planned a little holiday. With the help of Captain Zhou, I secured two precious train tickets, and we traveled east to Beidaihe and Shanhaiguan, where the Great Wall meets the sea. I sat back in the chilly train car and opened the *China Daily*, reading about an old Communist Party boss who had been indicted in a sex scandal with a twenty-year-old singer. "Look at this dried out old geezer," I showed Jin Lei the photo and story. "Can you believe this?"

"All cats eat fish," she recited a Chinese proverb, cocked her head, and ran her finger down the page to another headline, *Virility Tigers Confiscated.*

There were no other foreigners in this wintry seaside town. Jin Lei wore her gold chain, and I buttoned up a black wool topcoat I had purchased for Aunt Lil's funeral. People stared at us and made remarks—"Look at that woman with her rich *laowai*." Jin Lei was upset.

"If they only knew how broke I am," I tried to joke, but quickly recognized that any comparison in material wealth seemed ridiculous and patronizing.

At a little deserted hotel, the clerk refused to give us a shared room because we were not married. I pushed more money across the counter and the Party morals relaxed. We put our bags in our room, and Jin Lei stood by the foggy window and started to cry.

"It's okay," I held her. "Do you want to go back?"

"No," she said.

The day was cold and clear. We walked past dark government villas where cadres and their families spent summer vacations. German shepherds barked from behind high fences. We walked along the frozen beach and then found a steamy restaurant and a friendly waitress. My Chinese was good enough to order tea and fried peanuts and chat about the weather. Jin Lei smiled.

Back to the same place for dinner, the seafood was spectacular, including big white slabs of skate sautéed in leeks and ginger. After two days, the staff treated us like family, bringing platters of duck feet, small steamed clams, fried squid, and a cod and seaweed soup that I tipped and slurped like a fat mandarin. The cook poured me a glass of special *baijiu* infused with lizards. "Good for man," he said.

On New Year's Eve 1994, Jin Lei and I drank, feasted, and talked our hearts full. "They sure laugh a lot," the waitress told the cook, opening the door to a frigid night of stars. We walked home, gazing over gnarled pine trees and ice-glazed rocks into the sea, our mood turning mournful as I thought of Aunt Lil, and Jin Lei remembered a friend who died last spring. We sang Chinese and English versions of "Auld Lang Syne"—"Should old acquaintance be forgot and never thought upon"—while those lonely guard dogs howled. Up in our room, Jin Lei lit candles planted in wobbly seashells. I put music through a speakered Walkman, and our bed drifted out to sea.

In April, Jin Lei moved into my apartment, her thick black hair tied back, her light brown skin glowing as we finished the second trip with her bags up to the sixth floor landing. Doors cracked open, and some people said *Ni hao*. Jin Lei was friendly and polite, but these same neighbors began to gossip, and one trusted Chinese professor on the first floor told us that people thought Jin Lei was using me for a room and money. On the other side, it was leaked to Miss Li that an older couple on the third floor thought I was prostituting this poor Chinese girl and that I should be arrested. Nearly all the students and faculty lived inside the campus walls, and there was always gossip—"like a fish bowl," I tried to raise a smile—but this kind of talk was starting to hurt. Then the university dean called me into his office.

"You cannot live with Chinese woman unless you are married." The dean, a solidly built middle-aged man with jet black hair, was said to have been a Red Guard during the Cultural Revolution.

"We are consenting adults and . . ."

"It's political," he interrupted me. "You are a visiting American teacher."

I consulted seasoned colleagues and confirmed that there was a policy against unmarried cohabitation, but it had not been enforced in years. The tension nearly broke Jin Lei and me, but after a few nights cooking and eating together, talking over tea, and sharing a warm bed, we knew it was worth the risk. After a Friday night of listening to the *Butterfly Serenade* and drinking a bottle of Guihua, an osmanthus brandy that mellowed our heads and lacquered our stomachs, we decided to get up early and go fishing.

Fishing heals, I thought of Hemingway and Maclean. And though we were a long way from the wilds of Michigan and Montana, Beijing had fishing parks planted with willows and stocked with carp. We packed our gear and jumped on an early bus to the Happy Fish Compound, a dull plat of ponds opposite the east wall of the Summer Palace. They had not yet opened, but a twenty yuan note, about two dollars, convinced the guard to let us walk around. The pools dimpled with rising fish, and I tossed a piece of lint from my pocket that drew a curious nose. At the far end of the compound, an unused pond had sprouted into a marsh where a purple heron waded and stabbed. *Still some wildness in this old city*, I thought.

At 8:00 the guard yelled across the compound, we checked in, paid our ten-yuan fee, and began fishing. The common carp will eat almost anything—small fish, tadpoles, insects, vegetation, bread, and, conveniently for us, processed fish pellets. The guard, Mr. Qin, a thin man in a worn Mao suit and conical paddy hat—a bit Vietcong-like in my movie-haunted imagination—grew more loquacious and helpful, showing me how to secure a fish pellet onto my hook with a tiny rubber band you might use in orthodontia. He adjusted my quill bobber and directed my cast. Jin Lei translated. I tossed a few feet from the bank and watched. There were swirls all around but no takes. Mr. Qin talked on and on. He puzzled over my reel, and I showed him how the bail opened and closed. I was tempted to mention that the Chinese probably invented the first fishing reels in the fourth century, certainly the oldest writing about fishing reels comes from the Middle Kingdom.

Mr. Qin went on to adjust my bobber and gesture another cast to a slightly different spot. Nothing. "They don't like your stink," Jin Lei translated.

"What?"

"He say carp don't like your stink."

"You mean 'smell,'" I corrected and then laughed. "Come on. They're carp."

Mr. Qin went to his shed. The clerk yelled at him. Other customers were showing up, but Qin shouted back something with the word "*laowai*," perhaps explaining, *I'm busy helping this inept foreigner catch a carp*. He returned with a jar of star anise and directed me to rinse my hands in the pond, rub in some anise, and rebait. Finger tapping his nose, he reiterated that carp have a good sense of smell and don't like human odors.

"It must be hard on them," I muttered, imagining the world's suffering carp, living in our foulest waters, noses and barbells wrinkling in perpetual disdain for free-pouring humanity. The bobber went down, and I set the hook on a deep-bodied brassy carp. "Fantastic," I cried. "You were right." Even in this phony pond, I enjoyed the brief fight and landing. Qin put the fish, *li yu*, a common carp, in a wire mesh creel basket and set it back in the water. We could keep as many as we wanted. "Pay by the pound," Qin pointed to the sign.

I set up Jin Lei's rod, rubbed more anise on my hands, and she caught a *cao yu*, a grass carp like the one Captain Zhou gave me. The two-pound fish made some good runs before surrendering to the bank. More slender and round-headed, the grass carp is highly valued in Asia and Europe for its flesh and fight. Why were carp so disliked in the US? In his piscatorial paean "Golden Carp," American poet Antonio Vallone asks: "When did I learn to call them trash? When did I unlearn it?" Carp are typically maligned in the US as an invasive species with dull looks, too many bones, and mud-flavored flesh, but I had enjoyed catching them in Indiana and South Dakota and came to love them in their home waters of East Asia.

Jin Lei and I kept two carp for our dinner and went on hooking and releasing several others. When Qin came back to check on us, I asked about the carp's lifespan. He said those inmates at Happy Fish Compound might only live two years. They thrive much longer in the wild. "All the catching tires them," Jin Lei translated. It's good to remember that even catch-and-release stresses fish, particularly in oxygen-limited confines. "So they are not so happy," I tried to joke with Mr. Qin, who just squinted and scratched his head under the conical straw hat. I pinched the barb down on our hooks and was even more careful to wet my hands and unhook each fish while it was still in the water, not wishing to rub its nose in humanity any more than necessary. The heron squawked and flew over the wall, and I thought the carp a bit more like us, the crowded millions of Beijing, waking in our little concrete rooms, breathing the pollution, working in our walled compounds, elbowing each other at the market, eating, crapping, sleeping, breeding—for what? Maybe for another hour of life, maybe a day, week, month, or even a few lucky years under the hazy sun.

My comparison ended, however, when we pulled the creel basket, brained the gasping dinner carp, put a string through their gills, paid the clerk, thanked Mr. Qin, and stepped on a crowded homebound bus. Pressed against the backseat, people stared at us and our fishing poles, so I pulled the bloody carp from the plastic bag. An old couple smiled and nodded, some boys laughed, and a teenage girl slipped on her headphones and stared out the window.

Angling is as old as China, and it has a deep connection with the sage's escape from worldly stress. In the fifth century B.C., a frustrated

Confucius is advised by an old fisherman to always be "sincere" and not let "frets over human concerns" distract him from the Great Way. In "Yu Fu," "The Fisherman," collected in the second-century's *Songs of the South*, the banished scholar Qu Yuan learns from a fisherman that it is best to gracefully retire from public employment when the system is corrupt and troubled. Subsequent centuries are filled with poems, songs, and parables alluding to angling's virtues and lessons. The Tang dynasty poet and provincial governor Bai Juyi declares:

> But when I cast my hook in the stream,
> I have no thoughts of fish or men.
> Lacking the skill to catch either,
> I can only savor the autumn water's light

In Beijing more than eight centuries ago, Jin dynasty emperor Zhangzong, and his eccentric court official, Wang Yu, sequestered themselves as humble fishermen at a place called Diaoyutai, the Royal Fishing Terrace. Successive dynasties used these spring-fed ponds, but over the centuries the park fell in and out of regard. In the early twentieth century, the grounds and waters went wild—starving people speared fish and frogs and were caught and stabbed in turn by guards who were, themselves, constantly under the sword of unpredictable rule. Finally in 1958, celebrating the tenth anniversary of the Peoples Republic, Diaoyutai was restored and served as a Communist Party office and retreat for Chairman Mao and his associates, eventually opening up as a state guest house, hosting the likes of Richard Nixon, Queen Elizabeth II, Ronald Reagan, Tony Blair, Boris Yeltsin, Christine Lagarde, and Hillary Clinton. Elaborate pavilioned docks extend over willow-banked ponds, where one might take shelter from the sun and rain or some tense political discussion while enjoying a drink or a long cast into the clear water.

The guest rooms at Diaoyutai are open to the public, but the nightly rates exceeded my monthly salary in 1995. With the mention of a few famous Chinese professor friends at the university and a carton of Marlboro cigarettes, I secured a couple hours inside, and Jin Lei and I strolled down the poplar-shaded lanes and around the lovely ponds amid groves of apricot, lilac, and pear. Jin Lei was always graceful when she walked, sometimes blossoming into impromptu dance and song, and as she sang today a large carp leaped, as they often do, not to feed but perhaps to enjoy the lyrics of living. After witnessing and wondering over disporting fish on the Hao River, the ancient Taoist sage Zhuangzi described the "joy of fishes," while his skeptical companion asked, "How could you know the joy of the fishes? You're not a fish." Zhuangzi replied, "Since you are not me, how could you know that I do not know what makes fish happy?" This goes on for a bit, but Zhuangzi concluded that by standing beside the river he knows the joy of fish through the shared pleasures of vitality and water. A big epistemological leap but one that lands in the right spot. Indeed these waters and fish looked healthy and happy, and seeking further connection, I quickly strung up my fly rod.

Fly fishing has always been more difficult for me, but I recalled those Happy Fish Compound carp rising to the lint from my pocket, and here mosquitoes disappeared in splashes at the pond's edge. I glanced nervously at a couple blue-uniformed guards across the way and tied on the gray-hackled, black-striped mosquito pattern. Thoughts returned of my first hot night on campus in Beijing when my dirty room had no screens and mosquitoes sucked my tired blood, leaving my face hot and swollen. Things had gotten so much better.

My first cast fell short in a half loop, and I saw the submarine wake of a spooked fish. I re-aerialized the line, felt the even weight back and forward, and laid out a long, straight cast. The fly lay perfectly still on the surface—then a carp gulped it down. I stripped and arced a hook set. A thunderous splash echoed across the park.

This resort-rested carp exploded in a powerful run—nothing like what we experienced at the commercial fish ponds—and an imperial fight commenced. The carp ran right and then way left, clearly a Communist, around a rocky island and under a bridge. I held tight and tried to steer the fish into open water. Another carp leaped, and Jin Lei sang, "The carp jumps over the Dragon Gate," a popular verse about strong and determined golden carp that make it up the Yellow River's Longmen Falls and are transformed into noble dragons. The story celebrates ascent in educational, social, or professional status, perhaps even our own rising fortunes as a Sino-American couple in Beijing, certainly our brief splash atop classy Diaoyutai while the curious guards stepped closer to watch.

Jin Lei loved to raise stories from the depths of Chinese history, among them the legend of Jiang Taigong, a philosopher-angler from China's tumultuous Bronze Age, around 1000 B.C. Jiang, a minor court official disgusted with the brutal and corrupt Shang dynasty, found solace in angling, though he explained that he "would never deign to catch a fish with a crooked hook or deceiving bait." His living parable of patience and virtue caught the attention of the right people. In the end, Jiang mentored a virtuous prince on how to defeat the Shang and create a new and just government. It is said that shortly before his death at the age of eighty-five, Jiang caught an enormous golden carp using neither hook nor bait.

Jin Lei and I also aspired to a humble, honest life of study, teaching, and fishing. If we were keen on catching dinner, we'd spend a couple hours at a fish park close to campus, but we were most comfortable along public waters like the Nanchang River that flowed right behind the university into the frog-filled Purple

Bamboo Park and below the National Library. Unlike the enlightened Jiang Taigong, however, we dangled baited hooks.

Pedaling our bikes two miles to the National Library and trekking around the grounds and through the marble lobby with our fishing rods, we enacted our own dramatic search for meaning. Somewhere in here were the surviving volumes of the massive *Yongle Encyclopedia* of 1408 with its references to Jiang Taigong and the great fish of China. "May I please see any *Yongle Encyclopedia* volumes that discuss fish?" I asked the reference librarian in practiced Chinese, presenting her my credentials and letters of reference. "No," she replied.

Many Westerners live and work in China, learning the language and forging deep relationships with the people and culture. But for many of us *laowai* there remained that sense of being outside the walls, outside the deep knowledge and understanding that makes someone feel at home in a distant place. To ease my homesickness, a friend sent a box of books that included the Chicano classic, *Bless Me, Ultima*. I was moved by the story of the boy, Antonio, living in New Mexico and struggling with his identity and religion. Antonio goes fishing and discovers the golden carp, a local legend and god of nature that, for a time, outshines the Catholic traditions of his Mexican family. In all my travels and years living in East Asia, fish and fishing have brought me closest to that inner sense of belonging and receiving something rare and true.

One July morning a couple weeks after my bid for the encyclopedia, Jin Lei and I cycled back to the Nanchang River, started to unpack our gear, and heard a loud splash. Deep rings spread out from the middle of the river. "Dragon?" Jin Lei arched her eyebrows, and we talked again of those unflagging and triumphant golden carp of the Yellow River graduating into dragons. Then we gazed at the river before us. The Nanchang had been diverted, diked, dammed, and overfished for centuries, with runs providing sewerage for huge apartment complexes and the zoo. This old river rivaled the black ooze flowing from the pit of Tartarus, so any swimming survivors definitely deserved dragon status.

We had little expectation of catching a fish and no intention of eating our catch, but the stretch near the library was banked in stone and shaded in willow, pintail ducks paddled by, and there were charming old men who drowsily angled away the hours, bells tied to their rod tips, occasionally bringing in an anemic carp or a scrawny catfish.

I rubbed my hands with anise, baited up our hooks with juicy worms, and we sailed our bobbers onto the river. Hours passed and we were chatting about life. Jin Lei and I had been living together for months without any official challenge from the university, and the gossip seemed to be fading. I enjoyed teaching my classes, but I also wanted to go back to graduate school, finish a doctorate, and get a tenure-track job. Jin Lei's studies were going well, but she, too, dreamed of graduate school and a better job, possibly in the States.

"Let's go for it," Jin Lei said over and over.

"Let me look into it," I nodded. "It won't be easy."

We drifted to lighter subjects, like the price of tea in China (about twenty yuan for a pound of oolong) when Jin Lei's bobber vanished.

"Where is it?" she asked.

"Down," I cried. "Pull it!"

And when she did, her rod received and transmitted some serious news. The dark pages of the *Yongle Encyclopedia* needn't open, for a big-mouthed *li yu* rolled and splashed a living entry before us. The old men leaned off their chairs, people blinked up from their reading, and a small tai chi group froze facing us as Jin Lei screamed, cranking madly and futilely against the drag until I calmed her down.

We had no landing net, so I coached her to tire out the fish and bring it along the bank. "Take it easy," I said. "You're doing great." Quite a crowd had gathered by the time I reached in and grabbed the carp, easily five pounds, and set it flipping on the grass, the bewormed hook neatly pinned in the corner of its mouth. Some people took pictures, asked questions. The colors of the carp were exceptionally bright, golden even, and one man reckoned it escaped from the zoo. Jin Lei beamed and gave a press conference. I remembered the golden carp of *Bless Me, Ultima* and how young Antonio learns that he must never harm that sacred fish. I lifted Jin Lei's carp toward the river for release and was blocked by a throng of angry shouts. "*Bu, bu.* No, no. What are you doing? That's delicious." Jin Lei tried to explain catch-and-release, but two of the other fishermen were clearly upset. The fish had been caught in the people's river, and the people should eat it. The call was clear, even if the water wasn't. I held the fish out to the oldest man there, a venerable angler I had seen several times. With a quick, slight bow and a grunt, he took the golden carp. The crowd satisfied, the bereaved old river flowed darkly on through her city.

Law Abiding

For Spring Festival, China's biggest holiday, Jin Lei invited me home to visit her family in the city of Kunming, Yunnan Province. We were joined by two friends, Nancy, a sixty-four-year-old retired British nurse, and Robyn, a twenty-two-year-old fundamentalist Christian from Australia who was studying Chinese at Bei Wai. They were both good company as long as we stayed away from the subject of evolution. Nancy and I felt evolution was the most obvious and wonderful process in the world; Robyn believed it was a lie confected to undermine the Bible. Robyn asked me to read a book that discredited the fossil record, a record I cherished as my own family album. I try to be open about ideas contrary to my own, but the first pages proved so ridiculous—"all life on earth was created 6,000 years ago"—that I handed it back to her, imagining Peking Man standing in the very field we passed, laughing his hairy ass off half a million years ago.

"You know there's actually something called scientific method," I said. "Laws that govern how we figure stuff out."

"What about God's law?"

"Okay, Robyn. I'll leave your faith alone if you leave mine alone." She frowned and slipped the book into her bag.

It was late January, and the coal heater in our second-class train car was broken. We bundled up in our seats for the twenty-five hour ride to Kunming. The land south of Beijing was flat with a few bare trees bordering dormant fields, bleak factories, and brick *hutongs* turning orange in the fading light. We slurped noodles and talked ourselves tired, crawling into the cold bunks above. I listened to the deep, soothing voice of Pearl Jam's Eddie Vedder on my cassette Walkman and slept well but woke shivering as flute music piped passengers awake at 6:30 a.m.—a standard practice on Chinese trains. The steward brought hot water for tea, and first light revealed mountains, leafy trees, and the lush groves of our descending latitudes. At a stop somewhere in Henan around noon, I ran out to buy beer, a bag of nuts, and—I couldn't resist—a grilled fish that I shared with Robyn. We dozed and woke with the breath of cats.

The train crossed the Huanghe, the Yellow River, and I thought of the golden carp, the cradle of Chinese civilization, and Aunt Lil, wondering if this was the Orient of her imagination. Men and women in coolie hats unloaded sagging barges onto donkey carts and blue trucks. Every city seemed to be pouring cement and laying steel. Shining glass office buildings emerged behind bamboo scaffolding. There were sports cars and glamorous women on cell phones. China in transition. Even the Yellow River, with its turbulent history of flooding, had been tamed with dams and high dikes. China's Sorrow, they called this river, and many people had been washed away over the years. This afternoon things were placid, and a man fished with a long pole on a muddy tributary. I pushed my face against the dirty glass and thought he might be into something very unlike sorrow, but we sped by before I could know.

We were greeted at the train station by Mr. Lu, a handsome man in his late twenties who managed the travel agency employing Jin Lei. He hugged Jin Lei and shook our hands, driving us to a welcome party at a friend's apartment. There were the usual toasts and platters of marvelous food, people offering me cigarettes, and asking questions in Chinese and English. Robyn's Chinese was excellent, and she helped interpret for Nancy and me—but I was exhausted and soon dropped into bed.

I woke early before the others, as I usually do, stepped onto the cool concrete floor, and found my way to the concrete shower. After a few seconds of warmth, a column of freezing water shocked my body, sending me into a frantic scrub that lasted less than a minute. Clenching and tensing sharply under the icy downpour, I pulled a muscle in my neck that would plague me for days. My giggling host would later tell me that the bathwater was solar heated and early morning showers were not recommended.

Jin Lei had stayed with her parents, and she returned the next morning with Mr. Lu, both looking happy and bright. We spent the day relaxing along seagull-swept Green Lake and then arrived at the shabby, state-subsidized apartment of Jin Lei's parents. Chubby, wearing cardigans, and smiling, her kind folks offered tea and spoke to us like family. I asked questions. Mr. Jin, whom I called Jin Laoshi, Professor Jin, was an artist, painter, and set designer for the Kunming stage. He adjusted his heavy square glasses and asked if we were hungry. Ms. Lei, Lei Laoshi, as Chinese women often keep their surnames, was an opera singer who now directed small performances that toured rural areas as part of China's state culture program. During another program called the Cultural Revolution in the late 1960s, this creative couple was sent into the countryside to make school chairs and, it turns out, their first daughter, Jin Lei. Although a potential artistic and intellectual threat to the nation, the couple was restored after the death of Chairman Mao in 1976 to the city and the work they loved. They had another daughter, Jin Wei, who aspired to be on television.

Jin Lei's parents lived a simple life in this concrete flat—the chief luxuries being a television set and a loveseat draped in a dog pelt, where they read, watched their favorite TV shows, or gazed at lacy goldfish in a mossy aquarium. But they had gone to great expense preparing a Spring Festival feast. Hearing I loved seafood and fish, a bundle of crab legs came many miles from the South China Sea to this boiling pot high in Kunming and a scaled and scored carp was ready for the hot oil. They also served Yunnan delicacies of fried goat cheese and thick, peppery bacon. Lei Laoshi bought a bottle of champagne. "They never had it before. Would you open it?" Jin Lei asked me. I proudly took the bottle in my hands and made a big deal over the label while the family, Mr. Lu, Nancy, and Robyn looked at me in anticipation. The wire cage over the cap had a strange twist, and as I tilted the bottle toward me for a better look the cork blasted off and struck my forehead. I staggered a moment and apprehended the amazement of the audience. Someone grabbed the spuming bottle, and I collapsed into my chair, dazed and bleeding. Nancy examined my head and eyes, Lei Laoshi got me a Band-Aid, and Jin Laoshi poured me a glass of his special ginseng *baijiu*, explaining that it would calm me. "He's calm," Nancy said. "He's very calm."

I soon recovered, though I long contemplated the ironic possibility of surviving so many dangerous drinking exploits only to be killed by a cork. Robyn said grace, and the dinner danced along on ample glasses of beer and *baijiu*, toasts, and lively conversation in English and Chinese. Lei Laoshi sung an aria, Jin Lei recited a poem, Jin Laoshi showed us his new paintings, and Mr. Lu told a joke that everyone got but me. After dinner, the men shared a smoke from a long bamboo pipe, sort of a cross between a bong and a hookah. Mr. Lu passed it to me with a wink, and I found the cool, native grown tobacco smooth and stimulating.

"*Yu*," fish, Jin Laoshi said to me, pulling out a tea-stained book of seventeenth-century paintings by Bada Shanren. "*Yu*," I replied with attention. He pushed back his thick glasses and opened to plates featuring ink brush paintings of tear-shaped fish with deeply expressive upturned eyes. Without looking silly or overly cartoonish, Bada Shanren's fish seem to express the anxiety of disruption and danger—as if the river were dropping and heating up or a great flock of cormorants had just alighted. A young scion of the established Ming dynasty, Bada Shanren's world was turned upside down with the Manchu conquest and takeover of the Ming in the mid-seventeenth century. How would it feel to have your traditions, values, and laws suddenly challenged by "barbarian" outsiders? I studied the compelling images while goldfish lazily mouthed algae off the aquarium glass. Jin Lei and her mother washed dishes. Mr. Lu picked his teeth, and Jin Laoshi sunk into the dog fur and nodded off.

We spent several days touring Kunming, including Lake Dian, more than two hundred miles of rippling water hung with fishing nets pulled by thin men on wooden junks reefing bamboo-battened sails. We walked through colorful markets, ate spicy noodles, and sipped tea. Jin Lei bought mentholated plasters for my stiff neck, and I purchased a couple dried lizards designed for *baijiu* infusions. "Good for man strength," the apothecary said and grinned, while a tomcat on the shelf behind him licked its furry balls. It was cool and sunny in Kunming, and we lingered around monuments, smelled flowers and fresh fruit, and chatted with a family whose tin and plastic shack abutted a twelve-hundred-year-old pagoda. The grandfather had driven a few spikes into the Tang dynasty stone to string wire from the pagoda to his pantry for hanging and curing bacon—the dusty, sacred past tied to the profane and delicious present.

I watched Mr. Lu and Jin Lei talk together—sometimes in laughter and smiles, other times in obvious tension. I could catch words and phrases but could not understand what they were discussing. I asked Robyn, and her face squinched. "You should talk to Jin Lei. She's going through a rough time."

"What is it?" I asked.

"You're both my friends. I don't want to be a spy."

"You can help me a little, can't you?"

"Well, Jin Lei's courses are over next term. Lu wants her to come back to the travel agency. She doesn't want to."

"Okay. I figured that."

"Lu's in the Party. And I guess the travel agency is run by the State. I'm not sure. There's something about Jin Lei getting money to study, and now she must go back to work. I guess it's the law. Then there's family stuff. You better talk to her."

One night Jin Lei and her girlfriends wanted to go dancing. With the right amount of alcohol, I loved club dancing, and we had a couple hours of fun at a hotel disco. Just as things were winding down, Mr. Lu showed up in a polyester suit. I could see Jin Lei's smile change. I wanted Jin Lei to come home with me. We'd hadn't been alone together since the trip began.

"I can't," she said.

"Why not?" I asked. We had agreed to keep our relationship discreet in Yunnan, but I was feeling strange about her connection to Lu.

I went outside, where one of Jin Lei's friends was smoking, and asked her for a cigarette. She spoke a little English, and with my limited Chinese we could talk.

"Mr. Lu is a strange boss," I said.

"He is a good man," she said. "Very confused."

"About what?"

"He is Jin Lei's husband, but maybe changing," she said. A sickening wave washed through my chest, and I started walking, though I wasn't sure where. I heard Jin Lei's voice calling my name. She ran to catch me. I stopped.

"I'm sorry," she said.

"Forget it. I'm going home." I rubbed my sore neck, turned, and walked on.

"No. Henry. Listen."

I turned again to face Jin Lei. "So, Lu is your husband?"

"Yes, but not like you think. For apartment. It's hard for young peoples to get place to live. You sometimes must do this. We grew up together. He is like brother. He took care of me. You don't know."

"I know you're married."

"I don't love him the way I love you. I want to be with you at Bei Wai, and read books, and study English."

It took a couple days for me to understand and accept what was going on. But the sting of betrayal faded, and I believed Jin Lei when she said she wanted a new life with me.

As planned, Nancy, Robyn, and I flew back to Beijing. Jin Lei would return later by train. After we got in the air, Nancy dozed off, and Robyn and I sipped beer, talked about Yunnan, and played a game of gin, the creationist and the evolutionist leaving victory to chance and attention. Robyn never had more than one beer; I drained three and took a sip of *baijiu* from a bottle in my carry-on. White clouds reflected sun through the little curved window, and Robyn began to win in proportion to my rising elevation. When turbulence suddenly shook the plane, I touched her arm and assured her, "It's okay." Then I won a hand with a run of hearts.

"You devil," she said.

"Robyn, maybe God and the Devil, like you and me, have coevolved to get along."

She smiled and shook her head. "God likes you, Henry. You should figure out why."

Nancy woke, and we all talked about the journey, sharing some of our photos. I studied a picture of Lake Dian. "You know, I didn't do any fishing on this trip," I said with regret.

Nancy looked over her glasses and smiled. "Oh, I think you did plenty, sir. I hope you can handle what you've caught. Don't you dare mislead that girl. Her world's been turned upside down."

"I know," I said. "I'll help her."

"Well, you remember it's easy for you to go home and forget all this. But this is her home, and she needs her friends and family. I'm sure they're questioning her right now."

Robyn gave me a sympathetic look and set down her cards.

"I know," I nodded respectfully. Older, wiser, and genuinely concerned, Nancy could speak to me like this. She was right. I now had a great responsibility to Jin Lei.

Beijing was cold. Ice thawed off the lakes and canals, but the water was still too chilly to angle. I taught my classes and thought about Jin Lei. I wrote long letters to Eugene and tried to work out my feelings. Did I love Jin Lei? Yes. Did I want to be married to her? To anyone? I wasn't sure.

I didn't trust the institution of marriage. Like the sanctioning of churches and state, the marriage bond itself seemed to entail as much unnatural dogma and expectation and bring as much suffocation and misery as it ensured trust and the promise of lifelong joy. I saw few benefits and many risks. I knew tortured couples and happy couples and every sort in between. But my contract in China ended in July. What then? Jin Lei's dreams were limited by

Mr. Lu, the travel agency, Chinese law, and the Party. Would she get a divorce and free herself of those restraints? Then what? She might end up *persona non grata* in Kunming. Maybe like the heron in the fish compound we could fly over the wall. In the States, I thought, she could start fresh and pursue a new life. We could go back to school together, develop careers. But we'd need to get married. It would be an act of friendship, I finally reasoned.

"That's a green-card marriage," old Art told me as we sipped beers in the faculty dining room. "I think it's fine," he said. "But it's against the law. If they find it's a sham, you could go to jail."

"It's no sham, Art. I'm not getting paid. I love Jin Lei and feel she has a right to this chance. Governments be damned."

"Okay. Go for it," he looked away, wary of my cause.

After a few humiliating state counseling sessions, Jin Lei got a divorce. She returned to Beijing, and we completed interviews, medical examinations, and extensive paperwork toward a Chinese marriage license, which we received from the Ministry of Civil Affairs in a plush red case bearing the golden phoenix and dragon. The next step required me to interview with an official at the American Embassy. The embassy was located in a posh neighborhood along with other diplomatic missions and foreign-owned mansions shadowed behind high iron gates among armed guards and flagpoles. One wonders what peasants pedaling by with rice and bloody pig snouts thought about the world outside. After checking my papers and passport, the Marine on duty smiled and said, "Hey. We're having a party here on Friday. You should come."

"Sounds great," I said.

"You're at the university, right? Bring some chicks."

"Okay," I answered and laughed.

"But no Chinese."

"Really?"

"Chinese nationals can't come in. Don't get me wrong, I'd love to fuck a couple, but it's a security risk."

"Right," I said.

My name was called. I nodded to the Marine, crossed the lobby, and entered the emigration office. The American official looked over my papers, asked basic questions about how long Jin Lei and I had been together, if we had any children, and the nature of our plans. "To study together in the States," I said.

"So she'll be applying for a visa and green card?"

"Yes," I said.

There was a pause. Then he asked, "She has mole on her face. Where?"

"Uhh." It took me a second to register the question, and I had to visualize Jin Lei's face. I pointed to a spot on my own chin, but the mirroring transfer put me on the wrong side. "Oh," I corrected myself and moved my hand to the right. "On the right side of her mouth. It's very cute," I smiled. The man squinted and studied me. I smiled some more. A few tense seconds ticked away, then he stamped and signed the form.

I left China in July of 1996, arriving home to find my father watching the Mets and my brother, David, oiling a pair of Penn reels over newspapers on the kitchen table. I had been living in Asia for five years, had $375 in my bank account, no job, no car, two suitcases, and some worn-out fishing gear. "Well," my father said and smiled. "Start splitting wood and cutting the grass, and we might feed you." My brother hugged me with his greasy hands.

David had struggled through his freshmen year of college in Massachusetts after Aunt Lil died, but he transferred to Long

Island's Dowling College, lived at home with our father, and had a decent sophomore year. "I'm starting to like school," he said. "Especially the history classes." Dowling also led David to the nearby Connetquot River State Park, sheltering a beautiful six-mile spring-fed trout run flowing into the Great South Bay. David described the park's history as the South Side Sportsmen's Club, founded in the 1860s, with members including Teddy Roosevelt, J. P. Morgan, and the Vanderbilts. In addition to native brook trout, the club introduced rainbows and browns and constructed a fish hatchery. David took me to the Connetquot, and at first I was put off by the sign-in and payment process, the strict rules and restrictions: fly fishing only, barbless hooks, no alcohol, stay on your beat.

"You're at number fifteen. Stay on your beat," the man in the booth repeated.

"What if there's no one at the next beat?" I asked.

"You can't leave your beat. Those are the rules." He handed me a receipt and yelled, "Next."

Fishing should free us, but I understand that in heavily populated areas like Long Island somebody had to manage rivers, or they'd soon be trampled and empty. This model has worked well in Great Britain, and I imagined myself walking to a famous beat on the River Test, though at an affordable stateside rate of only fifteen dollars. We fish-walked a half mile down the wooded road, saw deer and wild turkeys, heard a rattling kingfisher and the music of moving water, and I felt even better. I told David about China's bleaker waters—the fishing parks and dirty canals—and it helped us both appreciate this clean refuge in suburban New York.

The river ran clear under bushes and through swaying mats of starwort. I could see trout nosing the current. A couple mayflies dipped and danced, and I tied on a small *Ephemera* pattern that I smeared with floatant squeezed from a small vial. I made an easy cast up and across the river and watched the fly drift down. A trout rocketed up and struck. It was a feisty ten-inch brook trout, and I marveled over its bright red spots haloed in pale blue. I caught a few more, let them go, and wandered off my beat to check on David.

My brother, an intractable lure and bait angler, tied on the meatiest imposter in his foam-filled box, a black spider. The spider threw a frightening shadow over the brown stones, but the fish loved it. I watched a big rainbow open his pink mouth and gulp the spongy spider. David played the fish with a smile and brought it to the net, its speckled olive back and silvery sides burning magenta. The park allowed anglers to retain two fish. "Keep that one," I said.

"Dad's gonna love this," David said, beaming.

I explored upriver past the hatchery, found an unattended beat, and made a cast beside a promising patch of wild celery. A small rainbow took the fly, and I slowly brought it in, admiring its silver flashes. David walked up behind me and shouted, "Holy shit." I turned to look at him and then felt a tremendous pull on my line. A monster brown trout swallowed my struggling little rainbow and powered downstream. What a run! The rod bowed and the reel pawl buzzed as I palmed the handle and reel's rim. David ran down the bank, whooping and pointing as the huge trout turned, flashing a golden, dark spotted flank that thrilled my heart.

"Hey, what's your beat number?" I heard a man's voice behind me, looked over, and saw the khaki-shirted official from the check-in both.

"Down there," I said. "But this brown ran me outta town."

My brother laughed. "Check out this fish."

"You're back at fifteen," he said. "Break it off."

"No way," I cried.

"You can talk to the ranger then."

"What? Give us a fucking break," my brother looked at him in shock. "The ranger? You gotta be kidding me. We're just fishing!"

The official walked off, yelling back over his shoulder, "Well, you won't be fishing here ever again."

"Some fucking place," I shook my head.

"Sorry," David said. I knew he wanted this to be a great day for us. Then the great brown trout made a great run and broke my tippet. "Great," I dropped my head. Perhaps in the stress of the moment I squeezed my reel too tightly, or maybe the brown—which wasn't really hooked at all—sawed the fragile line with his teeth. In any case, it was free. And I was free to turn the hassle and loss into a tale of suburban adventure. I slapped my brother on the back. "Oh man, wait'ta we tell Dad." We told the story many times over the years, animating the feisty dialogue and perhaps adding a couple pounds to the cannibal brown. My brother, Eugene, and I warily returned to Connetquot River State Park the following summer. A young woman was working the booth, and when I gave

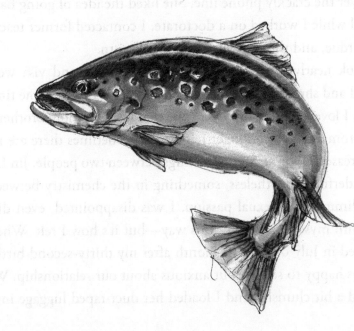

her my name, she smiled. "There's a note here about you," she said. But she let us in, and we angled as law abiding gentlemen with the exception of a nip of bourbon and puff of chowder.

I worked as a substitute teacher at my old high school and taught freshmen writing and literature classes at Dowling College and Hofstra University. I liked the university work. At Hofstra I became friends with Professors Dana Brand and John Bryant. "You should think about getting your Ph.D.," Brand told me after observing my class. He was a huge Mets fan, and I brought him a couple old *Daily News* "Go Mets" buttons my father had kept from the 1969 World Series. John Bryant and I had long talks about early American mariners, such as Amasa Delano, who went to China at the turn of the nineteenth century, and writers including Richard Henry Dana and the great Herman Melville. "You've got something in common with these guys," Bryant smiled. "I'll write you a recommendation." I brought him fluke fillets and a couple dozen oysters packed in ice. "Good *guanxi*," Jin Lei assured me when we talked over the crackly phone line. She liked the idea of going back to school while I worked on a doctorate. I contacted former teachers at Purdue, and they encouraged me to return.

It took nearly a year before Jin Lei's passport and visa were approved and she could immigrate to the States. This gave me time to think. I loved Jin Lei, but over time that love felt more brotherly and less romantic. It no longer felt erotic. Sometimes there are no obvious reasons for a change of feelings between two people. Jin Lei was wonderful. Nonetheless, something in the chemistry between us had dimmed my sexual passion. I was disappointed, even disgusted with myself for feeling this way—but it's how I felt. When she arrived in July of 1997, a month after my thirty-second birthday, I was happy to see her but anxious about our relationship. We embraced a bit clumsily, and I loaded her duct-taped luggage into my father's new pickup and drove her to our house in Port Jefferson. My father and brother hugged Jin Lei, Twain the cat jumped on her lap, and we sat and talked for hours. In bed at midnight, I kissed her cheek and said, "You must be tired."

"Not too tired," she whispered.

I kissed her forehead and rolled over on my back. "Goodnight, Jin Lei."

That Friday we threw a big welcome party. My brother and I picked a bushel of oysters, and my father splurged on two dozen lobsters. We took Jin Lei fishing for porgies—which were making a great comeback in Long Island Sound—and she loved it, reeling in fish after fish as the sun poured down on the calm water. I showed Jin Lei how to carefully handle the spiky porgy, holding it up to admire its pearly luster. She traced a finger over the scaled crosshatching. "Like a church window," she said. "Wow, yes," I smiled, seeing for the first time the porgy's skin and scales as stained glass. Later she helped me clean, butter, salt, and foil-wrap the fish for the grill. Jin Lei planned grand noodle dishes and several vegetable delights using local zucchini, tomato, and eggplant ignited with pickled peppers smuggled in from Yunnan. Eugene and his wife, Susan, delivered striped bass fillets from their trip off the Jersey coast. The kitchen filled with sizzling sounds, garlic aromas, and smoke from a Long Island duck we forgot in the oven.

As the band—three guys from down the street—warmed up with the Grateful Dead's "Brown Eyed Women," my brother wheeled in a keg of Coors and neighbors presented bottles of wine. With more and more guests gathered on the back patio, I unveiled a two-gallon jar of *baijiu* infused with the dried lizard I purchased in Kunming. The spotted creature had steeped for six months, turning the clear liquor a fossilly amber. I ladled up the first draft.

"Who wants to try? It's good for man power, if you know what I mean." People laughed, stared, and considered. But even among this group of intrepid drinkers, there were no volunteers. My father finally stepped forward. "At my age, I need some man power." He quaffed a jigger, tightened his mouth, and pronounced, "Not bad. A little brackish. But not bad." The lizard *baijiu* did, indeed, taste of the sea, perhaps redolent of our primal origins and storied past splashing around with dragons and leviathans. Jin Lei later explained that I should have rinsed the lizard of its preserving salts before bathing it in spirits. But by the end of the night half the jar was gone, the sea monster transubstantiated into early hour antics of howling, lewd dancing, and a tree climbing contest that ended with my brother falling into a mucky mulch pile of lobster shells and fish bones. He slept on a lawn chair, awakened by the highly aroused pawing and licking of a couple neighborhood cats.

The next morning my father went out to his flagpole, as he does every morning, but that day under the stars and stripes he raised the banner of the People's Republic of China, its red field flashing gold stars against the blue Atlantic sky. His old buddy from the Korean War, Tony, came by and turned furious—"That's the damn Red Chinese, Charley. What the hell you doing?" My father waved him away. "We're not at war with China. What's the matter with you?" They didn't talk much after that. "To hell with Tony," my father said. "I love Jin Lei."

Folks loved Jin Lei. She was outgoing, warm, bright, and funny, though some people disapproved of our arrangement. "Are they married or what?" a neighbor woman interrogated my father. "We got enough Orientals in this country," she hissed, and dad accidently backed over her petunias. And one of my brother's mentors, a retired teacher who owned a stamp shop in Stony Brook, went on about my deceiving the US government and disgracing the institution of marriage. My brother stood by me and told the man that this country could use a few more people like Jin Lei.

Jin Lei and I talked about being friends rather than lovers, and she thought we might just need more time to get to know each other again. "Maybe you are so afraid," she said to me. I just looked at her. She gently asked if I was afraid of losing the women in my life. She spoke of my mother's death when I was thirteen and the recent loss of Aunt Lil. "Maybe," I said.

We drove around Long Island, and Jin Lei asked about the fish glued to the backs of cars. "Jesus fish," I said and explained the revived symbol once used by early Christians to identify each other.

"Christians really like fish," she nodded.

I went on to talk about Jesus and the net-casting disciples, and the Greek word *ICHTHYS*, fish, that served as an acronym signifying "Jesus Christ, God's Son. Savior." Jin Lei listened then asked, "Do people think you strange to love fish and not God?"

"I love God, just not in the way most Christians do," I said. "God is fish. Fish is God."

Jin Lei shook her head in confusion. "I need some money for school. In China, we pray for money. Can you pray to your fish god for some money?"

I laughed and said we might have better luck harvesting some shellfish. So we picked and sold oysters to earn some extra cash, and Jin Lei quickly developed a knack for haggling with restaurant owners over the price. "Now I'm a real capitalist," she joked. It was wonderful watching her in America. Alone one afternoon when door-to-door missionaries showed up, Jin Lei accepted their free Bible, invited them into our living room for tea, and started telling them about Laozi, even offering to send them copies of the *Dao De Jing*.

"It's gonna take more than a prayer," my father said to us as he listened to the low compression cylinders of the '85 Buick Regal my uncle gave me. "Eight hundred miles to Indiana? I wouldn't risk it." But he had a friend with a low mileage 1986 Olds engine that would work in my Regal. We bought the Olds engine for two bushels of oysters. My father parked the tired Buick under the oak tree in the backyard, swung block and tackle over a thick limb, pulled out the clunker, and dropped in a smooth-running transplant that carried me for years.

In August of 1997, Jin Lei and I loaded the repowered car with boxes, suitcases, and some fishing gear, said goodbye, and drove west listening to Jin Lei's CD of the Nitty Gritty Dirt Band. She kept replaying "Fishing in the Dark," saying it was our song.

In West Lafayette, Indiana, we rented a second floor apartment at Williamsburg on the Wabash, a faux colonial complex beside the Wabash River and just a couple hundred feet from two flood ponds where had I fished many times as a master's student. It had been six years, and I'd seen a lot of strange and wonderful water around the world, but the Wabash basin held a special place in my muddy heart. Before we even unpacked, I pulled out a rod, walked through the sycamores and maples down the steep bank, and made a cast. After ten minutes a solid fish took my jig. Jin Lei stood behind me, "*Hen hao*," she cheered. "We have dinner."

"Well," I said, trying to ease her hopes. "There's a lot of pollution in this water."

"Worse than China?"

"Maybe not. No. But let's throw this one back." When I saw that the silvery gray fish was a drum, I howled, "Gaspergoooo," old times and old waters rising. I held up the fish for Jin Lei.

"I love this place," she said.

After long, hot days preparing for school, we'd have a light dinner of rice and vegetables and then cool off down by the river-linked ponds. Bordered by high banks and trees, the South Williamsburg Pond offered a wonderfully wild sanctuary for beavers, birds, turtles, and fish. There were constant splashes and rise forms. Longnose gar hovered a few inches below the surface, and the dark shadows of larger fish—bowfin, catfish, sturgeon, paddlefish—passed by as we cast or just watched. Jin Lei and I had been translating some Chinese fishing poems, and she recited the simple ninth-century verses of Bai Juyi, "Walking around the pond, I watch intently the fish as they swim." Jin Lei and I walked or sat together; sometimes I scribbled in a small notebook or wandered off, casting into the wooded cover or across the deep drop, just needing some time alone. One night I snagged, landed, and released a large paddlefish that reminded me of the one Ben Whitehorse caught from the Missouri almost twenty years before. Using three-inch floating Rapalas, I also hooked a few big gar, but their hard, toothy jaws always shed the lure or cut the line. A Mexican man in a cowboy hat told me to use yarn wrapped around the lure, claiming it would get stuck in the gar's teeth. "We do it down in Tamaulipas," he said. It was good advice, and one warm afternoon I landed a yard-long gar using, you might say, the fish's own teeth as hooks. I talked to the man from Tamaulipas now and then, and he once told me about catching fish from the backseat of a car.

"You were sitting in the backseat with your rod?" I asked, confused.

"No, no," he shook his head. "The car's in water. The fish like to hide there."

He pointed downriver to some sloughs and explained in vividly gestured English that he dropped his bait through the back window of a partially submerged car and caught some sunfish and a catfish "right off the backseat." In Mexico, he said, they always fished in and around sunken cars.

I retranslated this story to Jin Lei, who latched onto the automobile aspect, floating on the pond in an inner tube, kick-trolling a Ford Fender and a Dardevle spoon she dug out of my tackle box, miraculously picking up a three-pound channel catfish that she was determined to cook and eat. I called a biologist friend who explained the advisory.

"One or two meals a month of smaller catfish from the Wabash would be okay. Don't eat fish over ten pounds, and definitely fillet everything."

"Yeah," I said. "I'd give it a full oil change if I could."

Jin Lei and I did our best to carefully fillet the catfish, frying the pink blushed slabs of pale meat in virgin olive oil and freshly chopped garlic. "*Haochi*," Jin Lei said. "Delicious."

After a few days back in Indiana, I went to see my old friend, Sean McNerney. We had exchanged letters while I was in Asia, and I called him from New York. Sean had abandoned his degree program, but he worked his way up to head chef at C-Rays, a well-regarded restaurant in town. I stepped into the kitchen one night after closing, and Sean was sitting at the end of a steel counter, joking in Spanish with a couple Latino men in grimy aprons. He saw me and stood, heavier, wearier, his face shiny and red from the heat and labor of a hundred dinners. "*Salveo piscator*," hail angler, he greeted me in Latin and asked if I had seen the new translation of the *Odyssey*, lamenting that they still hadn't gotten the fishing scenes right.

Our friendship instantly renewed, we returned to our old angling spots below the Oakdale Dam on the Tippecanoe River, stopping at the bait shop to see bourbon-nosed Smitty and his cats, and caught our limit of silver bass and several large carp and suckers. I told Sean how in China we used anise to mask human odors, but these American carp seemed less discriminating. Asia had given me a new attitude about carp, and we kept a couple that Jin Lei prepared for a group of new friends, including two Chinese professors. "*Hao chi!*" the praise went up around the table as we plucked out cloves of pale, succulent flesh with our chopsticks. Everyone was asking how and where we caught the fish. There was a good Asian market in West Lafayette, but customers complained that their fish tasted muddy. "From fish farms, yes?" Professor Wang asked me, pushing back her long black hair.

"Probably," I said, explaining that the carp we were eating came from the clear, cool waters of the Tippecanoe River. The fish moved upstream to the dam, where there was an abundance of small shad and other forage. "And I clean the fish right away and pack them in ice. They're very fresh," I said.

"Yesterday?" Wang asked.

"Yes," I said, filling her glass with a little more white wine.

"So to get a fish like this you must catch it," she seemed to study my face.

"Yes," I said. "Or know a fisherman."

Jin Lei read the situation perfectly. The following week she collected orders and then sent Sean and me fishing. "We need six carp about this big," Jin Lei opened her hands to the length of her keyboard. "Or a little longer."

"Come with us, Jin Lei," Sean urged.

"I must study," she said without remorse.

Jin Lei liked to fish and play, but she loved to read and study. She took to the wide waters of an American university like a fish.

She made friends, connected with the Chinese community on campus, had her transcripts translated, and was enrolled in undergraduate classes that would qualify her for a master's program in comparative literature.

"What do you want to be?" I asked her one day.

"A professor like you," she said.

I smiled and nodded but knew her skills in English were a long way from a master's thesis or a doctoral dissertation. Just a few months ago, I spied her reading children's books pulled from the shelves of my father's house. She was sounding out difficult words, looking up vocabulary, and making notes. Now she stared at an online gloss of Twain's *Huckleberry Finn*, despairing over Jim's diction. "I'll help you when we get back," I said, kissing her cheek.

Sean and I scrubbed out his dirty cooler and filled it with ice from a local motel's ice machine. "Don't worry," Sean said. "Conchita—the housekeeper here—she's the sister of my line cook."

"Good *guanxi*," I commended Sean, explaining the term.

At the Oakdale Dam we set up our gear, and Sean pulled out bottle of ouzo.

"What the hell are you doing with that?" I asked.

"Anise, man. Let's rub some on our hands. Maybe we'll catch even more."

I laughed out loud and told him it was probably a waste of good booze. So we shifted East to West, and like old Greek fishermen, we took long pulls of ouzo, rolled up our sleeves, and got our lines in the water.

I started throwing a chrome Castmaster, thinking I'd pick up a silver bass, but I hooked a twenty-inch carp, took him down through the rock race and beached him on the gravel. I cut the gills, bled and gutted the fish, and tossed the entrails into the river. Then

Sean hooked one. "I can't believe they're taking lures," he beamed. I helped him land the fish, and when I pulled out my knife an old bearded man approached me with a bucket. "Gimme the guts, will ya?" he asked.

"Guts? Sure," I said. "For what?"

"Crayfish bait. You gonna have more? Heads, too. I'll leave the pail here." He put a rag over the pail and screwed it down into the gravel. The next carp Sean hooked was snagged in the back. Then I caught one in the mouth and then snagged a sucker. "Bite or get out of the way," we joked. There must have been a dense concentration of carp and suckers below the dam. In two hours we caught twenty fish; killed eight carp, four suckers, and three silvers; filled the old man's gut bucket; and packed our ice chest with one last fish.

"What the hell you doing with all them carp?" the old man asked.

"We gotta bunch of Chinese friends who really love them."

"Shit, them niggers and chinks can have 'em."

"What did you say?" Sean leaned into the man, but I put my hand on my friend's shoulder and addressed the crayfisherman.

"You don't know what you're missing, old-timer."

"Shit," he grumbled.

"Bug eater," Sean jabbed as we walked away.

Back at Williamsburg, Jin Lei gave us addresses of where we were to drop off the fish.

"So, am I collecting money for these?" I asked.

"No," she said. "Say they are gift."

"Okay," I shrugged.

We delivered the first brace of fish to Professor Wang. She thanked us warmly and handed me a couple books. "These are for Jin Lei. And tell her to come see me on Monday. I have an idea for her."

At another Chinese professor's house we got more books for Jin Lei, and the professor asked if Sean could do an East-West luncheon at C-Rays for an upcoming conference. "Sure," Sean said, and they talked menu and cost. At the barracks-like married student housing complex we called on Zou Zhen, a Chinese graduate student doing a doctorate in American literature. Zou Zhen and I had spoken about my idea for a dissertation on early American narratives about China, and when I gave him a fish, he handed me a bibliography of books by missionaries that were new to me. "This is gold," I said, thanking him over and over. This kind attention continued with a couple more fish lovers, and it soon became obvious that Jin Lei had tied into some serious *guanxi*.

The following week, Sean and I continued our carp fishing operations, landed twenty fish, delivered a dozen, and were left with a heavy surplus. "You wanna try the Asian market?" I suggested. West Lafayette and Lafayette both had Asian food stores. I knew the Taiwanese family that ran the West Lafayette market, and we told them about our haul of fresh fish. "Let me see," the man said. We stepped out to my car and opened the trunk and our ice packed cooler. He pulled a fish out, smelled it, and asked, "You have license?"

"Yes," I said.

"Okay. How much?"

Sean and I looked at each other. "Well," I said, "How about some trade?"

"Trade?" the man tilted his head.

"I'm looking for some *ma la* spice," Sean queried.

"Rice noodles, tofu, dried seaweed?" I added.

"Okay, okay," the proprietor said. And thus began our fish and grocery barter. We iced up at the hotel, Conchita adding little soaps and coffee packets to our pickups in exchange for a few fresh fish. Sean even considered a carp special for C-Ray's—"We'll call it *Cyprina*, after the Latin name." I applauded the idea, but the owner, Ray, scorned it away, "We're not gonna serve trash fish." Ray continued to offer farm-raised salmon and muddy tilapia when there was an abundant supply of fine carp swimming through the state.

One morning Sean collected me in his little Nissan pickup. I was terribly hungover, up half the night drinking with my major professor, Dick Thompson. Studies were going well, but it was hard to keep up with Thompson, a good scholar and teacher who, at twice my age, could put away a barrel of bourbon and never fumble a word. Thompson and I took a taxi home, and I was trying to remember where I left my car when Sean started reciting a litany of hangover cures, including two raw owl eggs prescribed by the Roman natural philosopher Pliny the Elder in the first century.

"Pull the fuck over, and I'll raid an owl's nest," I growled.

"I don't think it's the breeding season," Sean tightened his lips and clenched the wheel.

I was always happy to go fishing, but after a month of snagging carp and suckers out of the river and delivering them to friends and markets, I began to feel a little less like an angler. The hangover further soured my attitude. We caught several fish at the dam, walked up to the parking lot, and saw the old crayfisherman step out of his truck, toss an empty can into the bushes, and go into the Oakdale Inn. His Ford was plastered with rebel flags and bumper stickers like *Kick Their Ass, Take Their Gas.* I opened the cooler, pulled out a small carp, and shoved it up his tailpipe.

"What the hell's gotten into you?" Sean looked into my bloodshot eyes.

I took another fish from the ice and pointed it at Sean. "Look at this fish, Sean. Do we even know this fish?"

"I think you need some sleep, Henry."

"Listen to me. We used to love and remember every fish. Right? Every fish. Now we're hustlers."

"We're having fun. And people are eating our fish."

"I don't know, Sean." I shoved the stiff fish back onto the ice. Herbert Hoover, in a speech years after his presidency, praised fishing as a "mockery of profits and egos" and a "quieting of hate." I went over, pulled the carp out of the old guy's tailpipe, and threw it to a nest of cats gathered around the kitchen door of the inn.

Sean drove us home, and I leaned back in the seat, slipping into a foamy dream, tumbling through white water, feeling like I would sink and drown, but my body was held up by thousands of fish—carp, bass, catfish—their shiny bodies squirming beneath me. I was crowd surfing over a stadium of admiring fish. Then they vanished and I sunk, drowning in the darkening water. I woke gasping. "Take it easy, buddy," Sean said. When we got to the Asian market in West Lafayette the owner looked worried. "State man in here," he said. "Ask about carp. Come from where?"

"The Tippecanoe. You know that," I said.

"Need your license number to sell."

"I don't have any license to sell," I said.

"You tell me you have license."

"A fishing license, sure." I pulled out my wallet.

"No, no," he shook his head. "Stay away now. Maybe come back at Spring Festival," he looked around nervously, hustling us out with a case of expired bamboo shoots.

Although we still gave fish to people and made an occasional trade at the Asian markets, our fishing business folded. Like fishing guides and pin hookers who love their work, I never fished purely for profit, but our carp trade did get out of hand. Turning once again to fishing literature, I was refreshed by the fifteenth-century advice of Dame Juliana Berners that you must not use the art of angling for "increasing and sparing of your money only, but principally for your solace, and to cause the health of your body, and especially of your soul."

"We had to bribe the guards with a carton of cigarettes, but yeah, we got in and caught some carp on flies," I told this incredulous hawk of a man who had flown down the hallway, questioning the veracity of one of my China stories. And when he saw me cast a nymph below the Oakdale Dam one morning, he smiled: "You caught fish in China with that cast? Must've been a mix up in the language." Willard Greenwood, a fellow graduate student in the English department, was a Maine-raised fly fisherman with family roots back to seventeenth-century colonial New England. "Imagine all the brook trout, all the Atlantic salmon," he mused on ancestral anglings. Willard urged me to read Thomas McGuane, Nick Lyons, Margot Page, and Ted Leeson, and he showed me how to tie flies and prepare leaders. We sat at our desks in Heavilon Hall, pushed the ungraded freshmen compositions aside, and wrapped soft Woolly Buggers and spiky Muddler Minnows, trying to think like fish. Willard was a good teacher, and he read aloud passages from McGuane, "I try to tie flies that will make me fish better, to fish more often, to dream of fish when I can't fish . . ." Willard glanced at the clock, wondering if there was still time to get on the river after office hours. Then he continued, ". . . and to take further steps toward actually becoming a fish myself." Just as that bug in the vise was looking pretty yummy—like tempura between my chopsticks—a girl came in to talk about her paper. She saw the scalps of fur and hair, put a hand to her Greek-lettered chest, and cried, "Oh my God, did you eat those?"

I led Willard to the south fork of Wildcat Creek near Monitor, where I had caught many smallmouth bass on jigs and live minnows. He parked his dented Mazda in the public access lot, and we suited up, entered the water under the State Road 26 Bridge, and waded downstream. "Nice place," he praised. At first I just watched Willard work his magic. The Woolly Bugger can be a clunky fly to cast, but he sent out graceful rolls of line that dropped the heavy black charm into moving pockets between roots and rock. Fishing without an indicator, he mended and felt for tension through the line and soon hooked a foot-long smallmouth that skied like a copper rocket. Backed up against the bushes, Willard executed smart roll casts, showing me how to pinch line and power the rod with my thumb.

We spread over the river. I plucked some plastic trash from the willows, shoved it down my waders, and then just took my time casting, mending, feeling, and eventually catching a ten-inch small-mouth with fiery red eyes. The pressures of school seemed far away, and I thought again of McGuane, "Angling is where the child, if not the infant, gets to go on living." I listened to the water and birds, played at casting, caught another small fish, and enjoyed the flowing world.

We worked our way downstream through the holes, took a break together, and ate some cookies while I told him about my old Indiana girlfriend, Caitlin, and how we tumbled out of the canoe and made love against a mossy trunk. Willard smiled and told me that despite all the proverbial warnings, he and his girlfriend had sex in a canoe—in Maine—"And that water is cold, man. So we took it real easy, and it lasted forever."

"Sounds like good tantric training," I said.

"Every teenager should do a little canoe screwing," he professed.

Willard and I walked back to the bridge and started upstream to what I remembered as the best water on the Wildcat. A sign planted in the middle of a gravel bar read *No Trespassing*. I was puzzled. Could it refer to the houses high above the bank? We were wading in the middle of the river. How could we trespass? I told Willard that I had fished this stretch many times and guided him to a deep, long, bassy cut. Willard started casting, and I saw a man walk across his shaggy lawn. "Didn't you see the sign?" he yelled. "This is private property."

"Good morning, sir. We're just passing through. Sorry." I signaled Willard to reel up. "We'll walk on by. Sorry."

"Hey, you're on my property. Go back the way you came."

I looked back at him and waved. "Sorry," I said again. Courtesy and a willingness to move on usually worked in these situations.

"I'm calling the sheriff," he yelled.

I finally turned to him and raised both hands in exasperation. "I've fished here many times. I don't understand. We're in the middle of the river."

"You'd understand if you picked up all the trash. This is private property. Those aren't your fish to catch. We'll get the sheriff down here if that's want you want."

I felt anger rise inside me. "Go ahead, call the sheriff." I turned to Willard, "Come on." Willard looked unsure, but we walked the edge of the sandbar against the shallow riffles and the man's wishes. "Hey," I heard him yell one more time, but we pushed through the water until we were out of sight. This stretch of the Wildcat held a lot of memories that suddenly felt brittle and stained like photos in a neglected album. How could a man own a wild river or its wild fish? It was a members-only law against the higher laws of nature of which we were all members.

We continued fishing, but the mood was tense. My fly kept snagging in the bushes, and Willard was worried about his car. I knew a way up through the pasture back to the road, and we returned to the access lot with no signs of the sheriff. "Let's get out of here," Willard said and pulled out his keys. "Hold on." I set my rod against the side mirror, bent down to reel up the slack, caught of glimpse of myself, and knew what I had to do. I heard a mower over at the property owner's house and walked toward it. He was on a green rider, and when he saw me coming, he looked alarmed. He turned off the engine and dismounted. I took off my hat, bowed a little, and said, "I just wanted to say sorry. I fished that river so many times. I just couldn't believe it was closed." He was silent for a moment before repeating his complaint about the trash. "I'm the last person who would drop trash. In fact, I picked some up," I said. The man stared, "Well I don't know you." I thought of introducing myself but just said, "It won't happen again." I put my hat on and walked away.

China, Too

When my father and brother drove out to visit the following Thanksgiving, they brought me a twelve-foot jon boat like the one I had as a boy. "Why don't you call it *Number Two China*," Jin Lei suggested. She'd heard about my old boat, *China Cat*, and thought it prophetic that I eventually traveled to China and made it a part of my life. Walking around the docks on Long Island, she also noticed that people often carried cherished names to their second loves—*Annie II, Cricket II, Day Off II*. So on a golden November afternoon, my brother, Jin Lei, and I launched the *China, too*, and the chilly waters of the North Pond gave up a few silvers that we admired and gently released.

China, too freed me to row around the ponds and up and down the river when flows were manageable. An hour of steady rowing against the current worked my chest and back, and after a few weeks muscles reappeared in my upper body. I also took longer jogs along the river trails, jumping over sinkholes, garbage, and dead beavers. I did a lot of thinking during these long runs and hours spent fishing. Jin Lei and I hadn't made love in many months, and it was clear to me that our relationship was in a platonic state. It was a form I could live with. We got along well as friends, roommates, and colleagues, and I was happy to stay together and safeguard her green card application. But I was also desirous of more erotic contact with women.

Feeling better about my body always gave me the confidence to talk with women, and so I did. A couple of the younger secretaries in the office, including the very cute Debbie, were reading Mary Karr's *Liars' Club,* and they asked me if all fishermen exaggerated and lied. "Never," I lied. I quickly read the engaging memoir and learned that one of the happiest moments in Mary Karr's hellish childhood was an afternoon out fishing with her father.

"Wanna go fishing?" I asked Debbie as she put mail into the department boxes.

"I heard you were married," she cocked an eyebrow.

"Not really," I said.

"Well, I only date men who are *really* single," she shot another envelope into a pigeon hole. "Besides, I haven't been fishing since I was a girl. I wouldn't know what to do."

"I could teach you," I persisted.

"I'm sure you could," she answered with a smile but never accepted.

One of the great joys of my sport was taking people out who didn't fish or hadn't fished since they were young. Matthew Vollmer, an emerging writer at Purdue, told me stories about fishing as a boy in North Carolina's creeks, but it had been years since he'd wet a line.

Matthew, Willard, and I planned an afternoon on the North Pond, but Willard had a terrible argument with his wife and had to cancel. Matthew and I unchained the *China, too* from the tree where I kept it locked, wiped off the seats, and slid the boat down the bank into the coffee-colored water. I rowed out to the middle of the pond, and we jigged near the bottom, talking about school and writing, wondering about Willard. Then I hooked a fish. The rod doubled and line peeled off the reel. It was a light Shimano bait casting outfit low on eight-pound test and I dared not tighten the drag. Holding on and smiling, I tried to regain a few feet of line when the fish came off the bottom, but the shallow spool was emptying fast. "Here, take this." I handed Matthew the rod. His eyes widened, and he squared his shoulders behind the run. "Keep tension and reel if you can." Coaching—even useless coaching— relieved some of the nervousness I felt when a friend was fast to a big fish. "That's it. Stay with him," I said, pulling gently on the oars and following the force.

"Maybe it's a turtle," Matthew ventured.

Over the years, I've hooked big snapping turtles, but they didn't swim this fast. I've caught snakes, bullfrogs, bats, birds, and boats. I even snagged one scuba diver who was safely released. But this was a fish.

"It's a fish," I said. "Sturgeon, paddlefish, maybe a big carp."

"Maybe a catfish?" Matthew added.

"Could be," I nodded, watching him raise his rod against the strain and then reel down to the fish. "That's it," I coached on. "You're doing great." I rowed after the fish for fifteen minutes, then shipped the oars and watched Matthew—mid-twenties, fit, with a Tintin haircut and a handsome farm-boy face that blushed between delight and panic when the fish made a move. For the next half hour the creature towed our boat around the pond, bolting suddenly for the river inlet and taking line. "Oh, no you don't," I said aloud. "See if you can rein him this way, Matthew."

"How?" He tightened his face into confusion.

The fish steamed halfway through the channel then suddenly turned tail in the opposite direction.

"Crazy," Matthew laughed. "This is incredible."

I took the rod for five minutes while Matthew rubbed his hands and slaked his thirst with a soda. We heard the university's six o'clock bells and a flock of geese somewhere downriver. I handed the fish-bent rod back to Matthew. "It's all yours." After an hour and a half, we had to get tough. "Steady lift of the rod, and then reel down to the fish," I went back to my coaching.

Soon the fish was directly below our boat, and we got the first glimpse of a long dark form. "Catfish"—I identified the creature. These moments are important in a fisherman's life. To see the hooked fish—just to see it—is often enough. If the line breaks or the hook comes free, at least we have witnessed the miracle of connection. The fish sounded, line rolled off the reel, and I advised Matthew to tighten the drag slightly.

We had seen the back of a huge catfish, but was that enough?

"I want to hold this guy," Matthew said, as if desiring consecration by touch.

"Hell, let's bring it to Burnham's," I went further. "We'll make the papers."

I normally never worried about records or trophy photos taped to the walls and counters of tackle shops or printed in the newspaper, but this fish might be a record. Would I be willing to kill an old fish just for the record? Toxins accumulate over time in the fatty tissues of some fish, and it wouldn't be wise to eat a portly old catfish from the Wabash River—but a state record might fill us with pride.

Matthew lifted the rod and reeled, lifted and reeled. There it was again—easily four feet long, a massive dark head tapering to a mustard mottled body. I told Matthew about the mythical *Onamazu*, a giant catfish that lives under the islands of Japan, guarded by the god *Kashima*.

But not even a god can manage complete control over *Onamazu,* and the fish's periodic thrashings caused terrible earthquakes. Our catfish rolled, and its tail thumped the boat like a drum. "Jesus," Matthew gasped, thrilled and amazed. "My God, that's a fish." It was a flathead catfish—the largest I had ever seen. "You've caught a god," I said.

Matthew was raised in a strict Adventist family, but he had gone his own way. When he moved to Indiana, he started visiting a different church each week—Presbyterian, Church of Brethren, Episcopalian, Quaker, and Unitarian—and found the varieties of worship fascinating and enriching. He even explored other mystical paths, such as Buddhism and Taoism. His mother grew worried. "She cried," Matthew told me, "fearing for my wandering soul." Matthew's mother felt he had jeopardized his promised place among the family when Christ returned and raised the faithful dead. "I just want us all to be together in the end," his mother wept.

The catfish came up, the little gold jig pinned to the side of his monstrous head. Small eyes and thick whiskers trembled on the surface in a grotesque, fearsome, beautiful display of the aquatic primitive. Matthew touched its back and smiled. The fish measured forty-eight inches, an estimated fifty pounds. If it were a channel catfish, we'd have the Indiana state record, but the record flathead catfish, I'd later learn, tipped the scales at seventy-nine pounds, eight ounces in 1966. "We gotta let it go," Matthew said. "This guy has lived such a long life."

"You finally catch a god, and you're gonna let him go?"

"Let him live. Yeah."

I reached down with my pliers, easily removed the hook, and we watched the great leviathan return to the murky depths.

I told Jin Lei that my visions came true. "God is a fish. And we saw him today."

"Where is he?" her brown eyes widened in delight.

"Back in the water," I said. "Where he belongs."

When we told Willard the whole story—God and all—he said, "That catfish had great *prana*." He was writing a dissertation on the sublime in nature and used the Sanskrit word, *prana,* a kind of *élan vital,* to describe the fighting life force of fish. Different species of fish fight differently. Cod come up like old tires; steelhead rage like burning maniacs. But even among the same species of the same size from the same waters, there can be individuality in the way a fish fights. Anglers sometimes receive these exceptional exertions as divine messages. I can't tell you exactly what Matthew heard over the line, but his blue eyes glowed, and with the zeal of the newly converted, he repeated Willard's pronouncement, "That catfish had great *prana.*"

Matthew, Willard, and I shared long talks about fishing, religion, literature, and life. We talked about relationships and women. Matthew got along well with his wife, Kelly. Willard and his wife, Maddy, were having troubles. They had years of happiness and a beautiful young son, but their union was on the rocks. My drifting

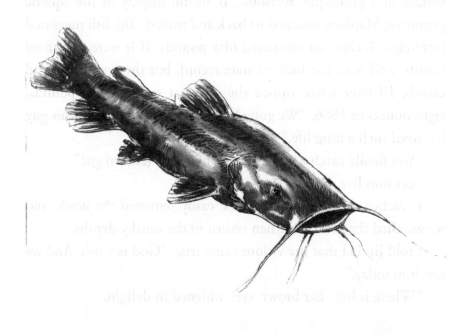

relationship with Jin Lei did not seem as painful, but Willard told me that Jin Lei and he walked back from the library, and she cried and confided her heartache. "She really loves you, man. It wasn't just an arrangement for her. She wants to be your wife."

The Indiana winter of the new millennium was very cold, and in January the Williamsburg Ponds froze over. I walked along the bank and a few feet out on the ice and marveled at the crystal transformation. Crows chipped away at frozen shad; feathers, leaves, flecks, and bubbles glistened in suspension; I traced a long blue subway trail that suddenly darkened with the chugging engine of a beaver. Life under the ice. I called Willard, who knew ice-fishing from his years growing up in Maine.

"Come on over and show me how to do this," I urged.

He sounded depressed. "I'm not really into it," he said.

"Come on," I pleaded. "Get out of that damn apartment. Imagine pulling a walleye through the ice."

Willard came over with a hand augur and a dozen tip-ups. We slide-stepped out on the ice, testing its thickness, and I followed his cues, eyeing the pale cracks like veins in granite. Our drill gnawed through six inches before the dark rush of water. "Good," Willard said, scooping out the chips and shavings with Jin Lei's dumpling ladle. He showed me how to rig the tip-up, setting the cross over the hole, the red flag tucked-in and ready to snap up and signal *Fish!* when the spool ran. Jin Lei came out on the ice in her beige wool coat and red scarf. "It's like trapping rats!" she exclaimed. She walked around for a while, peered down into the holes, said we'd turn the pond into "swede cheese," then went inside. Willard and I set tip-ups baited with nightcrawlers and mealworms, sat on overturned plastic buckets, and looked at each other. Cold and windless, winter spoke in crows, whale-like booms, and moans that startled me. "It's just the ice," he said.

Willard started talking about his wife. She left with their son, Max, a few days ago.

"I'm sorry, brother. I didn't know."

"It's been bad for a couple years. I kept thinking it was being in school and just the changes we were going through with Max. But she hasn't been very loving. Then she met someone."

"Damn," I said.

"Shit, one night she went out to get groceries. I was home waiting with Max. And it was like hours. She was probably at this guy's house. I almost fuckin' lost it, man. That kind of anger is scary. One of us had to leave."

Thin panes closed around our lines. No bites. We patrolled each hole, broke up and skimmed the fresh ice with the dumpling ladle. Back at our station in the middle of the pond we tried jigging little blue teardrops. Nothing. Willard talked about catching big lake trout through the ice in Maine and how sometimes they had cigarette butts in their stomachs. I told him that New Orleans catfish will also eat cigarette butts. "Why would such a beautiful creature eat such filth?" he wondered. We speculated that the warm water fish of central Indiana had tucked themselves in for a long winter's nap. In summer, these ponds were full of biting game, but today we aroused nothing but the pain of our relationships.

"You were right about Jin Lei," I said. "We had an agreement, but she took things much more seriously—more emotionally— than I did."

"Wake up, man," Willard looked at me with something like disgust. "She's in love with you. The marriage is real to her. Or was real."

"But I told her from the beginning . . ."

"You *told* her? I think you need to listen to yourself."

"I feel terrible about it." I dropped my head. "She's such a good woman."

We fell silent. "Should we get a bottle of something?" I asked.

"I think we'd better." Willard jigged a little more.

I walked up to our apartment on the second floor and pulled a half-empty bottle of Old Crow from the cupboard. Jin Lei was typing away at something. "Catch anything?" she asked without looking up.

"No," I said, then I went over and put my hands on her shoulders.

I looked out of our sliding glass doors and saw Willard standing there alone on the ice. I had gazed at the ponds so many times, and now it seemed bizarre to see a man standing on water simply because it was cold.

A month later I slept with a friend, a graduate student in psychology who liked to drink and talk at the Knickerbocker Saloon in Lafayette. I avoided drinking and driving, and one night walking her home she invited me up to her room where we just consumed each other. It felt great to have those carnal passions reignited in my body and mind. I left her place at six in the morning, took a shortcut across the still-frozen South Pond, and plunged through the ice. Blue shock and fear. Water over my shoulders. Ice cutting my neck and arms. But my toes touched bottom, and I thrashed madly through the remaining ice to the shore. Cold, bleeding, head ablaze, and suddenly confused about what I'd done all night, I stumbled into the apartment. Jin Lei woke in a panic and helped me undress and get into bed. I slept until two in the afternoon and woke to find her reading. She put down her book and asked where I was all night. I told her some of the truth. "I don't want to be with you anymore," she said and started to cry.

"I know," I said. "I'm sorry. You don't deserve this."

Jin Lei moved out of our Williamsburg apartment. I helped, dividing our meager possessions and lifting the heavy end of her desk onto Sean's truck. She avoided my eyes and was quieter than I'd ever known her to be.

A couple months went by, and we didn't talk. Then I saw her in the library, and she smiled. Our friendship slowly healed. I read and edited her essays and put up shelves at her new place; she translated Chinese sources for my research and taught me how to braise eggplant, Yunnan style, with soy sauce, vinegar, sugar, and garlic. Jin Lei finished her master's in comparative literature, secured an assistantship teaching Chinese, and was well on her way to the doctorate.

"You're really doing it, Jin Lei," I raised my glass over lunch at Harry's Chocolate Shop. "To you!"

"To you and America," she revised the toast.

These days no one ever toasts America, I thought.

On September 11, 2001, I was finishing my dissertation and looking out over a painful highway construction project that had filled part of the South Pond when a knock rattled the door. It was Jin Lei. "Did you see what's happening? We need to call your family and see if they are all right."

"What are you talking about?"

We followed the news on the web and then went to Sean's house to watch CNN. My father and brother were safe on eastern Long Island. I tried calling Eugene and a couple other friends who did business in lower Manhattan. They were also safe, but thousands were dead, and another war over religion, power, and oil had begun.

Like Jiang Taigong at the bloody end of the Shang dynasty, Guy de Maupassant during the senseless Franco-Prussian War, and Ernest Hemingway after the earth-shattering World Wars of the twentieth century, Jin Lei and I looked to water and fishing for a little healing. I borrowed Sean's pickup, hauling us and the *China, too* toward the Tippecanoe, turning off the radio news. "Don't think about that right now," I said. We arranged for a shuttle and launched into the clear running river, drifting and rowing downstream, casting and swinging lures and flies. "Tippecanoe and *China, too*," I sang, enjoying the word play, then realizing it was another paean to battle and slaughter.

The air and water were still warm, and I rowed up on a gravel bar where we stepped into the river wearing our shorts and old sneakers. It had been a while since Jin Lei and I fished together, and she was happy to see me using a Yuanwei fly reel that her father sent me. The reel was made in Shandong, the home province of Confucius, and it felt good to be pulling line from another legacy. The first mention of fishing reels comes from Chinese writing in the fourth century, and now the Chinese were making them again.

"Can I try the fly rod?" Jin Lei asked.

"Of course," I said, showing her the basics. She soon found the rhythm, looping out a decent cast that placed the streamer behind a swirling logjam where a bass waited. The fish struck, ran, tailed-danced, and then disappeared. "Whoa!" she yelled.

We worked our way downstream, raising a few small fish but mostly our presence with each other. Jin Lei climbed atop a large rock, made a long cast, watched, and retrieved with jaguar concentration. She looked beautiful and strong. A lady of limitless reach.

By spring we would be legally divorced but good friends. Jin Lei was heading back to China to visit her family, and I was leaving for a teaching job in Oregon, but I felt close to her in words and feelings. The poet Seamus Heaney visited the university in late April, and Jin Lei and I went to the hall early to help setup. Mr. Heaney was warm and friendly, offering us a glass of whiskey from a bottle he'd just received. I accepted an amber inch in a plastic cup and told him that I loved his poems, reciting a couple lines from "The Salmon Fisher and the Salmon." He gave us that squinty smile.

"Thanks," he said. "Are you a fisherman?"

"Oh, yes."

"It's good to get out," Heaney said. "I'm not much at it these days. Do you know Ted Hughes' work? Now he was a real angler—heart and soul."

We talked about Ted Hughes and his son, Nick, fishing for pike in Ireland. Then Mr. Heaney turned to Jin Lei. "Do like to fish, my dear?"

"Yes," Jin Lei said and recited a couple lines from a Tang dynasty fishing poem we were translating together. Heaney chuckled and sipped his whisky. "You two are perfect for each other."

It was painful to hear the great bard pronounce us "perfect for each other." But we formed a near perfect friendship that endures to this day. Indiana was in full May bloom when Jin Lei handed me a folder and floppy disk of those Chinese fishing poems. I turned to our translation of "Green Creek" by Wang Wei, an eighth-century master of many arts.

> In the clear, stilling waters,
> My heart and the river are equally at peace.
> Let me sit upon a large, flat rock
> And drop my line and hook forever.

Jin Lei was high in my heart, above the river on that shining stone, making impossible casts and raising fish after fish. "*Zai jian, lao pengyou*," she whispered and hugged me. "Goodbye, old friend."

"*Zai jian*, Jin Lei," I said.

"And don't be afraid," she told me. "Our lives are starting over again. Keep your heart open."

Thinking I'd take the *China, too* for one last trip, I got my oars out of the closet and walked down to the pond. Over the weedy berm and down through the trees I looked and looked again. The boat was gone. Then I saw that someone had cut the rusty chain from which she depended, leaving only a flat trail through the mud toward the ever-giving and taking water.

Arc and Pulse

Fishing an Oregon river with my wife, Chloë, turns to dancing. I touch her back and shoulders, leading her gently. She smiles, follows my gesture, swings back, and sees in the bubbly kiss of this emerald tailout a big slivery flash. A fish that's come from the ocean. Chloë has taught me a lot, but today I'm teaching her to cast for steelhead. We met a few years after I arrived at Western Oregon University. She was coming through a divorce, and I was surfacing from a drowning relationship. At Richard Bunse's art studio in Independence we used pencil and charcoal to draw nude women and men, sipping wine and learning about each other. We talked, explored ideas and the tastes and positions that shape them, and I remembered old Herbie Clark's crude adage, "Head before tail," in a new way—that you must love a person's mind and personality if you hope to continue loving his or her body and place beside you. Chloë and I dated, shared our histories, took her children fishing, spent a night and a few months together, and fell in love. A good bit of Roman poetry is worth repeating, "Let your hook always be cast," Ovid tells us in *The Art of Love*. "In a pool where you least expect it, there will be a fish."

We had fished this coastal river once last year in early September. The woods were dry, the water low and clear, and the fish wary of our shadows as if they were the smoky dances of fire. The fires of any romantic relationship can burn in the wrong direction. As Chloë and I got to know each other better, we had our first arguments. The issues were familiar—my excessive time spent fishing, long days on the water without a phone call, or just my need to be alone when Chloë said she needed me around. And when plans for marriage firmed up, we had our first disputes about money. Most disagreements worked themselves through to a place of better understanding, but some clashes turned red and sore. One quarrel over my debts exploded into harsh words, slammed doors, and days of silence. When I emailed Chloë to ask if she still wanted to go fishing on Friday as we planned, she typed back, "Okay, but no champagne."

We walked deep into the warm canyon, whispering about the Siletz Indians who once speared, trapped, ate, laughed, and lay along these basalt ledges. What is it we really want and need from the world, from other people? The Indians surely worried about many things before the ships and wagons arrived but not loans and credit cards. They needed each other; they needed fish. Hours into the canyon, Chloë and I didn't see another person, and when we found a sun-drenched stone over a deep pool, we stripped down and plunged into the cold water. Wild awake with just the river and ourselves, it felt so easy to see, touch, and love completely. Would I ever need anything more?

I would need this October when rains bring more fish and the opportunity to catch them. Chloë swings the rod forward and sends the blue spinner into the riffles. It has a nice vibratory resistance, and she's steering it right into the sweet spot. No bobber or bells for this woman. She likes to "feel it," she tells me. I glance up at the narrow gray sky, the rocky canyon lush in moss, fern, and fir—a great cathedral echoing wonder and promise. She brings the spinner across the deep tongue and there!—the arc and pulse of the rod, a splash, line tearing out—she's into a fish.

There are many ways people grow closer, and each way comes with the risk that it will lead inversely to pain and undoing. We learn each other's burning passions and dull apathies, the consistencies and idiosyncrasies of our minds. We count on each other, raise children, take care of a house, garden, even a pet. A couple years ago a skinny gray tabby cat jumped in our boat while I was cleaning up in the driveway. The cat gobbled some leftover prawn baits, rubbed against my leg, and purred. Chloë called him Shrimp and said we should take him in. I was reluctant. Just another thing to worry about. But she and the boys convinced me. We love the cat, of course. And yet I do worry sometimes when he's out at night—will he get bit by a raccoon or hit by a car? Then that worry seems silly in light of the children's health, the life concerns of our family and friends, a leaky roof, bills, work. So much matters. But during exciting moments of possibility—diving into water, reaching for someone you love, hooking a great fish—nothing else seems to matter.

Chloë is focused, excited, anxious. I touch her flexing back and say, "Great." There's nothing quite like a big, bright, sea-run fish in a rushing river. She keeps her balance on the slippery rocks, stepping back into the shallows. I coach, and she retrieves a little line, and then there's a confused moment of slack and a rocketing burst of steelhead, its body completely out of the water in an electrifying silver somersault.

This fish left the river as a small smolt two or three years ago, returning heavy, handsome, and hard to hook—until now. Steelhead may be the sexiest gamefish in the world—and it's taken me a lifetime to find them. When this fish splashes back and disappears, the

rod resumes its pulsing arc. "It's still on. It's coming," she says. A chrome steelhead streaking through the blue-green river.

And then it's gone.

"Oh no! What happened?" she groans. My jaw clenches and eyes squeeze shut as I exhale a tremendous sinking disappointment. You can't pray for everything. Like young Huckleberry Finn, who prayed hard for fishhooks but never got them, concluding "there ain't nothing in it," I had long ago replaced divine entreaty with high hope. My hopes were sky high that Chloë would hook a fish today. And she did. Long ago, I got over losing fish on my line, but only recently have I dealt with what it means to lose the women in my life. Chloë's never caught a steelhead, and she's worked hard at it for days, the river rising and falling, the fish constantly on the move. Today's conditions are ideal, her rod-work perfect. I examine the line and hooks. Everything is fine. "Sometimes it just happens," I say. "You did great. What a gorgeous fish. Cast again."

The endless, repeated promise of fishing—the hope that the next cast will be the one that connects you to a fish, a magnificent fish, the fish of a lifetime—can lead to a hobby, obsession, addiction, healthy emotional and physical persistence, the faithful practice of something like religion, even passion and love. It has to lead somewhere. "The craft of angling is the catching of fish," the writer Ted Leeson wrote after wading these same Oregon rivers. "But the art of angling is a receptiveness to these connections, the art of letting one thing lead to another until, if only locally and momentarily, you realize some small completeness." And then you start over.

West and east, open ocean and weedy ponds, urban canals and pristine springs, hot swamps and arctic lakes, rowing into a fresh breeze and motoring through outboard fumes, drunk and sober, serious and silly, swinging baits, lures, and flies for hits and misses, landing little sprats and lead-bellied leviathan, eating some fish and letting others go—it's been an endless journey of angling. And along the way there were relationships of every variety—backseat and front seat, crazy and calm, primal and cerebral, one night stands and lifetime friendships, years of dating and nights of being alone, divorce and marriage. The endlessly repeated, recurring, predictable, surprising, erratic, and bizarre experiences that are so much a part of fishing can drown in an instant or, over time, become the sustaining forces of our existence. Like the constant and constantly changing river that we wade in today, you never know what will happen.

"Take a step upstream," I say, "and cast again."

Acknowledgments

In a book about relationships over many years I owe tremendous thanks to many people. Thanks to Barbara Davenport, who reminisced with me at Ralph's Fishing Station near the sandy mouth of Long Island's Mt. Sinai Harbor about her late husband, Ralph, and the old station that flourished from 1961 until 1977 at the muddy back of that harbor. Ralph's Fishing Station and Caraftis' Fishing Station in neighboring Port Jefferson represent great legacies of angling and boating culture for many Long Islanders, from the late Herbie Clark to parents taking their children snapper fishing for the first time this summer. Thanks to old Long Island friends, especially Eugene Jones, my angling and cocktail companion for more than thirty-five years.

Prairie praise for the folks at Dakota Wesleyan University, South Dakota, and special thanks to those that assisted with my research: Jennifer Ditmarsch, Birch Hilton, John and Patti Duffy, Joseph and JoAnn Ditta, and Ben Janis, director of Lower Brule Sioux Tribe Department of Wildlife, Fish and Recreation. Gratitude to the many people at Purdue University, Indiana, that cultivated my riverside education, especially Colleen Morton Busch, Rob Davidson, and the anglers Sean McNerney and Willard Greenwood.

The Japan and China years were supported and seasoned by many wonderful people, including Carl Delaney, Jon Trachtman, Yano Tadayoshi, Sugiura Takao, Chen Lin, and Lou Guangqing. I am beholden to Ishikura Naoko for reading and commenting on the Japan chapters. Deep gratitude to my dear friend and continuously generous colleague, Jin Lei, currently an associate professor of Chinese at the College of Charleston, South Carolina.

Thanks to my Oregon fishing buddies: Bob Fultz, Jackson Stalley, Wayne Harrison, John Larison, Mark Weiss, Tom Friesen, Paul Shirkey, Ted Leeson, Peter Betjemann, and the consummate angler-artist Richard Bunse.

Thanks to Celeste Thompson, who keeps the fish flags flying, and to Paul Gentry, who pours tall drinks and ideas.

A wave of continued appreciation for my wonderful colleagues at Western Oregon University, especially those who waded though drafts of this book and offered superb suggestions for revision: Karen Haberman, David Hargreaves, Dennis Eddings, and Curtis Yehnert.

I am truly beholden to the distinguished literary angler-friends who read, commented on, and supported this book, even when light was fading and there were no bites: Marjorie Sandor, James Hepworth, Nick Lyons, Ted Leeson, Margot Page, Charles Rangeley-Wilson, and David James Duncan.

Much of this story is about family, and I offer thanks back through time to my late mother, Marion Spies Hughes, and her sister, my aunt, Lillian Spies. Love and thanks to my father, Charles, who didn't like to fish but took me fishing and kept our boats afloat. To my brother, David, a cherished angling friend and supporter.

And finally and most powerfully, an ocean of thanks to my closest reader, best friend, wife, and lover, Chloë—with you I rise and jump.

Research for this project was made possible through a Faculty Development Award from Western Oregon University.

Some parts of this book first appeared in slightly different form in *Harvard Review, Japan Quarterly, Adventures NW, Marine Quarterly*, and in the introduction to *Fishing Stories* from Knopf's Everyman's Library.